# "Mr. President"

*President George Washington*

# "Mr. President"

## GEORGE WASHINGTON AND THE
## MAKING OF THE NATION'S HIGHEST OFFICE

# HARLOW GILES UNGER

DA CAPO PRESS
A Member of the Perseus Books Group

Designed by Trish Wilkinson
Set in 11.5 point Adobe Garamond Pro by The Perseus Books Group

Library of Congress Cataloging-in-Publication Data

Unger, Harlow G., 1931–
    "Mr. President": George Washington and the making of the nation's highest office / Harlow Giles Unger.
    pages cm
    Includes bibliographical references and index.
    ISBN 978-0-306-81961-2 (hardcover)—ISBN 978-0-306-82241-4
(e-book)  1.  United States—Politics and government—1789–1797.
2.  Washington, George, 1732–1799.  3.  Executive power—United States—
History.  I.  Title.
E311.U54 2013
973.4'1092—dc23
[B]                                                              2013024235

First Da Capo Press edition 2013

Published by Da Capo Press
A Member of the Perseus Books Group
www.dacapopress.com

Da Capo Press books are available at special discounts for bulk purchases in the U.S. by corporations, institutions, and other organizations. For more information, please contact the Special Markets Department at the Perseus Books Group, 2300 Chestnut Street, Suite 200, Philadelphia, PA 19103, or call (800) 810-4145, ext. 5000, or e-mail special.markets@perseusbooks.com.

10 9 8 7 6 5 4 3 2 1

*To*
*Gay Hart Gaines*
*and*
*James C. Rees*

# Contents

# List of Illustrations

# Acknowledgments

My deepest thanks to my friend and mentor John P. Kaminski, one of America's outstanding constitutional scholars, who was kind enough to review the manuscript of this book. Historian, author, educator, lecturer, documentary editor, and patriot, Dr. Kaminski was founder and director of the Center for the Study of the American Constitution at the University of Wisconsin (Madison), and the longtime editor-in-chief of one of the nation's most important historical treasures: *The Documentary History of the Ratification of the Constitution.*

I am most grateful, as well, to Da Capo Press publisher John Radziewicz; to my editor Robert Pigeon, the executive editor at Da Capo; and to Lissa Warren, Vice President and Director of Publicity (and an author herself). Many others at Da Capo Press and the Perseus Books Group have made enormous contributions to the production and distribution of this book, among them Kevin Hanover, Director of Marketing and the extraordinary Perseus Books Group sales force; marketing executive Sean Maher; Cisca L. Schreefel, Manager of Editorial Production; and copyeditor Martha Whitt. To all of you, I thank you not only for your professional help but for your warm friendship and patience.

One last expression of gratitude and acknowledgment for his contribution to this and all my other books goes to the late Edward W. Knappman, my literary agent since I started writing books on American history. A brilliant scholar, publisher, and editor before he began representing authors, Ed founded New England Publishing Associates with his wife Elizabeth Knappman, and the two were instrumental in introducing dozens of authors to the public. I owe my career as an author to Ed and shall always miss him.

# Introduction

Most Americans were still celebrating their Revolutionary War victory when fresh sparks of rebellion flared in Philadelphia. By 1786, they had burst into flames and spread northward to New York and Massachusetts, then southward into Pennsylvania, Maryland, Virginia, the Carolinas, and Georgia. By 1791, they lapped onto the Blue Ridge, across the Shenandoah, and over the Appalachians, where they engulfed the entire frontier, as angry mobs swelled into an army ready to fight for independence . . . and not from Britain—but from the United States!

Goaded by the press, foreign agents, and ambitious home-grown demagogues, tens of thousands of American farmers vilified President George Washington, his government, Congress, the courts, and the army—much as they had vilified King George III, the British Parliament, and the Redcoats two decades earlier in 1776.

"If ever a nation was debauched by a man," growled a correspondent in Philadelphia's *Aurora*, "the American nation has been debauched by WASHINGTON! Let the history of the federal government instruct mankind that the masque of patriotism may be worn to conceal the foulest designs against the liberties of a people." Another writer urged

1

the President to "retire immediately; let no flatterer persuade you to rest one hour longer at the helm of state."[1]

Only two decades earlier, Washington and members of Congress had led Americans in rebellion against British taxation, calling it "the horror of all free states, wresting your property from you . . . and laying open to insolent tax-gatherers, [your] houses, the scenes of domestic peace and comfort."[2] Washington growled to a British friend at the time, "I think the Parliament of Great Britain hath no more right to put their hands in my pocket, without my consent, than I have to put my hands into yours for money."[3]

Now, Congress was sending its own "insolent tax-gatherers" across the nation to wrest properties from those who wouldn't or couldn't pay taxes. Even more appalling: George Washington, "the father of our country," was ready to lead an army to enforce American tax laws, assailing his fellow citizens "for creating discord"—just as the British government had assailed him "for creating discord" after Parliament had passed the Stamp Act in 1765.

"The Constitution and laws must strictly govern," Washington thundered as he prepared to call up troops to crush farmer opposition to taxes in western Pennsylvania. It was every American patriot's worst nightmare come true—George Washington turned tyrant—a George IV.[4]

Only four years earlier, in 1788, Virginia governor Edmund Randolph, who had been Washington's aide-de-camp at the beginning of the Revolutionary War, warned that the new American Constitution was a "fetus of monarchy."[5] His fellow Virginian Patrick Henry agreed, insisting that the Constitution would simply replace Britain's parliamentary and royal tyranny with homegrown congressional and presidential tyranny. "Liberty will be lost and tyranny must and will arise," Henry protested. "As this government stands, I despise and abhor it."[6]

But President Washington remained firm in his determination to preserve the government and the Union, insisting that "the daring and factious spirit which has arisen to overturn the laws and to subvert the

Constitution ought to be subdued. If that is not done . . . we may bid adieu to all government in this country. . . . Nothing but anarchy and confusion can ensue. . . . If the minority . . . are suffered to dictate to the majority . . . there can be no security for life, liberty or property."[7]

Then, in one of the defining events in the creation of the U.S. presidency, Washington startled his countrymen by ignoring constitutional limits on presidential powers and ordering troops to crush tax protests by American citizens—much as the British government had tried, and failed, to do in the years leading up to the American Revolution.

It was not the first time—nor would it be the last—that Washington would assume—or as critics charged, "usurp"—powers not granted by the Constitution. Indeed, from the moment he took office in the spring of 1789, Washington had been obsessed with establishing the President as "a supreme power to govern the general concerns of a confederated republic."[8] Fearing anarchy, disunion, and an end to American freedom if he failed to act decisively, he transformed himself—and the presidency—from a relatively impotent figurehead into America's most powerful leader, creating what modern scholars have called the "imperial presidency."[9] Although often associated with twentieth- and twenty-first-century presidents, the imperial presidency was George Washington's creation over eight tumultuous years, as one by one, he raised seven pillars of power that sustain the mighty American presidential edifice today—the power to control executive appointments, foreign policy, military affairs, government finances, and federal law enforcement, along with the power to legislate by presidential proclamation and to issue secret fiats under the cloak of executive privilege.

Washington's steady assumption of ever more extra-constitutional powers during his years in office came as no surprise to tens of thousands of Patrick Henry's followers. After the Constitutional Convention, Henry—and at least five delegates to the convention itself—condemned the secret proceedings and the Constitution they produced as nothing less than a bloodless coup d'état.

The Confederation Congress had called the convention "for the sole and express purpose of revising the Articles of Confederation . . . [to] render the federal constitution, adequate to the exigencies of government and the preservation of the union."[10] Instead, convention delegates—the so-called framers—ignored the instructions. "That they exceeded their power is perfectly clear," Patrick Henry roared. "The federal convention ought to have amended the old system. For this purpose they were solely delegated. The object of their mission extended to no other consideration."[11]

With George Washington presiding, the Constitutional Convention voted not only to proceed in secret, but to discard the Articles of Confederation and overthrow the old U.S. government. Still operating in secret, they then wrote a new constitution that established a *new* form of government, with a legislature armed with most of the powers of the British Parliament that Americans had struggled to destroy during eight torturous years of rebellion. Only thirty-nine of the fifty-five delegates who came to the convention stayed to the end, and three of them refused to sign the document. Virginia planter George Mason, a neighbor of George Washington, raged that the document gave the government "dangerous power" and that it would end "in monarchy or a tyrannical aristocracy." He affirmed that he "would sooner chop off my right hand than put it to the Constitution as it now stands."[12]

The framers made a tacit recognition of republicanism with a disingenuous assertion in the preamble that "We the people" had ordained and established "this Constitution for the United States of America," but Mason, Henry, and other "antifederalists" saw through the ruse. "The Constitution has been formed without the knowledge or idea of the people,"[13] Mason growled. Patrick Henry was equally furious: "Who authorized them to speak the language of *We, the People*? The people gave them no power to use their name.

"The new form of government," Henry argued, "will oppress and ruin the people. Our rights and privileges are endangered . . . the rights of conscience, trial by jury, liberty of the press, all your immunities and franchises, all pretensions to human rights and privileges are rendered insecure, if not lost."[14]

Within a year after Washington's new government had assumed power, Virginia Governor Henry ("Light-Horse Harry") Lee declared Patrick Henry a prophet: "His predictions are daily verified. His declarations . . . on all the doings of government already have been undeniably proved . . . we can be relieved, I fear, only by disunion."[15]

Those were not words Washington had hoped to hear. After leading the war of independence for eight years, then struggling for six years to unite the states into a republic, Washington believed that "no morn ever dawned more favorably than ours." With chaos and anarchy abounding about him, however, Washington proclaimed, "Wisdom and good examples are necessary at this time to rescue the political machine from the impending storm."[16]

# *Prologue*

"My country," John Adams barked, "has in its wisdom contrived for me the most insignificant office that ever the invention of man contrived or his imagination conceived."[1]

Adams had won election as the nation's first vice president, but within days of taking office, the hyperactive little lawyer from Quincy, Massachusetts, found himself with so little to do of any consequence that he grew furious. George Washington, however, was even more furious. Having slain the British lion, he had won election unanimously as the new nation's first president and had even less to do than the vice president. To his consternation, the Constitution he himself had helped write had given the vice president specific obligations, but not the president.

Although they were an incongruous pair, the two men were better friends than most historians seem to think. As farmers, they had much in common, enjoyed each other's company, and trusted each other. They had met for the first time at the First Continental Congress in the fall of 1774 and dined together—even went to church together—several times. A brilliant attorney, the serious-faced Adams did most of the talking when they were together, and Washington, true to form, listened—to the intense pleasure of both. Five feet, six inches tall—admittedly "short, thick, fat"[2]—Adams invariably tilted his head back to look up and bark at the huge, soft-spoken Virginian, who looked down quizzically.

Onlookers sometimes held their breaths, fearing the two were arguing, when in fact it was Adams's stature—or lack thereof—that made him bend his head back uncomfortably and grimace as he talked to his tall friend. As experienced farmers, however, they were completely at ease talking weather, soil, crops, and livestock with each other. Adams had some difficulty relating his 40 acres to Washington's 20,000, and Washington puzzled over the viability of a 40-acre vegetable plot. Both loved horses, hunting, and "ducking." Washington admired men of learning—Adams was a Harvard man—and Adams admired soldiers and deeply regretted not having served in either the French and Indian War or Revolutionary War.

"Oh that I was a soldier!" he had wailed to his wife, Abigail, after learning of the slaughter at Bunker Hill. "I will be," he pledged, not realizing he was far more valuable to the nation in the Continental Congress than on the battlefield.[3] It was Adams who would engineer the critical congressional decision that united northern and southern colonies in war by naming the southerner Washington to command the largely northern troops of the Continental Army. Next to Washington himself, Adams had garnered the most votes for the presidency and the two joined to form the nation's—indeed, the world's—first freely elected government. Both quickly realized, however, that neither had any powers to act effectively. Indeed, the Vice President seemed to have more power than the President.

The Vice President presided over the Senate and could cast a vote to break ties. Adams, therefore, could amble into the Senate every day when it was in session, mingle with a few garrulous senators, then display his authority by pounding his gavel, clearing his throat ostentatiously, and calling out to the twenty-two senators, "Gentlemen, please! Please, gentlemen!"

Washington, on the other hand, presided over no one but himself, sitting alone at his empty desk each day, staring at walls or out the windows of an otherwise empty office. He was a man of action—a superb horseman, hunter, and soldier who spurred his huge steed over tall fences in the chase, dodged arrows and bullets in battle. Now he sat at an empty desk, idle, bored. Having answered every letter, he stared at the walls, wondering how to spend the rest of the day.

He often wrote to his nephew George Augustine Washington, who had agreed to supervise the farms at Mount Vernon in his uncle's absence. What often followed were pages—sometimes ten at a time—of detailed instructions on virtually every aspect of the enterprise: fish, timothy seed, rents, use of the mules, brick work, harvesting, cow pens, sheepfolds, stables, gullies, tobacco, rum, flour, barley . . . the list ran on and on, before concluding in typical Washington understatement: "The general superintendence of my affairs is all I require of you, for it is neither my desire nor wish that you should become a drudge to it—or that you should refrain from any amusements, or visitings which may be agreeable . . . I am ever your warm friend and affectionate uncle."[4]

After writing to his nephew, however, Washington had nothing better to do than wander through the house to find his wife, Martha. As often as not, his diary detailed his having "exercised with Mrs. Washington in the coach the 14 miles round," referring to a popular dirt carriage road that rambled northwards through the woods to Harlem Heights and back along the eastern edge of Manhattan island.

"Walked around the Battery in the afternoon," read another diary entry, referring to the decaying fortress guarding the harbor entrance at the southern tip of Manhattan.

"Exercised with Mrs. Washington and the [grand] children," he wrote on another page.

"Went to St. Paul's Chapel in the forenoon," he wrote one Sunday.

"Wrote private letters in the afternoon."

On several days, Washington rode his horse in the morning before the family's midday meal, then spent afternoons walking from the presidential mansion to the Battery. After exploring the battlements, he returned home to read. One morning he accompanied Martha to an exhibition of

John Trumbull paintings, and on the next they rode off in the coach with the grandchildren again—this time for a picnic in the country.

Nor was the Constitution of any help. In creating the presidency, the framers had made every effort to prevent him from metamorphosing into another British-style monarch.

"The executive power shall be vested in a president of the United States of America," said the Constitution—without defining or identifying "executive power" or indicating what the President was to do with it other than "execute the office of president."

It mentioned how long he could serve, how he'd be elected, how he could be removed; it said he had to be "a natural born citizen" and that he'd be paid for his services. It even specified, word for word, the oath he had to take—but it gave him almost nothing to do. He was to be commander in chief of the armed forces "when called into action," but only Congress could call the armed forces into action—which left Washington commander in chief of nothing and no one when the nation was at peace. And the nation was now at peace, with no navy and a minuscule army of only 560 men and officers.

Other presidential powers—making treaties, appointing judges, executive department heads, and so forth—were similarly limited. The Constitutional Convention—and Washington himself—had made it clear that "the powers vested in the federal government are particularly defined," and that no federal official could exercise any power "not particularly delegated to the government of the United States." Thus, the Constitution ordered the President to "take care that the laws be faithfully executed" and to "preserve, protect, and defend the Constitution of the United States," but when he took office, there were no federal laws to execute—"faithfully" or otherwise—and had there been any to execute, the Constitution gave him no law-enforcement arm or powers to do so—or to arrest or punish miscreants.

In fact, the Constitution that he had been first to sign in Philadelphia two years earlier, in 1787, failed to give the president any measurable executive functions or aides to help him. He stood—or sat—alone as the entire executive branch of the new government. That had not been his intention. Indeed, his eight years leading the Continental Army had taught him that he needed more, not less power to govern and that he had come perilously close to losing the Revolutionary War because of his impotence as commander in chief. The Articles of Confederation—a constitution of sorts in effect during the Revolution and six years thereafter—gave him no powers to raise troops—or money to pay them. He could not deal with foreign powers to seek military or financial aid—or war against Indian tribes if they attacked his troops. He could not even appoint an aide, issue an order, or take a breath that was not subject to congressional oversight—and the result had been near-chaos that often left him flirting with defeat in the war for the nation's independence.

# CHAPTER ONE

❧

# *A Mutiny over Bounties*

High winds and bitter cold had paralyzed the nation; solid ice encased the island of Manhattan for the first time since white men had landed, while Chesapeake Bay froze from its head to the mouth of the Potomac. Washington's army was close to "dissolution or starving. . . .

"The soldiers eat every kind of horse food but hay," Washington had complained bitterly from his Morristown, New Jersey, quarters in January 1780. "Sometimes it has been five or six days together without bread . . . at other times as many days without meat, and once or twice two or three days without either."[1]

His appeals for relief from the Confederation Congress went unheeded. Washington—as furious as his troops—found it useless to explain to them that the Articles of Confederation the states had approved in 1777 for their "common defense" had failed to give the Continental Congress powers to tax the people for the moneys to feed the armies it put into the field. And the Articles left him, as commander in chief, powerless to do anything about it. Far from creating the "perpetual union" of its preamble, the Articles asserted that each state retained "its sovereignty, freedom and independence and every power, jurisdiction and right . . . not delegated to the United States"—including collection

13

of import duties, the largest single source of revenues in the Americas. States with the best port facilities, however, had a virtual monopoly on those revenues, and they vetoed every effort to force them to share their revenues with the Confederation—even if it meant starving the troops in the Continental Army. Virginia proposed a compromise with a federal tariff on imports limited to 5 percent and lasting only twenty-five years, with *all* federal receipts earmarked for wartime expenses. New York, however, rejected it, arguing that its effects would be patently unfair: States that bought the most imports would pay the most taxes, regardless of actual war debts, while states with the greatest war debts could pay the least taxes by simply reducing imports.

In the field, however, the army had little patience for the arguments of posturing politicians in Congress. After languishing for months with no pay and too little food and clothing, troops in Pennsylvania and New Jersey mutinied. "Officers and men have been almost perishing for want," Washington explained to New Jersey officials. "Their distress has in some instances prompted the men to commit depredations on the property of the inhabitants."[2]

With powers bordering on the mystical at times, Washington was able to calm the mutineers, appealing to them not to discard the "time, blood, and treasure" they had invested in the war. The British, he said, had "distressed millions, involved thousands in ruin, and plunged numberless families in inextricable woe." Calling the enemy "wantonly wicked and cruel," he rallied the army behind him and marched them southward to Virginia, where they joined a French army under General Rochambeau and encircled British forces at Yorktown. With a French fleet lurking offshore to block British escape by sea, the allied army, about 9,000 Americans and 7,800 Frenchmen, laid siege to the British fortifications. After an eight-day storm of shells had reduced Yorktown to rubble, the allied troops penetrated the outer British works. Two days later, on October 17, 1781, British commander Lord Charles Cornwallis sent a message to Washington under a flag of truce: "Sir,—

I propose a cessation of hostilities." And two days after that nearly 8,000 humiliated British soldiers laid down their arms as "prisoners of Congress."[3]

Although victory at Yorktown ended major fighting in America and forced British diplomats to the negotiating table, the peace talks dragged on for more than a year. Unable to disband until the British signed articles of peace, thousands of American troops remained in encampments, at the ready to resume fighting, but overwhelmed by boredom as diplomats in Paris tried working out acceptable peace arrangements.

Without money for adequate food or clothing, let alone amusement, they were as much "prisoners of Congress" as the British troops who had surrendered at Yorktown. When Congress failed to respond to an army ultimatum for overdue pay and adequate pensions, the troops resumed their mutiny—this time with the support of outraged officers, including General Horatio Gates, the celebrated commander at the Battle of Saratoga.

In Newburgh, New York, where most of Washington's Continental Army lay encamped, an unsigned leaflet appealed to officers to take up arms and lead the troops against Congress if and when Britain signed a peace agreement ending the war. If, on the other hand, Britain resumed fighting, the leaflet urged officers to abandon their posts and "set up a new state in the wilderness," thus leaving Congress and the coastal states defenseless.

"My God," Washington shuddered at what he saw as a call to treason. He ordered officers to assemble immediately, and, in a rare appearance by any commander in chief, he addressed them personally. After reading the letter aloud, he acknowledged the hardships officers and troops had faced, but called the contents of the letter "something so shocking that humanity revolts at the idea." He reminded officers that "I have never left your side one moment" and then pledged his name and honor that "you may command my services . . . in the attainment of complete justice for all your toils and dangers."

Washington knew he commanded the love and respect of his troops. He had, after all, served without pay and remained with them in camp through the most severe winters. Most officers in the world's armies routinely left their men in winter quarters and returned to the comforts of their own homes or suitably comfortable rented quarters. On March 15, 1783, he pleaded with them "to express your utmost horror and detestation of the man . . . who wickedly attempts to open the flood gates of civil discord and deluge our rising empire in blood."[4]

Washington paused, his eyes evidently faltering. He laid his paper down and fumbled in his pocket for a pair of glasses that evoked murmurs of surprise from his men. They had never seen him use an aid of any sort.

"Gentlemen," Washington's voice quavered. "You will permit me to put on my spectacles, for I have not only grown gray, but almost blind, in the service of my country."[5] All remembered the great warrior who had soared unscathed through storms of British shells on winged steed and inspired them to impossible acts of valor. In their minds, they could still hear his commands above the fray at Monmouth in June of '78: "Stand fast, my boys! Stand fast!" Shifting his horse to the right, the left, and rearing back, he charged at the British Redcoats—a vengeful titan risen from some netherworld.

"General Washington was never greater in battle," the French Major General Lafayette marveled as he rode back from battle. "His stately appearance on horseback, his calm, dignified courage . . . secured the victory."[6]

Almost five years had passed since Monmouth; the perils and privations of war had aged Washington noticeably as he stood before his officers in Newburgh. With his health apparently failing, a sadness crept into his voice, which captured their hearts. His address, said one officer, "with the mode and manner of delivering it, drew tears from [many] of the officers."[7] "He spoke," said another, "and the tide of patriotism rolled again in its wonted course." The mutiny ended with a unanimous resolution of confidence in Congress and an appeal to Washington that he represent the interests of all army officers in peace as he had in war.[8]

There was, however, little that Washington or Congress could do to ease the army's plight. In June 1783, a month after Congress ratified the provisional treaty of peace with Britain, soldiers in and around Philadelphia mutinied and, bayonets fixed, they marched to the doors of Philadelphia's Independence Hall. Unable to address the soldiers' demands, Congress fled to Princeton, New Jersey.

Washington fulfilled his promise to his officers with a blistering condemnation of Congress and the states for mismanaging the nation's finances during the war. In what was called "Washington's Legacy," he issued a 4,000-word "Circular to the States" demanding full payment of all debts to soldiers and officers, pensions equal to five years' pay for officers, and lifelong pensions for those "who have shed their blood or lost their limbs in the service of their country. . . .

"Nothing," he declared, "but a punctual payment of their annual allowance can rescue them from the most complicated misery . . . without a shelter, without a friend, and without the means of obtaining any of the necessaries or comforts of life; compelled to beg their daily bread from door to door." Warning that "the eyes of the whole world" were watching the United States, he also called on Congress to repay foreign and domestic creditors, declaring,

> This is the moment to establish or ruin our national character forever. This is the favorable moment to give such a tone to our Federal Government as will enable it to answer the ends of its institution or this may be the ill-fated moment for relaxing the powers of the Union, annihilating the cement of the Confederation, and exposing us to become the sport of European politics, which may play one state against another . . . to serve their own interested purposes.

Washington went on to demand that Congress and the states reform the Confederation, with the states ceding "a larger proportion of power to Congress" and creating "an indissoluble union of the states under one federal head." Failure to do so, he predicted, would "very rapidly tend to anarchy and confusion.

> It is indispensable . . . that there should be lodged somewhere a Supreme Power to regulate and govern the general concerns of the confederated republic, without which the Union cannot be of long duration. . . . There must be a faithful and pointed compliance on the part of every state with the demands of Congress, or the most fatal consequences will ensue. Whatever measures have a tendency to dissolve the Union, or contribute to violate or lessen the Sovereign Authority, ought to be considered as hostile to the liberty and independency of America, and the authors of them treated accordingly.[9]

As commander in chief of the Continental Army, Washington had near-dictatorial powers at the end of the Revolution. He could have seized control of government—with the support of many in Congress and most of the military. He chose instead to retire and trust in America's elected leaders to reform the government of the Confederation. He himself had tired of command and of governing others and longed to return home to his farm and family. Indeed he had promised his wife, Martha, he would be home for Christmas dinner—their first at home in nine years. Washington had remained with his troops during the winter cessation of hostilities since the first year of the war, and Martha—like the wives and sweethearts of the lowest-ranking soldiers—had dutifully appeared at winter encampments to bring a measure of comfort to her husband during the cold, lonely days of nonengagement—at Valley Forge, Morristown, and other ice-bound northern camps.

"I never in my life knew a woman so busy from early morning until late at night as was Lady Washington, providing comforts for the sick soldiers," one camp follower wrote. "Every day, excepting Sunday . . . knitting socks, patching garments and making shirts for the poor soldiers. . . . Every fair day she might be seen, with basket in hand, and

*General George Washington, commander of the
Continental Army.* (LIBRARY OF CONGRESS)

with a single attendant, going among the . . . most needy sufferers, and
giving all the comforts to them in her power."[10]

At noon on December 23, 1783, Washington strode into the Maryland State House in Annapolis to surrender his commission as commander in chief to Congress before a gallery packed with former officers,
public servants, relatives, and friends. Mutinous soldiers had chased
Congress form Philadelphia, and it had found a temporary refuge in
Annapolis.

"Sir," intoned President Thomas Mifflin, a prominent Philadelphia
merchant who had been a major general in the war, "the United States
in Congress assembled are prepared to receive your communications."

"Mr. President," Washington replied, "the great events on which my resignation depended having at length taken place; I have now the honor of offering my sincere Congratulations to Congress and of presenting myself before them to surrender into their hands the trust committed to me, and to claim the indulgence of retiring from the service of my country." As he recalled the "services and distinguished merits" of his officers and "the Gentlemen who have been attached to my person during the War," he choked with emotion and paused. Spectators held back their tears.

> Having now finished the work assigned me, I retire from the great theater of action; and bidding an affectionate farewell to this August body under whose orders I have so long acted, I here offer my commission, and take my leave of all employments of public life.[11]

Washington then "drew his commission from his bosom and handed it to the president." After Mifflin had replied, "the general bowed again to Congress . . . and retired. After a little pause . . . Congress adjourned. The general . . . bid every member farewell and rode off from the door, intent upon eating Christmas dinner at home."[12]

A few days later, Washington wrote to his friend Lafayette: "At last, my dear Marquis, I am become a private citizen on the banks of the Potomac and under the shadow of my own vine and fig tree, free from the bustle of camp and the busy scenes of public life. I am solacing myself with those tranquil enjoyments of which the soldier who is ever in pursuit of fame . . . can have very little conception. . . . Envious of none . . . I will move gently down the stream of life until I sleep with my fathers."[13]

As passionate as he was in his devotion to his family and farm, however, Washington's fear and abhorrence of social disorder would not let him ignore the turmoil and chaos engulfing the nation beyond the idyllic fields and forests of Mount Vernon. Neither Congress nor the states had been able or willing to respond to his "Circular to the States," and their failure became evident in the growing national unrest.

By emasculating Congress, the Articles of Confederation not only left the national government without funds, they all but bankrupted the nation by crippling foreign trade and the economy. Foreign nations that tried negotiating trade agreements with the "united" states found any agreement with Congress meaningless without agreements from each of the individual states through whose territory the goods would have to travel. Rather than negotiate so many separate agreements, overseas merchants simply stopped trading with the United States. America's foreign trade plunged 25 percent, while farm income, which depended on exports, dropped 20 percent.

"Persuaded I am that the primary cause of all our disorders lies in the different state governments," Washington wrote to his son-in-law David Stuart.

> Whilst independent sovereignty is so ardently contended for . . . incompatibility in the laws of different states and disrespect for those of the general government must render the situation of this great country weak, inefficient, and disgraceful. It has already done so, almost to the final dissolution of it—weak at home and disregarded abroad is our present condition, and contemptible enough it is.[14]

Britain compounded the young nation's economic woes by closing the British West Indies to American vessels, and blocking exports of lumber and foodstuffs to one of America's most lucrative markets. Spain strangled trade still more by banning American shipping on the Mississippi River, which had been the primary route for farmers and merchants west of the impenetrable Appalachian Mountains to ship goods to market.

Unlike Congress, individual states could levy import duties and property taxes—and send small armies of sheriffs to collect them. Indeed, political leaders in almost every state capital had quickly transformed the former colonies into independent fiefdoms after the Revolution, often enriching their own business interests and amassing personal fortunes from the flow of government revenues.

To retain control of government, they set excessively high property qualifications for voting and for holding office. South Carolina, for example, required assets of at least £10,000 (about $750,000 today)[15] to vote or stand for election. In the end, a small group of the most powerful northern merchant-bankers and southern plantation owners held a tight collective grip on the reins of their respective state governments. Their powers to tax and appoint sheriffs and judges gave state governors and their cronies in the legislatures control of trade, market prices, and lending rates—in effect, an economic stranglehold over shopkeepers, craftsmen, farmers, and every other group of working-class citizens.

Making matters worse—indeed, tragic for tens of thousands of the least affluent Americans—was the near-absence of money. The national government and state governments, along with most merchants, had exhausted their supplies of specie, or "hard" money—silver and gold coins, ingots, and so on—by the end of the war. They had spent most of it to buy arms and ammunition during the war and used up the rest buying badly needed imports immediately after. Forced to rely on barter, small farmers, craftsmen, and workers found themselves at an enormous disadvantage with merchants and other employers who bargained from a position of strength. The small farmer had to sell his perishables on market day for whatever price (or merchandise) he could get or watch his produce spoil.

Major merchants, on the other hand, could not only determine market prices at home, they could accumulate enough quantities of any given commodity to export by the shipload overseas and obtain specie in payment. The net result was to leave American farmers, who made up the vast majority of the population, with no money and a relatively small clique of wealthy merchants with hordes of gold and silver in their vaults.

Farmers, craftsmen, and other economically disenfranchised Americans—almost all debtors—demanded that their state governments print paper money for farmers to pay their taxes and debts.

Merchants—almost all of them creditors—opposed issuance of paper money and, in Rhode Island, many closed their shops rather than accept paper money that the state began issuing in the spring of 1786. When the legislature responded by making it illegal *not* to accept paper money, some merchants fled the state. Debtors rioted and broke into shops to force shopkeepers to accept paper money—all to no avail.

It was not long before discontent with state governments threatened to erupt into rebellion. Promised individual liberty and representative government when they went to war, war's end left many without money to pay their debts and often barred from voting and holding office by the same property qualifications that had disqualified them under British rule. Even more distressing, independent state governments levied far higher taxes than those of British colonial governments, which could count on British crown subsidies to cover many expenses.

Farmers—thousands of them veterans who had yet to be paid for wartime services—were first to rebel. Out of money, with no way of paying their assessments, most had no protection against government seizures of their properties for nonpayment of debts or taxes—and few ways to appeal. Indeed, most of the courts where lien holders filed claims were usually in far-off cities along the Atlantic Coast; by the time most farmers inland could appear, the courts had already declared them in default and sent sheriffs to seize their properties.

Hundreds of farmers saw their lands and homes confiscated and their livestock and personal possessions—including tools of their trade—auctioned at prices too low to clear their debts. Hysterical wives and terrified children watched helplessly as sheriffs' deputies dragged farmers off to debtors' prisons, where they languished indefinitely—unable to earn money to pay their debts and without the tools to do so even if they obtained release. Printer Isaiah Thomas, who had fought as a Minuteman at Lexington and Concord before starting the *Massachusetts Spy*, reported prisoners dying in small, damp, moldy cells of a Massachusetts debtors' prison—"a place which disgraces humanity." Samuel Ely, a Massachusetts farmer, testified of his suffering "boils and putrefied sores all over my body and they make me stink alive, besides having some of my feet froze which makes it difficult to walk."[16]

Enraged farmers across the nation took up rifles and pitchforks to protect their properties, firing at sheriffs and others who ventured too near. Reassembling their wartime companies, they set fire to prisons, courthouses, and offices of county clerks. New Hampshire farmers marched to the state capital at Exeter, surrounded the legislature, and demanded forgiveness of all debts, return of all seized properties to former owners, and equitable distribution of property. A mob of farmers in Maryland burned down the Charles County courthouse, while farmers in Virginia burned down the King William and New Kent county courthouses.

In western Massachusetts, former captain Daniel Shays, a destitute farmer struggling to hold onto his property, convinced his neighbors that local lawyers and judges had conspired with Boston merchants, bankers, and state legislators to raise taxes and seize farms for nonpayment. Calling on farmers to "close down the courts!" Shays led a force of five hundred men to Springfield to shut the state supreme court and seize the federal arsenal. As his cry echoed across the state, farmers marched to courthouses in Cambridge, Concord, Worcester, Northampton, Taunton, and Great Barrington—and shut them all down.

"The commotions . . . have risen in Massachusetts to an alarming height," Virginia's congressional delegate Henry ("Light-Horse Harry") Lee wrote to Washington from the Confederation capital in New York. "After various insults to government, by stopping the courts of justice etc., the insurgents have taken possession of the town of Springfield. . . . This event produces much suggestion as to its causes. Some attribute it to the weight of taxes and the decay of commerce . . . others, to British councils."[17]

As rumors spread that British spies and provocateurs were behind the farmer uprisings, Congress grew alarmed and urged Lee to seek help from Washington, who remained the living symbol of national unity. As Lee explained to the former commander in chief,

> A majority of the people of Massachusetts are in opposition to the government and their leaders *avow* the *subversion* of it to be their object together with the abolition of debts, the division of property and reunion with Great Britain. In all the eastern states, the same temper prevails. . . . The malcontents are in close connection with Vermont, and that district . . . is in negotiation with the Governor of Canada. My dear General, we are all in dire apprehension that a beginning of anarchy . . . has approached and have no means to stop the dreadful work.[18]

Lee proposed calling a convention of state leaders "for the sole purpose of revising the Confederation" to permit Congress to act "with more energy, effect, and vigor."[19] To everyone's amazement, even Patrick Henry, Virginia's first governor and patron saint of state sovereignty, agreed. Henry now predicted that "ruin is inevitable unless something is done to give Congress a compulsory process on delinquent states."[20]

Learning of Henry's declaration, Washington grew optimistic: "Notwithstanding the jealous and contracted temper which seems to prevail in some of the states, I cannot but hope and believe that the good sense of the people will ultimately get the better of their prejudices."[21]

As popular dissatisfaction with government swelled, a surge in land speculation added to the national disarray by provoking territorial disputes between the states. New York and New Hampshire were ready to go to war over conflicting claims to lands in Vermont; Virginia and Pennsylvania both claimed sovereignty over lands in present-day western Pennsylvania and Kentucky; Massachusetts claimed all of western New York; and Connecticut prepared to send its militia into Pennsylvania after Pennsylvania militiamen fired on Connecticut farmers who had claimed vacant lands in the Wyoming Valley of northeastern Pennsylvania.

In addition to territorial disputes, six states were involved in fierce economic disputes over international trade. Maryland and Virginia each claimed their borders lay across the Potomac River on the opposite shoreline, thus giving each the right to collect fees and duties from ships traveling the waterway.

Farther north, states with deep-water ports such as Philadelphia, New York, and Boston were bleeding the economies of neighboring states with heavy duties on imports that passed through their harbors on their way to inland destinations. "New Jersey, placed between Philadelphia and New York, is like a cask tapped at both ends," complained James Madison, another Virginia delegate in Congress, "and North Carolina, between Virginia and South Carolina seems a patient bleeding at both arms."[22]

Other factors such as geography and language also contributed to the nation's internal frictions. Philadelphia, the nation's largest and most important cultural and commercial center, lay more than three days' travel from the national capital in New York, about ten days from Boston, and all but inaccessible from far-off cities such as Richmond or Charleston during various times of year. Foul winter weather and spring rains isolated parts of the country for many months each year and made establishment of close cultural ties difficult at best and often impossible. In many respects, the South—and southerners—was as foreign to most New Hampshiremen as China and the Chinese. Indeed, only 60 percent of Americans had English origins. The rest were Dutch, French, German, Scottish, Scotch-Irish, Irish, and even Swedish. Although English remained the common tongue after independence, German prevailed in much of eastern Pennsylvania, Dutch along the Hudson River Valley, French in Vermont and parts of New Hampshire and what would later become Maine. As early as 1750, Benjamin Franklin complained that Germantown was engulfing Philadelphia and that Pennsylvania "will in a few years become a German colony. Instead of learning our language, we must learn theirs, or live as in a foreign country."[23]

With Congress impotent and New York City so distant, delegates to the Confederation Congress from far-off states appeared only intermittently. A few states even stopped appointing delegates. When Congress did meet, its members often had little in common and barely fathomed each other's thinking. Without money or means to raise any, Congress stopped repaying principal and interest on foreign debts, disbanded the American navy, and reduced the army to a mere eighty privates.[24]

Secretary of War Henry Knox, who had been a major general in the Revolutionary War and Washington's chief of artillery from their early days in Cambridge in 1775, warned his old friend,

> Different states have . . . views that sooner or later must involve the Country in all the horrors of civil war. A neglect in every state of those principles which lead to union and national greatness—an adoption of local in preference to general measures appears to actuate the greater part of the state politicians. We are entirely destitute of those traits which should stamp us *one Nation*, and the Constitution of Congress does not promise any alteration.[25]

Knox's letter alerted Washington to the likelihood of a bloody civil war and that he was probably the only man in America who might prevent it. Although he despised deviousness in others, he would have to use all his wiles and those of his most trusted friends to trick state leaders into ceding their powers to the central government.

❦

## CHAPTER TWO

# A Coup d'État in Philadelphia

Although Washington had stepped off center stage of public life at the end of 1783, he could not resist slipping into the prompter's box the following summer as his concerns mounted over "the disorders engulfing the nation." Clearly, the freedom engendered by independence from Britain had failed to produce the utopian republic Washington had envisioned. With Americans apparently unable to govern themselves, he hinted at his possible return to the political theater in a letter to his friend Virginia Governor Benjamin Harrison:

"The disinclination of the individual states to yield competent powers to Congress, their unreasonable jealousy of that body and of one another . . . will, if there is not a change in the system, be our downfall as a nation."[1]

He invited Harrison to visit Mount Vernon with Mrs. Harrison, who was Martha's cousin by marriage. Their visit inspired Washington to write to political leaders in other states to goad them into more responsible behavior.

For several years, Washington had envisioned organizing a project to build a gigantic transportation route linking the Ohio River Valley to Chesapeake Bay. By building a series of canals, waterways, and portages, the project would tie the headwaters of the Potomac River on the east slope of the Appalachians to the headwaters of the Monongahela River on the west slope, where it flows to the Allegheny River to form the Ohio River. The connection would allow grain, furs, pelts, and the wealth of the West, where Washington owned 100,000 fertile acres, to travel quickly to East Coast ports and trade routes to Europe, eliminating the long trip down the Mississippi River and across the Gulf of Mexico. He believed that the huge waterway would yield its investors enormous profits and spur an economic boom that would unite the nation with unbreakable economic, geophysical, and political bonds and end the tax riots and interstate border disputes that threatened to erupt into anarchy and civil war. The Potomac River waterway project had taken on even more significance in 1784, when Spanish authorities in New Orleans closed the lower Mississippi River to American shipping.

"Extend the inland navigation of the Eastern waters with those that run to the westward," Washington explained, "open these to the Ohio and Lake Erie, we shall not only draw the produce of western settlers, but the fur and peltry trade to our ports, to the amazing increase of our exports, while we bind those people to us by a chain that can never be broken."[2]

Knowing that states bordering the waterways stood to prosper most, Washington invited four political leaders each from Maryland and Virginia to confer near Mount Vernon at Alexandria, Virginia, in March 1785. A few weeks later, the two states agreed to join in funding the project and named Washington its president. The two states went beyond expectations by adopting uniform commercial regulations and a uniform currency—in effect, establishing a commercial union. In but a few months, Washington had succeeded in organizing the greatest public works project in North American history and, more importantly, uniting two states that had been ready to war with each other over rights to the very waterway they would now develop together.

But Washington's vision was wider: "We are either a united people or we are not," Washington asserted to James Madison, who had served for three years as a Virginia delegate in the Confederation Congress. "If the former, let us, in all matters of general concern act as a nation which has national objects to promote and a national character to support. If we are not, let us no longer act a farce by pretending to it."[3]

Responding to Washington's plea, Madison urged Virginia's legislature to expand the scope of its waterway agreement by inviting all states to participate in a convention the following year, in September 1786, at Annapolis, Maryland. Although delegates from only five states showed up on time, they called for a second, more substantial convention in Philadelphia, in May 1787. The Confederation Congress agreed and gave its official sanction to a convention of delegates from the thirteen states that was to meet in secret "for the sole and express purpose of revising the Articles of Confederation . . . [to] render the federal constitution, adequate to the exigencies of government and the preservation of the union."[4]

Washington had other, farther-reaching ideas, however. He favored nothing less than scrapping the Articles of Confederation and writing a new constitution to create a powerful national government with "legislative, executive and judiciary departments concentered."[5]

---

In contrast to the anonymity of many other delegates who drifted into Philadelphia unnoticed, cannons fired continuously and church bells pealed their welcome as Washington rode into the city on May 13, 1787. A committee of three generals, two colonels, and two majors who had served under him in the Revolutionary War had met him at Chester, Pennsylvania, earlier that morning, and, after a festive luncheon and appropriate toasts, they escorted him to a hero's welcome at the Philadelphia city line. With a chorus of huzzas, hundreds of mounted citizens awaited with the City Light Horse to greet the general and lead him through cheering throngs to the Pennsylvania State House,* where the great convention was to assemble the following morning.

---

*Now Independence Hall.

*The Pennsylvania State House, Philadelphia, where the Second Continental Congress met on July 4, 1776, and declared independence from Britain.*

"The joy of the people on the coming of this great and good man," the *Pennsylvania Packet* reported, "was shown by their acclamations and the ringing of bells." Although gentle of voice, he was an intimidating figure—a near-giant at six feet, three inches tall, 200 pounds, soldier-straight, towering above most people of his era. Several years at Mount Vernon had restored his health and soldierly bearing. Enhancing his physical stature was the aura of his legendary exploits—his superb horsemanship, his courage in battle, his genius as a military commander and entrepreneur.

First and foremost in the pantheon of American heroes, Washington was not only the most revered figure in America, he was one of the wealthiest. His estate included more than 120,000 acres in eastern and western Virginia, more than 300 slaves, and a vast agro-industrial enterprise of 20,000 productive acres in and about Mount Vernon. "I fancy," said a visitor to Mount Vernon, "he is worth £100,000 sterling [$6 million today], and lives at the rate of three or four thousand a year [between $200,000 and $250,000 today]."[6]

By the time the convention got under way, Washington had virtually shredded the instructions of Congress, and few delegates dared oppose him at first. All knew his temper: Three dozen of the fifty-five delegates had served under him in the Revolutionary War—four of them as close personal aides. Seven other delegates had served with him in the Continental Congress of 1774 or 1775 or both. Everyone at the convention revered him as father of their country and progenitor of their individual liberties, but as much as they revered him, they feared him in the sense that most sons fear a powerful father.

All knew Washington could have seized power as a military dictator during the Revolutionary War. Although he had opted to retire to "the shadow of my own vine and fig tree," the tens of thousands of tax protesters across the nation—almost all veterans of his army—stood prepared to rally around him if he opted to reverse his decision and seize power. To no one's surprise, delegates unanimously elected him convention president. Few, if any, could match his broad knowledge or vast experience in public life, and, whether impelled to vote for him by reverence or fear, all knew he was the only man qualified for the job.

Washington had spent eight years as a member of Virginia's House of Burgesses and was thoroughly familiar with convention procedures, rules of order, and the legislative process. Unlike other delegates, he came to the convention with a grasp of virtually every issue facing not just his own state and region but the entire nation and, indeed, the western world. As a surveyor in his youth, then as an officer in and commander of the Virginia militia, and finally, as commander in chief of the Continental Army, he had traveled the length and breadth of the nation as few other Americans of any station had done—from the streets of Boston to the Ohio River Valley wilderness. As commander in chief, he had worked with subordinates from all parts of the nation and coordinated grand military strategies with commanders of every state militia and with the French army and navy. An obsessive autodidact, he alone came to the convention with a vast knowledge of history, law, economics, agriculture, national and international commerce, foreign affairs, and military affairs. His library at Mount Vernon was legendary, with more than 1,000 works on law, economics, history, international affairs, political science, natural science, agriculture, literature, and more, from which he could quote almost at will.

Washington had studied crown law, criminal law, libel laws, property law, bankruptcy laws, the laws of nations, the laws regarding war and peace—and all the laws of the United States and each of the states. Complementing his law books were more than fifty books on history— among others, Gibbon's six-volume *History of the Decline and Fall of the Roman Empire*—and more than sixty on political science and economics, including well-worn copies of John Locke's *On Human Understanding* and Adam Smith's then-new, three-volume *Inquiry into the Nature and Causes of the Wealth of Nations*. All contained ample marginal notes in Washington's own handwriting to testify to his having studied their contents. Nor did the range of his knowledge stop with the practical. Over the years, he had accumulated seventy works of literature—all Shakespeare's plays among them, along with Joseph Addison's *The Tragedy of Cato*, Laurence Sterne's *Tristram Shandy*, Homer's *Iliad* and *Odyssey*, Alexander Pope's works, Voltaire's letters, and endless books of poetry and literary periodicals.

"His mind was great and powerful," Thomas Jefferson, would recall years later, "though not so acute as that of a Newton, Bacon, or Locke."[7] John Adams, who would serve as vice president during both of Washington's two terms in office, listed Washington's "talents" in order as "genius, experience, learning, fortune, birth, health."[8]

As he gaveled the convention to order, no one outside his own Virginia delegation knew his plan of action, but all soon found out. He recognized Virginia Governor Edmund Randolph, who had been his aide in Cambridge, Massachusetts, at the beginning of the Revolutionary War. Randolph presented a scheme of government that shocked the convention and left most delegates in stunned silence. The "Virginia Plan," as they called it, urged scrapping the Articles of Confederation in favor of a new constitution with a strong new national government made up of three "supreme" branches: a legislature, an executive, and a judiciary.

South Carolina's Charles Pinckney, a Revolutionary War hero and prominent attorney, shot up from his seat, demanding to know whether Randolph "meant to abolish state government altogether."[9] Pinckney's second cousin, the equally prominent Charles Cotesworth Pinckney—also an attorney and war hero—all but shouted that "the act of Congress recommending the Convention" did not "authorize a discussion of a system founded on different principles from the Federal Constitution [i.e., the Articles of Confederation]." The Virginia plan, he argued, violated the mandate of Congress to "revise" the Articles of Confederation. To violate that mandate would represent a usurpation of authority not granted by Congress or the Articles of Confederation.[10]

Elbridge Gerry, a Massachusetts merchant who had signed the Declaration of Independence, agreed, protesting that

> it is questionable not only whether this Convention can propose a government totally different or whether Congress itself would have a right to pass such a resolution as that before the house. The commission from Massachusetts empowers the deputies to proceed agreeably to the recommendation of Congress. This is the foundation of the convention. If we have a right to pass this resolution [the Virginia Plan] we have a right to annihilate the confederation.[11]

Scattered applause greeted Gerry, as delegates suddenly realized that Washington and the Virginians had redefined the mission of the convention and indeed intended to "annihilate the Confederation"—in secret, without the public's knowledge, let alone approval. Most delegates

*Elbridge Gerry of Massachusetts opposed George Washington's plans to write a constitution creating a new type of federal government.* (LIBRARY OF CONGRESS)

had voted to keep proceedings secret—not to undermine the existing government, but to allow delegates to speak more openly and change their minds on different issues without fear of political reprisal for ignoring local in favor of national interests. The Virginians, however, had taken advantage of the secrecy rule to violate the mandate of Congress and propose what amounted to a bloodless coup d'état to replace the old government with a new "supreme" national government.

Enraged delegates immediately attacked the plan, calling it nothing less than a revolution. In the days that followed, they argued about every resolution and almost every word and punctuation mark, including whether to include the word "supreme" in the phrase "supreme Legislative, Executive and Judiciary." The explosive question of how many votes to give each state in each house left big states and small states outraged at each other. All states agreed on proportionate representation for the lower house, but big states favored the same in the upper house. Irate delegates from small states charged that the three states with the largest populations—Virginia, Pennsylvania, and Massachusetts—would be able to outvote and therefore control the rest of the country. They demanded parity, with the same one-state, one-vote system of the Confederation Congress. Now it was the turn of delegates from heavily populated states to express outrage, charging that a one-state, one-vote system would give eight small states, with a total population smaller than Virginia's alone, the power to dictate to the majority of the American people.

Delaware's delegates charged big states with trying to "crush the smaller states" and threatened to walk out of the convention before submitting to proportionate representation in both houses. Indeed, tiny Rhode Island had refused even to send delegates to the convention.

"Sooner than be ruined," a Delaware delegate cried out, his government would find "foreign powers who shall take us by hand. I say this not to threaten or intimidate, but that we should reflect seriously before we act."[12]

Adding to the intensity of the debate was the question of whether to include blacks in the population count that would determine the number of votes each state would have in Congress under proportionate representation. "Why," Elbridge Gerry demanded, "should the blacks, who are property in the South, be in the rule of representation more than the cattle and horses of the North?"[13] Rufus King, also of Massachusetts, protested that the four New England States had more white people than the southern states combined. If slaves were included in the population count, however, a handful of southern planters who own most of the slaves would have more congressional representatives than the entire New England population. "No principle would justify giving them [the southern states] a majority."[14]

When Pennsylvania's Quaker delegate introduced the word "abolition" into the debate, former South Carolina Governor John Rutledge, the owner of a great plantation and a hero of the Revolution, threatened to walk out. "The true question at present," he warned, "is whether the Southern States shall or shall not be parties to the Union. If the northern states consult their interest, they will not oppose the increase of slaves which will increase the commodities of which they will become the carriers."[15]

The convention also divided on whether to invest executive powers in one man or several. Veering away from Washington's point of view, Virginia Governor Edmund Randolph called a single executive the "fetus of monarchy," while South Carolina's Charles Pinckney agreed that a one-man executive would render the office "a monarchy of the worst kind";[16] Gerry of Massachusetts also favored a multiple executive, saying that "a Council [would] give weight and inspire confidence."[17]

"The *mode of appointing* the executive was the next question,"[18] Madison noted, as Pennsylvania's Scottish-born James Wilson called for popular elections, but balked at the question of appropriate pay for such a figure. Too weakened by age and gout to stand, Benjamin Franklin nonetheless gained recognition and gave his speech to Wilson to read. Franklin argued for limiting executive pay to "necessary expenses" and not paying any "salary, stipend, fee, or reward whatsoever for their services. . . .

> Sir, there are two passions which have a powerful influence on the affairs of men . . . the love of power and the love of money. . . . [but] have we not seen, the most important of our offices, that of general of our armies executed for eight years together without the smallest salary, by a patriot whom I will not now offend by any other praise. . . .* And shall we doubt finding three or four other men in all the United States, with public spirit enough to bear sitting in peaceful council for perhaps

---

*George Washington had refused "pecuniary consideration" as commander in chief during the Revolutionary War, asserting to Congress, "I do not wish to make any profit from . . . this arduous employment" (Address to the Continental Congress, June 16, 1775).

*Benjamin Franklin supported the new Constitution. "With all its faults," he said, "there is no form of government but what may be a blessing to the people if well administered."*
(LIBRARY OF CONGRESS)

an equal term, merely to . . . see that our laws are duly executed. Sir, I have a better opinion of our country. I think we shall never be without sufficient number of wise and good men to undertake and execute well the office in question.[19]

As the debate raged over the shape of the new government, delegates grew increasingly mean-spirited, often losing their tempers—and almost their sanity. They rejected good motions, yielded to bad ones, postponed both good and bad. As the process of the Convention spiraled into the same abyss of futility that had emasculated the Confederation Congress, Washington, New York's Alexander Hamilton, Virginia's James Madison, and others stepped in to calm the atmosphere.

"This country must be united," pleaded Pennsylvania's Gouverneur Morris, a close friend of Washington. "If persuasion does not unite it, the sword will," he warned. "The scenes of horror attending civil commotion can not be described, and the conclusion of them will be worse. . . . The stronger party will then make traitors of the weaker; and the gallows and halter will finish the work of the sword."[20]

A puzzling figure to many, Morris had been born and raised in luxury on his father's baronial estate, which covered most of what is now the Bronx, the huge borough just north of Manhattan Island on the New York mainland. A graduate of King's (now Columbia) College and a lawyer, Morris had opposed independence at first, but eventually adopted a moderate stance favoring both independence and tolerance towards loyalists. In 1777, he won election as a New York delegate to the Continental Congress, where he helped draft a 1778 declaration that made American independence the price that Britain would have to pay for peace. Although his obsessive, public pursuit of women cost him reelection to Congress in New York in 1779, he remained in Philadelphia and won election as a Pennsylvania delegate to the Constitutional Convention. Clearly annoyed at the increasingly bitter exchanges, he urged delegates to "take out the teeth of the serpents" and adopt a nationalist point of view in what he called "the true interest of man. . . . Who can say whether he himself, much less whether his children, will the next year be an inhabitant of this or that State."[21]

Hamilton took a different, more pedantic approach, lecturing to the delegates as if to schoolchildren: "The general power, whatever be its form, if it preserves itself, it must swallow up the state powers. Otherwise it will be swallowed up by them. . . . Two sovereign powers cannot co-exist within the same limits. . . . Give all power to the many, they will oppress the few; give all power to the few, they will oppress the many."[22]

*Gouverneur Morris of Pennsylvania was the brilliant wordsmith who penned the preamble to the Constitution, beginning, "We, the people of the United States, in order to form a more perfect union . . . "* (LIBRARY OF CONGRESS)

In the end, Washington brought the convention to heel. "Every state has some objection," he barked in frustration. "That which is most pleasing to one is obnoxious to another and vice versa. If then the union of the whole is a desirable object, the parts which compose it must yield a little in order to accomplish it. . . . There are seeds of discontent in every part of the Union ready to produce disorders if . . . the present Convention should not be able to devise . . . a more vigorous and energetic government."[23]

With the convention stalemated over congressional voting, a few delegates walked out in disgust and went home. Two of the three New York delegates quit after New York Governor George Clinton called the proceedings an illegal usurpation of power. Roger Sherman, the mayor of New Haven, Connecticut, calmed the remaining delegates by proposing what seemed a fair compromise on the voting issue: "Let voting in the lower house be proportionate to each state's population, and give each state parity . . . in the upper house. Otherwise a few large states will rule. The smaller states would never agree to a plan on any other principle than an equality of suffrage in this branch."[24]

A majority of delegates agreed and went on to propose "a national government . . . consisting of a supreme Legislative, Executive and Judiciary," with the national legislature consisting of two branches: a popularly elected lower house and an upper house elected by state legislatures. Each state in the lower house would cast votes proportionate to the total of its free population and three-fifths of its slave population, while each state in the upper house would have two votes. They gave the national legislature almost all the powers of the British Parliament—namely, to tax the people directly without consent of state legislatures; to raise troops for a federal force; to declare war; and to enact any laws it deemed "necessary and proper." All national laws would "negative" all state laws that contravened the federal constitution. They barred states from printing or coining money, giving all such powers to the federal government, and, to keep the South in the Union, the North agreed to prevent Congress from interfering with the importation of slaves for twenty years.

The convention decided on a one-man executive chosen by electors appointed by state legislatures. Although he could serve for an indefinite number of four-year terms—a condition that seemed to open the way for him to turn tyrant—the other conditions of his service left him little more than a figurehead. Although it named him commander in chief, it gave Congress sole powers to declare war, raise troops, or send soldiers into action. Although it charged him with faithfully executing the laws,

*Roger Sherman, the mayor of New Haven, Connecticut, was master of the art of compromise at the Constitutional Convention, suggesting the solution to the conflict between large states and small states over voting in the new Congress.* (LIBRARY OF CONGRESS)

it gave him no evident enforcement powers to do so. In token obeisance to Washington's stature as a national icon, delegates gave him a veto over legislation, but empowered the legislature to override his veto by a two-thirds majority. It allowed him to propose candidates for judgeships and key executive posts, but placed approval of such appointments in the hands of the Senate and gave him no authority over appointees once they assumed office.

Some scholars today suggest that the convention's failure to "carefully define and limit the executive power" stemmed from recognition that "they could not see the future" and wanted to give the president wide latitude to act "with speed, decision and vigor to guide the nation through war and emergency."[25] Their argument, however, ignores the clear assertions of almost all the signers, including George Washington, that the federal government had no "latitude to act" beyond those specifically granted by the Constitution. As Connecticut's Roger Sherman put it, "The powers vested in the federal government are particularly defined, so that each state still retains its sovereignty . . . and a right to exercise every power of a sovereign state not particularly delegated to the government of the United States."[26]

Apparently satisfied with the shape of the legislative and executive branches, the convention went on to create a national judiciary consisting of "one supreme tribunal" and gave the national legislature the option of creating lower courts at its discretion. A proposal that judges be appointed for life on condition of "good behavior" drew no objections, but the question of appointment—by the legislature or by the executive—provoked a heated debate. Franklin tried to respond, but found it still too painful to rise from his seat. Again, he gave his comments to Wilson, to read in his amusing Scottish brogue.

Lifetime appointments of judges, said Wilson in Franklin's words, were working well in Scotland, where "the nomination proceeded from the lawyers, who always selected the ablest member of their profession" to serve as a judge—"in order to get rid of him and share his practice among themselves."[27] After the roars of laughter subsided, delegates approved lifetime appointments for the Supreme Court. Twenty-nine of the forty-two remaining delegates at the convention were lawyers.

Delegates found something to debate to the very last day, including how many states should ratify the Constitution for it to take effect among those states. Maryland argued for all thirteen, but Pennsylvania's Wilson retorted, "It would be worse than folly to rely on the concurrence of the Rhode Island members of Congress in the plan. . . . After spending four or five months in the laborious and arduous task of forming a Government for our country, we are ourselves at the close throwing insuperable obstacles in the way of success."[28]

As Washington drummed his huge, impatient fingers on his desk, delegates compromised by requiring ratification of the Constitution by nine states for it to take effect.

Before the debate ended, Elbridge Gerry of Massachusetts moved for a committee to prepare a bill of rights to protect freedom of speech, freedom of the press, and other individual rights. Virginia planter George Mason—a neighbor of Washington—hailed the proposal and seconded. Connecticut's Roger Sherman argued that most states protected individual rights in ways that obviated the need for a federal bill of rights. Seven states already had bills of rights in their constitutions, and, although five had established state religions, every state protected freedom of religious choice. Every state guaranteed the right to trial by jury in criminal cases, and eleven states guaranteed freedom of the press. Eight states protected freedom of assembly, although only three guaranteed the right of free speech. Sherman concluded, "The immediate security of the civil and domestic rights of the people will be in the government of the particular states. State declarations of rights are not repealed by this constitution, and being in force are sufficient."[29]

As written, he added, the Constitution did not delegate any authority to the federal government to establish a state religion or to abridge freedom of speech or the press, or limit the right of peaceable assembly, and there was, therefore, no need to impose limits on nonexistent powers. Mason, however, scoffed at Sherman's arguments, asserting that the power of Congress to pass any laws it deemed "necessary and proper" to the fulfillment of its constitutional obligations might mean passage of laws limiting individual rights, and if it did so, the Constitution made "the laws of the United States . . . paramount to state bills of rights." He then issued his famous pledge to "chop off my right hand" rather than sign the Constitution as it had been written.[30]

Mason's appeal provoked a roar in the convention hall, as delegates turned to each other to argue for or against the Gerry/Mason proposal for a bill of rights. Connecticut's Oliver Ellsworth found it ironic that Mason would champion a bill of rights. "Mr. Mason has himself about

*George Mason, the wealthy Virginia planter whose properties neighbored those of George Washington, refused to sign the Constitution, declaring, "I would sooner chop off my right hand" than sign the document before it included a bill of rights guaranteeing individual liberties.* (LIBRARY OF CONGRESS)

three hundred slaves, and lives in Virginia, where it is found by prudent management they can breed and raise slaves faster than they want for their own use, and could supply the deficiency in Georgia and South Carolina."[31] Virginia Governor Edmund Randolph added to the turmoil by announcing that he, too, had broken with George Washington and would join Gerry and Mason in refusing to sign the document.

Clearly angry at the defections by members of his own delegation, Washington had the presence to regain control of the convention before it deteriorated any further. Without allowing any more debate, he put the Gerry motion to an immediate vote and ten states voted to quash it, with Massachusetts, Gerry's home state, abstaining.

Before delegates could resume the debates, Benjamin Franklin decided to end the proceedings. Struggling to rise with a speech in hand, he again found it too painful to proceed and handed the paper to Wilson. Whether or not the two Federalists had rehearsed the scene, it made for effective drama that drew the attention of every delegate. "Mr. President," Wilson mouthed Franklin's words,

> I confess there are several parts of this constitution which I do not at present approve, but I am not sure I shall ever approve them. The older I get, the more apt I am to doubt my own judgment, and to pay more respect to the judgment of others. Most men indeed as well as most sects in religion, think themselves in possession of all truth and that wherever others differ from them it is so far error. Steele a Protestant . . . tells the Pope that the only difference between our churches in . . . the certainty of the doctrines is the Church of Rome is infallible and the Church of England is never wrong.

Franklin went on to proclaim his support for the constitution "with all its faults . . . because I think a general government necessary for us, and there is no form of government but what may be a blessing to the people if well administered." He said he doubted whether another convention could write a better constitution.

"Thus, I consent, Sir, to this constitution because I expect no better, and because I am not sure it is not the best."[32]

Only thirty-nine of the forty-two delegates signed the Constitution, although Gouverneur Morris's disingenuous statement at the top of the signatures—"Done in Convention by the Unanimous Consent of the States present"—used the unanimity of one-state-one-vote balloting to mask divisions between delegates within many states.

Even Washington, who was first to sign the document, was less than pleased. "I wish the constitution . . . had been more perfect," he admitted, "but I sincerely believe it is the best that could be obtained at this

time. And, as a constitutional door is opened for amendments here-
after, the adoption of it . . . is in my opinion desirable."[33]

The Constitution was admittedly a compromise. The men who
wrote it came from every part of the country and represented conflicting interests—farmers vs. merchant-bankers, big states vs. little states,
northern vs. southern states, easterners vs. westerners, slave holders vs.
opponents of slavery. Someone invariably wanted some power that deprived someone else of power. Convention delegates eventually resolved
some of their differences. Instead of majority rule, as in a democracy,
the Constitution created a republican government that bowed to majority rule in one house of the legislature, while protecting the rights of
the minority in the other by giving each state two votes, regardless of its
size or population. In the end, every state won something and no state
won everything it wanted.

Even Washington was unable to obtain most of his major goals. Although the Constitution gave the national legislature powers to tax
Americans directly to pay for national defense and to raise an army to
defend the nation, it failed to create a powerful executive—a "federal
head," as Washington called it. After decades of perceived oppression
by an autocratic British monarch and his often megalomaniacal royal
governors, convention delegates created a union with what seemed to
be a relatively impotent chief executive.

As written, the Constitution severely restricted the president's authority over the military, his participation in foreign affairs, and his
overall executive authority. Although commander in chief, he could not
declare war, raise troops, or send them into action. The troops would
be his to command only *"when called into action"* by Congress. Although the Constitution entitled him to make treaties, he could only
negotiate with the *advice* of two-thirds of the Senate and convert the
finished treaty into law with the *consent* of two-thirds of the Senate.

Although the Constitution directed the President to "take care that
the laws be faithfully executed," his inability to raise troops left him

powerless to do so. And in one of the most curious "powers" assigned to the President, he was to appoint judges and other important government officials—but again, only with the *advice* and *consent* of the Senate. Although chief executive, he would have little executive authority over his appointees—and no specific power to discipline or dismiss them once they took office.

As written, the Constitution would have left the heads of key executive departments—finance, war, foreign affairs, and so forth—serving indefinitely, as judges would, until their retirement or removal for cause by Congress—and they would have been responsible to Congress—that is, "We the People"—rather than to the President.

The finished document cloaked differences—some of them bitter differences—between individual delegates at the convention with a paean of joyous unanimity crafted by the brilliant, if disingenuous, wordsmith Gouverneur Morris of Pennsylvania:

WE, THE PEOPLE OF THE UNITED STATES, in Order to form a more perfect Union, establish Justice, insure domestic Tranquility, provide for the common defence, promote the general Welfare, and secure the Blessings of Liberty to ourselves and our Posterity, do ordain and establish this Constitution for the United States of America.

What followed were seven articles, with the first three defining the shape and powers of the national legislature, the executive, and the judiciary and the methods of selection and qualifications for serving (and removal) in each. It gave Congress, *inter alia*, powers to raise taxes and levy duties, borrow money, regulate foreign and interstate commerce, maintain a standing army and navy, and declare war. It gave the President power to make treaties with the advice and consent of the Senate, and it stripped the states of rights to deal with foreign nations. Article IV forced the states to recognize each other's laws and to give all citizens the rights of citizenship in every state.

*One of the engrossed (handwritten) copies of the Constitution that was approved by the Constitutional Convention and sent to the legislatures of the thirteen colonies for ratification.* (LIBRARY OF CONGRESS)

The same article also provided for admission of new states and guaranteed establishment of "a republican form of government" in each. Article V provided for amending the Constitution, and Article VI ranked laws by category. The Constitution and U.S. laws and treaties ranked as "the supreme law of the land," and local laws ranked lowest, with little or no consequence for the rest of the nation. Article VII required approval by ratification conventions in nine states for the Constitution to take effect among those states and create a new national government.

After signing the Constitution and sending it on to the Confederation Congress, Washington returned to Mount Vernon—clearly fatigued by the trial of keeping peace among squabbling delegates. Left with but one tooth, his lower jaw in pain from ill-fitting tooth implants, shoulders and hips racked by arthritis, the fifty-five-year-old Virginian seemed intent on resuming his retirement and letting others govern the nation. Passionate about farming, he found the simple act of digging his fingers into the soil to insert a seedling or root cutting a spiritual act—at once a part of the earth but apart from the world, his intellect and emotions at one with nature.

"No pursuit is more congenial with my nature and gratification than that of nature," he purred, "nor none I so pant after as to again become a tiller of the earth."[34]

After four months of isolation with largely pro-Constitution delegates in Philadelphia, Washington assumed the rest of the nation would be at one with Convention decisions. In fact, even Virginians were divided—and, indeed, most Americans favored amendments to guarantee individual rights. Richard Henry Lee, Virginia's delegate to Congress who had been first to proclaim American independence in 1776, wrote to George Mason, warning, "I think it is past doubt that if it should be established, either a tyranny will result . . . or a civil war."[35]

Patrick Henry, who had been Virginia's first governor after his state declared independence from Britain, was even more irate. Also predicting tyranny as an inevitable result of the new Constitution, he railed at its failure to limit national government powers.

"Congress," he predicted, "will have an unlimited, unbounded command over the soul of this commonwealth," with powers to pass any laws it deemed "necessary and proper." The president would have all-but-free rein to exercise whatever he defined as "executive power." The

*Richard Henry Lee, Virginia's delegate to Congress,
who resolved in June 1776 that "the United Colonies
are, and of right ought to be, free and independent
states," refused to sign the Constitution binding the
states in union under a strong federal government.
"Tyranny will result," he predicted, "or a civil war."*
(LIBRARY OF CONGRESS)

Constitution offered no specifics. And, Henry concluded, the federal judiciary had all-but-supreme power over every state and local court in the land and could hear cases without juries—a right guaranteed in the English-speaking world since 1215, when King John had signed the Magna Carta.[36]

Nor did the Constitution provide term limits for the president, members of Congress, or the judiciary. All could serve indefinitely and collude to establish tyranny. Henry feared the president and senate could plot to sell American territory or territorial rights to foreign governments for their own profit. Henry also objected to granting the national government powers to maintain a standing army, to impose taxes without the consent of states, to "negative" state laws, and to enforce

*Patrick Henry led the struggle against ratification of the
Constitution and establishment of a big federal government,
predicting, "Liberty will be lost and tyranny must and will
arise. . . . As this government stands, I despise and abhor it."*
(LIBRARY OF CONGRESS)

federal laws with troops. Calling "the sword and the purse" the two
greatest powers of government, he raged that "the junction of these
without limitation in the same hands is . . . despotism." He demanded
that the federal government share these powers with the states.[37]

Among his other objections: The Constitution stripped states of their
sovereignty and failed to protect individual rights. Although Virginia's
Declaration of Rights guaranteed them, he declared, the Constitution
gave the new national government power to "negative" state guarantees.

Henry argued that the Constitution would establish a national government with powers to impose the very tyranny from which Americans had freed themselves in their revolution against Britain.

The objections of Lee, Mason, and Henry helped sway anti-Constitution sentiment far beyond Virginia.

"Beware! Beware!" warned the *Massachusetts Centinel*. "You are forging chains for yourself and your children—your liberties are at stake."[38] Philadelphia's *Independent Gazetteer* predicted that the Constitution would create "a permanent ARISTOCRACY,"[39] while *Freeman's Journal*, another Philadelphia newspaper, warned of congressional powers "to lay and collect taxes."[40]

Despite press attacks on the Constitution, conventions in six states—Delaware, Pennsylvania, New Jersey, Georgia, Connecticut, and Massachusetts—ratified the Constitution by February 6, 1788. The three smallest states—Delaware, New Jersey, and Connecticut—had favored ratification because the Constitution would give the federal government sole rights to collect duties on imports. States with deep-water ports such as Philadelphia, New York, and Boston had been bleeding the economies of neighboring states with heavy duties on imports that passed through their harbors on their way to inland destinations. Sparsely settled Georgia—beset by Indian raids from Spanish-held Florida—ratified the Constitution to ensure itself a strong federal force to protect settlers. To eke out a victory in Massachusetts, Federalists pledged to "recommend" to the First Congress nine amendments to the Constitution to guarantee individual rights.

In Pennsylvania, Federalists simply stole victory. Despite widespread popular opposition to the Constitution in inland farm country, powerful banking and trading interests in Philadelphia controlled the majority of delegates at the Constitutional Convention. After the convention, Benjamin Franklin, of all people, ignored all principles of self-government by marching into the Pennsylvania Assembly with the delegation from the Constitutional Convention the day after the Constitution was signed. Interrupting the assembly's proceedings, he all but promised that Philadelphia would be the new federal capital if Pennsylvania was first to ratify the Constitution and ceded the federal government an appropriate tract of land for the federal capital. Like other major property owners in the city—along with bankers, merchants, and business owners—Franklin stood to reap enormous profits if the new government established its capital in Philadelphia.

Ten days later, after Congress sent the Constitution to the states, the federal majority in the Pennsylvania assembly insisted on an immediate call for a state ratification convention—without delay for debate. Angry back-country Antifederalists refused to appear at the assembly, however, and left it two members short of a quorum. Speaker Thomas Mifflin, the wealthy Philadelphia merchant, ordered a sergeant-at-arms and a clerk to find at least two absent members and order them to the hall. A mob of Federalists followed the two to the boarding house where many Antifederalists lodged and physically dragged them back to their seats in the State House. Despite their shouts of protest, sentries restrained them in their seats while Federalists voted to hold the ratification convention on November 20.

In the days and weeks that followed, back-country Antifederalists rioted to protest the assembly's actions, attacking Federalists and burning effigies of Federalist leaders and copies of the Constitution.

"The whole county is alive with wrath," a reporter wrote from Cumberland County to Philadelphia's *Independent Gazetteer*, "and it is spreading from one county to another so rapidly that it is impossible to say where it will end or how far it will reach."[41]

French consul-general Louis-Guillaume Otto was appalled, writing to his foreign minister in Versailles that "the legislative Assembly of Pennsylvania imprudently . . . revived the jealousy and anxiety of democrats.

In a blunder that is difficult to explain, Pennsylvania limited its delegation to the Constitutional Convention to Philadelphians; the other counties, whose interests have always been different from those of the capital, were hardly satisfied. . . . In forcing the minority to ratify the new government without debate, the legislature has acted so harshly and precipitously as to render any new government suspect. . . . It could strike a fatal blow.[42]

Former Virginia governor Patrick Henry was equally offended, saying that Pennsylvania had been "tricked" into ratifying the Constitution. "Only ten thousand were represented in Pennsylvania," he charged, "although seventy thousand had a right to be represented."[43]

Ironically, by the time the Pennsylvania ratification convention finally met and ratified the Constitution, Delaware had already become the first state to ratify the Constitution—on December 7, 1787.

In March 1788, Rhode Island became the first state to reject ratification—largely because it refused to give up the right to print paper money to pay off state debts. In addition, its land mass was too small to support a viable agricultural industry, forcing the state to depend on import duties for the bulk of its revenues. State leaders refused to surrender those revenues to a new federal government as the Constitution would have required.

Despite rejection by Rhode Island and a setback in North Carolina, where the ratification convention recessed rather than commit itself, the ratification juggernaut continued gaining momentum elsewhere. By the end of April, Maryland became the seventh state to ratify, followed by South Carolina two weeks later. New Hampshire became the ninth state a month later, thus ensuring ratification of the Constitution and establishment of the new republic. Virginia, however, was the nation's wealthiest state with the largest population and the second largest territory. Unless it ratified the document, national unity would remain difficult, if not impossible to achieve. Patrick Henry—still the state's titular political leader—seemed to hold the future of the republic in his hands.

Although Henry and New York Governor George Clinton hoped to forestall their respective state conventions long enough to prevent ratification, George Washington worked behind the scenes with James Madison and other Virginia Federalists to try to thwart Henry and other

*Edmund Randolph, the governor of Virginia, opposed the
Constitution at first, then supported ratification after George
Washington promised him a key role in the first administration.*
(LIBRARY OF CONGRESS)

Virginia Antifederalists. The Virginia ratification convention met on
June 2, and, to the astonishment of Federalists and Antifederalists alike,
Governor Edmund Randolph, who had refused to sign the Constitution
in Philadelphia, declared, "The Union is the anchor of our political salvation . . . I am a friend to the Union."[44]

As Randolph rambled on, Henry and other Antifederalists grew convinced that Washington had offered the governor an enticement for
switching political camps. "It seems to be very strange and unaccount-
able," Henry said of Randolph, "that that which was the object of his

execration should now receive his encomium." Although he stopped short of suggesting bribery, Henry told the convention that "something extraordinary must have operated so great a change in his opinions."[45] What had "operated so great a change" became clear later when George Washington offered Randolph the post as attorney general in Washington's cabinet.

After Randolph's defection to the Federalists, James Madison was able to convince enough moderate Antifederalists to switch sides by all but guaranteeing passage of a Bill of Rights in the First Congress. Despite Henry's dazzling eloquence, Virginia ratified the Constitution by a comfortable majority of ten votes, on June 25, and New York followed suit a month later.

Although Washington had evidently enjoyed manipulating events that brought down the Confederation of American states and ensured ratification of the new constitution, he feigned disinterest in assuming leadership of the new government he had been instrumental in creating. Washington was a master at obtaining and retaining authority by either feigning reluctance for power or threatening to step down once he attained it. Although eminently qualified to be the nation's first president, he had elevated surrender of his commission as commander in chief to high drama by publicly pledging to retire from public life. To announce for the presidency would be to renege on a promise to the American people and cast suspicion on every one of his future public promises. If he assumed the presidency, he would need the unquestioned, unanimous support of the American people.

Nor was this his only concern. His physical condition had deteriorated again: his false teeth made it difficult—and painful—for him to speak and eat in public, and his arthritis had become so painful that he had partially immobilized one of his arms in a sling.

Still another factor in his considerations was his personal happiness. He adored life at Mount Vernon, surrounded, as he was, by his beloved Martha and their grandchildren. Actually, they were hers but did not know the difference. For whatever reason—perhaps his bout with smallpox as a young man—George Washington was unable to have children of his own. Martha was a widow with two children when he married her in January 1759. He was just about to turn twenty-seven; she was a year older—a widow with two children, four-year-old Jacky and two-year-old Patsy. George Washington raised both as his own—and they returned his love. On the eve of battle in June 1776, as he and his small army faced annihilation by 25,000 British and Hessian troops, Jacky wrote his stepfather a letter that Washington had committed to memory:

> *Few have experienced such care and attention from real parents as I have. He best deserves the name of father who acts the part of one. I first was taught to call you by that name, my tender years unsusceptible of the loss I had sustained knew not the contrary; your goodness (if others had not told me) would always have prevented me from knowing I had lost a parent. I shall always look upon you in this light. . . . I shall with the greatest eagerness seize every opportunity of testifying that sincere regard and love I bear you.*[46]

Jacky had died of "camp fever" (typhus) two weeks after the Battle of Yorktown in the fall of 1783, leaving his wife with four children. Unable to cope, she settled into a house in Alexandria, Virginia, with her two oldest—both of them daughters—and surrendered the two youngest—five-year-old "Nelly" (Eleanor) and three-year-old "Washy" (George Washington Parke Custis)—to the Washingtons to raise at nearby Mount Vernon. For fifty-two-year-old Martha, the children were a cherished new beginning. She wanted more from retirement than running a household and planning dinners. Though somewhat less expressive than his wife, George Washington adored children—none more than little "Washy." Washington did not want to leave what seemed an idyllic life— and Martha didn't want him to leave, insisting he was too old to assume the presidency.

But Henry Knox, whom Washington had plucked from the obscurity of a Boston bookstore to command the Continental Army artillery in the war, knew how to manipulate his patron after eight years of close

*George Washington surrounded by his family—his wife, Martha, and grandchildren "Nelly" (Eleanor) and "Washy" (George Washington Parke Curtis)—at the Mansion at Mount Vernon, Virginia.* (VIRGINIA HISTORICAL SOCIETY)

association. After assuring Washington he would win election to the presidency by unanimous acclaim, he predicted that the role would be "highly honorable to your fame . . . and doubly entitle you to the glorious republican epithet—'The Father of Your Country.'"[47]

Washington responded with deep misgivings: "So unwilling am I, in the evening of a life . . . to quit a peaceful abode for an ocean of difficulties. I can assure you . . . that my movements to the chair of government will be accompanied with feelings not unlike those of a culprit who is going to the place of his execution."[48]

Other Federalist leaders supported Knox with pleas to Washington that the nation's survival would depend on his assuming the presidency. After the discord at the Constitutional Convention and state ratification conventions, political leaders in both North and South agreed—and in his heart Washington also knew—that only he would command enough support from the American people to hold the Union together as president during the formative years of the new government. Even in retirement, he remained "Father of Our Country" and the only man whom almost all Americans trusted implicitly.

"I should be deeply pained, my dear Sir," wrote his protégé Alexander Hamilton, "if your scruples in regard to a certain station should be matured into a resolution to decline it. . . . Every public and personal consideration will demand from you an acquiescence and that will certainly be the unanimous wish of your country."[49] One of Washington's friends in London was more blunt: "The happiness and prosperity of the thirteen United States depend on your acceptance of the President's chair. . . . Allow me to add that it is the general opinion of the friends to the new government that if you decline being at the head if it, it never can or will take effect."[50]

On February 4, 1789, presidential electors in ten states voted unanimously for George Washington as first President of the United States. He agreed to take the office in response to "the voice of my countrymen" and to preserve "a good name of my own . . . but what returns will be made for them, heaven alone can foretell. Integrity and firmness are all I can promise. These, be the voyage long or short, never shall forsake me although I may be deserted by all men."[51]

George Washington's election to the presidency crushed Martha Washington's hopes and dreams of leading a peaceful, normal family life at Mount Vernon. "That we should have been left to grow old in solitude and tranquility together," she wrote to a friend, "was the first and dearest wish of my heart. But in *that* I have been disappointed . . . yet I cannot blame him for having acted according to his ideas of duty in obeying the voice of his country."[52]

A few days later she told her nephew, "I am truly sorry to tell that the General is gone to New York. When or whether he will ever come home again, God only knows. I think it was much too late for him to go into public life again, but it was not to be avoided. Our family will be deranged [disarranged] as I must soon follow him. I am grieved at parting. . . . The same horses that carried the General are to return for me to carry me to New York."[53]

Martha's sorrow weighed on Washington for days. He had tried unsuccessfully to comfort her before he left their bedchamber the morning of his departure, and he almost believed he had succeeded when she smiled like a good soldier at the door as his carriage pulled away. But he knew better. He himself had mixed feelings about leaving, but was now convinced that only he could unite Americans behind the new federal government, and if he failed to do so, civil war and anarchy would engulf the nation. He was not about to bequeath a land in turmoil to his grandchildren as long as he had the power to transform it into a land at peace.

"About ten o'clock I bade adieu," he wrote in his diary that evening, "I bade adieu to Mount Vernon, to private life, and to domestic felicity; and with a mind oppressed with more anxious and painful sensations than I have words to express, set out for New York . . . to render service to my country in obedience to its call, but with less hope of answering its expectations."[54]

His ride to New York fulfilled any and every ambition for glory he—or any other leaders, for that matter—might have harbored. Over the next eight days, every city and village greeted Washington and his party with elaborate—often interminable—festivities, complete with church bells, fireworks, bands, marches, floral arches, balls, and, of course, speeches—endless speeches, often late into the night. Washington was hard put to rise before daybreak, but he had no choice if he was to cover enough ground to get to New York in time for his own inauguration.

A white horse awaited at the outskirts of Philadelphia for him to ride at the head of mounted troops to City Tavern and an elegant banquet with 250 of the city's most prominent citizens, followed by an evening of fireworks. The extravagance disquieted Washington, and he asked himself in his diary, "How would those same mobs react if I failed?"

"I greatly apprehend," Washington wrote, "that my Countrymen will expect too much from me. I fear, if the issue of public measures should not correspond with their sanguine expectations, they will turn extravagant . . . praises which they are heaping upon me at this moment, into equally extravagant . . . censures."[55] Washington wanted to write to Martha, but decided against adding his own fears to those he knew she already harbored.

Washington's election to the presidency temporarily united Americans with hopes that he could lead them to victory in peace as he had led them to victory in war, but he recognized that one misstep would reignite the people's wrath. He knew he would not have much time to build an effective governmental structure before they turned on him. To do so, however, he would need more powers than the Constitution had granted him, and any attempt to implement them would almost certainly set off another revolution.

# CHAPTER THREE

## His Highness, the President

As Washington was on his way to New York to assume the presidency, Vice President Adams struggled to bring order to the newly minted U.S. Senate. Six weeks earlier, the first senators had straggled into New York and found an angry crowd milling about New York's magnificent City Hall, at the intersection of Wall and Broad Streets. City fathers had transformed it into the nation's most stunning public building and renamed it Federal Hall to house the First Congress of the United States.

Restored, redesigned, and refurbished by French architect Pierre Charles L'Enfant, Federal Hall was the first example in America of the Federal style of architecture: a two-tiered portico in front, crowned by a pediment with a great American eagle perched in relief, its wings spread, ready to soar over Broad Street. Crowned by a graceful cupola, Federal Hall enclosed both houses of Congress—the House of Representatives on its ground floor and part of the second, and the Senate on the rest of the second floor. Although Senate proceedings were to be secret, spacious galleries overlooked the House floor for the public to view debates in that chamber.

Pealing church bells had signaled the opening of Congress on the morning of March 4, 1789. Cannons had fired eleven symbolic blasts to

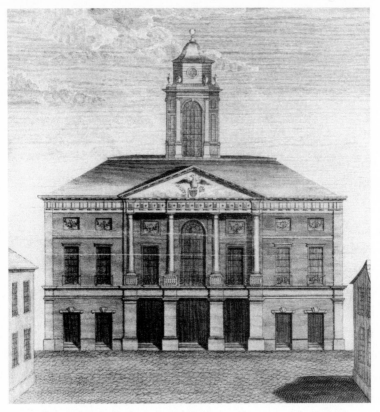

*Federal Hall in New York City, where the First Congress of the United States convened in April 1789.* (LIBRARY OF CONGRESS)

welcome congressmen from the eleven states that had ratified the Constitution and herald the dawn of a new, self-governing republic. A gleeful gathering of citizens waited to greet the arriving congressmen, but, to the disappointment and anger of welcomers, only thirteen of fifty-nine members of the House of Representatives and eight of twenty-two senators had found their way to New York for the scheduled call to order. Each house required at least a majority of its members for a quorum.

With both chambers still under construction, members had left for their lodging houses, and the crowd had dispersed. Pessimistic onlookers muttered their collective contempt for the new government and promised to return each day to protest the failure of the elected government to assemble.

"A very great loss of revenue is running upon us every day by means of the delay of the members to attend," groused Connecticut Representative Benjamin Huntington, while New Jersey Representative Elias Boudinot wrote an angry letter to his wife calling New York a "dirty city" and complaining, "The difference of the wholesome country air from the stench of the filthy street was so apparent as to effect our smelling faculties greatly."[1]

In London, British king George III and his ministers rocked with laughter when they learned how America's leaders had demonstrated the benefits of self-government.

A month passed until enough members of the House reached New York to form a quorum and another week before the Senate counted twelve of its twenty-two members. Their long and often difficult journeys to New York evidently ruffled more than a few of their feathers and left them in foul moods as they made their way into Federal Hall. Not surprisingly, the first calls to order in each house produced nothing but disorder, as members clawed for power over committee memberships and chairmanships. Southerners elbowed northerners, westerners argued with easterners, delegates from small states growled at delegates from large states. . . . Anything they could fight about they did, with South Carolina slave holders threatening to walk out at the mere whisper of the words "abolition" or "emancipation" by Pennsylvania's Quaker abolitionists. Both Rhode Island and North Carolina had refused to ratify the Constitution and didn't send delegates. Although North Carolina had at least called for a convention to consider ratification, Rhode Island preferred remaining an independent sovereign state outside the Union for the time being.

Indeed, the bitterness of the ratification struggle had not abated when the First Congress finally came to order. Twenty members—nine of the fifty-seven in the House and eleven of twenty-two Senators—had been members of the Constitutional Convention and had every intention of continuing their debates when they took their seats in Congress. As they had at the Constitutional Convention, America's wealthiest white males made up almost all the Congress, with the owners of the largest southern plantations representing the South, and prominent lawyers and merchant-bankers representing the North—"sober, solid, old-charter folks," according to Federalist Representative Fisher Ames, a Harvard graduate and prominent Massachusetts lawyer.

Although pro-ratification Federalists had won a significant majority in both houses (fifty of the fifty-nine House seats and eighteen of the twenty-two Senate seats) they represented but a minority of the American people—namely, those who met each state's property qualifications for voting. But a majority of Americans either owned no property or owned too little to vote, and most had opposed ratification because it not only failed to guarantee all citizens the vote, it failed to include a bill of rights guaranteeing such individual liberties as freedom of speech and freedom of the press. South Carolina's Charles Pinckney warned that the Constitution would "abolish state government" and accrete popular participation in government affairs.

The few Antifederalists who managed to win election to Congress, therefore, came to New York prepared to fire a barrage of more than one hundred proposed constitutional amendments to emasculate the federal government, restore state sovereignty, and guarantee individual rights.

It was not until April 20—six weeks after the scheduled opening of Congress—that John Adams completed a week-long journey from his Massachusetts home and crossed the bridge onto the northern end of Manhattan Island. President Washington had just started his own journey to the nation's new capital. Alerted to the Vice President's imminent arrival, a New York cavalry troop awaited with Foreign Affairs Secretary John Jay and leading members of Congress to escort him southward to the city and his temporary lodging at Jay's magnificent mansion. The next morning, the Senate's president pro tempore greeted him at the door of Federal Hall, led him up the flight of stairs, and escorted him into the Senate chamber to his chair, where he assumed the presidency of that body without ceremony. Although the Constitution required the incoming President to take a specific oath, it required no comparable commitment by the Vice President. His election automatically installed him in office.

After calling the Senate to order, Adams immediately threw off conventional procedural restraints as presiding officer and pressed the Senate to consider as its first order of business how to address the President. Infatuated by the pomp of European courts he had visited as an American minister during the Revolutionary War, he suggested "Your Highness" or "Your Most Benign Highness" as appropriate titles for the President. In a scene that would have delighted Lemuel Gulliver in Lilliput, twenty-two of America's most learned and powerful statesmen responded with complex arguments supporting "His Exalted Highness," "His Elective Highness," "Most Illustrious and Excellent President," and even "His Majesty the President." When one senator proposed calling the President "George," another snapped in response, "Why not George IV?"

A few senators protested Adams's intrusion in the debate as a blatant violation of customary procedures, with one protestor ridiculing the Vice President as "His Rotundity." Others were less oblique, stating that the President was neither a king nor an emperor and entitled to no title but "George"—certainly not "George I." Vice President Adams suggested that the Senate and House name special committees to resolve differences. He warned that the United States would earn "the contempt, the scorn and the derision" of Europe's monarchies if Congress persisted in calling America's national leader "General" or "President."

"You may depend on another thing," he warned Federalists. "The state government will always be uppermost in America in the minds of our own people till you give a superior title to your first national magistrate."[2]

Cowed by Adams at first, the eighteen Federalists yielded to Adams's suggestion: "His Highness, the President of the United States, and Protector of the Rights of the Same." After a few more days of debate, one

*Vice President John Adams complained to his wife Abigail that the vice presidency was "the most insignificant office that ever the invention of man contrived." (LIBRARY OF CONGRESS)*

senator reminded his colleagues that the Constitution prohibited titles, and members finally adopted the republican simplicity of "Mr. President."

Having ended the debate on how to address the President, senators began debating how to address each other and whether any of them were honorable enough to warrant the title of "The Honorable Member," let alone "The Honorable Gentleman."

The titles debate proved only a prelude to similarly Swiftian arguments over other elements of protocol, without which the pompous princes of polity refused to proceed with the important business of governing the nation. Senators insisted theirs was the "upper house" of Congress and demanded that two *members* of the "lower house" deliver all House communications to the Senate, while the Senate would send its communications to the "lower house" with a secretary. After the howls of protest subsided, the House resolved—rather vociferously—to send its communications to the Senate via the clerk of the House.

Although the Senate had no choice but to abandon its concept of upper and lower houses, it nonetheless insisted that its members be paid a dollar more per day than the $6-per-day remuneration for representatives. Facing an impasse at a time when tens of thousands of Americans were threatening to rebel if Congress did not make good on worthless government currency, the House and Senate compromised: Congress would pay each senator $1 a day more than House members for seven years, after which Congress would pay all its members the same amounts.[3]

By then, the congressional focus on petty issues began to draw public criticisms. "The slowness with which the business is carried on [in Congress] is a cause of complaint," Washington's son-in-law David Stuart warned Washington. "Congress, it is said sit only four hours a day and, like schoolboys, observe every Saturday as a holiday. If this be true, it is certainly trifling with their constituents in the extreme, who pay them liberally and have, therefore, a right to expect more diligence from them." The average American, Stuart noted, lived on a mere $2 a day, or less than one-third the amount paid Congressmen.

Congress finally ended its protocol debates by actually passing the nation's first law—the Oath Act—which provided words for the oath required in the last paragraph of Article VI of the Constitution. Without prescribing the actual oath, the framers of the Constitution had required that all members of Congress *and* state legislatures, along with "all executive and judicial officers, both of the United States and of the several states shall be bound by oath . . . to support this Constitution."[4]

Passage of the Oath Act did not come a moment too soon. President-elect Washington was already approaching New York after his festive, eight-day journey from Mount Vernon. After the tumultuous welcome in Philadelphia, he had sailed north on the Delaware River to Trenton to revisit the site of his Revolutionary War heroics before riding cross-country to Elizabeth, New Jersey, on the western shore of New York Bay, across from Manhattan.

A breathtakingly beautiful barge—fifty feet long, bedecked by flowers, and powered by thirteen oarsmen—awaited to carry the President across the bay to Manhattan. A special committee of congressmen joined him aboard as an armada of decorated ships and boats of all sizes sailed alongside, colors flying, their sailors firing salutes and cheering as they crossed the harbor. A huge crowd stretched one-half mile along the Manhattan waterfront to cheer as he stepped ashore onto the appropriate red carpet. Eleven cannons fired a salute before a huge band struck up the solemn—and ironic—notes of *God Save the King*, with the crowd intoning its new words:

> *God Save Great Washington,*
> *Our nation's noblest son,*
> *Long to command. . . .*

The ostentation disturbed Washington, who knew how quickly mob hysteria could devolve from veneration to execration. "The display of boats," he penned in his diary later, "the decorations of the ships, the roar of cannon, and the loud acclamations of the people . . . filled my mind with sensations as painful . . . as they are pleasing (considering the reverse of this scene)."[5]

On the morning of April 29, the thunder of eleven cannon blasts awakened him and the rest of the city, and George Washington arose to prepare for his inauguration as the first President of the United States of America. "At twelve, the troops of the city paraded before our door," Washington's secretary Tobias Lear wrote in his diary, "and soon after, the committees of Congress and heads of departments came in their carriages to wait upon the President to the Federal Hall."[6] Washington rode to the hall in what could have passed for a royal chariot, pulled by six cream-colored Belgian draft horses. His wife, Martha, had remained home in Mount Vernon until the President settled into permanent quarters that could accommodate her, their two grandchildren, and their servants.

Vice President John Adams wore an absurdly long ceremonial sword at his side as he welcomed Washington at Federal Hall. Then, as he tried to keep from tripping over his scabbard, the Vice President led Washington onto the second-floor portico overlooking Wall and Broad Streets. Samuel Otis, the Secretary of the Senate, lifted a red cushion that held a Bible on which Washington placed his huge right hand, and New York Chancellor* Robert R. Livingston administered the constitutionally prescribed oath, as thousands looked up from the streets below. It was one in the afternoon:

"Do you solemnly swear that you will faithfully execute the office of President of the United States and will, to the best of your ability, preserve, protect, and defend the Constitution of the United States?"

"I solemnly swear that I will faithfully execute . . . " and he repeated the oath.

"It is done," declared Livingston, who turned to the crowd, raised his arms, and shouted, "Long Live George Washington, President of the United States."[7]

According to Lear, "The air was rent by repeated shouts and huzzas,—*'God bless our Washington!' and 'Long live our beloved President!'*"

Never known for his great oratory, Washington pursed his lips to contain his false teeth as he stepped inside to address a joint session of Congress. Superficially implanted into his gum sockets, his teeth often shifted as he spoke, and he kept his speeches short. His inaugural address—the nation's first—lasted but twelve minutes and ended with a solemn prayer "to the benign Parent of the human race . . . to favor the American people, with . . . the security of their Union, and the advancement of their happiness."[8]

"It was a touching scene," said one Congressman. Another described it as "elegant." But a third noted that Washington trembled. "This great

---

*Chief judge of the court of equity.

*The inauguration of George Washington as first President of the United States, on the porch of Federal Hall in New York City.* (LIBRARY OF CONGRESS)

man was agitated and embarrassed more than ever he was by the leveled cannon or pointed musket."[9] New York celebrated the inauguration with fireworks, illuminations, and festivities that resembled a coronation, but it was Congress that had ordered most of the day's regal events—not Washington. In contrast to many congressmen, the President dressed in a plain brown suit made of "superfine American broad cloth" that he had seen advertised in the *New York Daily Advertiser*.[10]

After the inauguration, the President dined rather hurriedly before going to the residence of his former artillery commander, General Henry Knox, to watch a display of fireworks that combined with extravagant—almost terrifying—accolades and left Washington embarrassed and uneasy.

"Absorbed and agitated by the sentiment which our adored leader and ruler inspired," the editor/publisher of the *Daily Advertiser* rejoiced, "the printer apprehends that he cannot with perfect precision describe the various scenes of splendor which this event exhibited."[11] The *Gazette of the United States* described Washington as "Saviour of his Country," who, with those around him were "exalted to be Gods among men," with Washington to be "the God of Gods.

> The attentions shown on this occasion were not merely *honorary*, they were the tribute of gratitude, due to a man whose life has been one series of labors for the public good upon a scale of eminence that Heaven never before assigned to a mortal. These labors have been achieved so perfectly that future ages shall acknowledge the justice of the poet when they read,

> *So near perfection that he stood*
> *Upon the boundary line,*
> *Of finite, from infinite good,*
> *Of human from divine.*[12]

Still uncertain what he was to do in his new job, Washington rode back to the President's house and found it filled with well-wishers, job seekers, hangers-on, and gawkers intent on seeing "the great man" for the first time. He and his invited guests fought their way through the crowd trying in vain to find a quiet room for themselves, to toast the health of the President and the nation.

In the fortnight that followed, throngs continued surging in and out of Washington's home each day, devouring his food and drink and threatening to bankrupt him—until he finally exploded with rage and ordered the mansion doors shut, locked, and barred to visitors.

"I was unable to attend to any business whatever," he growled as he recalled his first days in office, "for gentlemen consulting their own time rather than mine were calling from the time I rose from breakfast—often before—until I sat down to dinner."[13]

In the days that followed, his anger subsided, and he regretted his decision to lock himself from public view. He grew melancholy as he thought of Martha, the grandchildren they were raising, and his beautiful home and farm at Mount Vernon. Martha and the children were not expected to arrive in New York until June 8, more than five weeks after Inauguration Day. "Nothing but a conviction of duty could have induced me to depart from my resolution of remaining in retirement," he complained to his friend Edward Rutledge of South Carolina—a signer of the Declaration of Independence. "I consider . . . this last great sacrifice . . . made for the good of my country. . . .

> You know, my dear sir, I had concentrated all my schemes, all my views, all my wishes, within the narrow circle of domestic enjoyment . . . but it was my duty to embark again on the tempestuous and uncertain ocean of public life. . . . With this last great sacrifice . . . I gave up all expectations of private happiness in this world.[14]

After emerging from his melancholy mood, Washington reckoned that, in a republic, the people who had voted him into office had a legitimate right to confront him. As with almost every other aspect of his presidency, however, the Constitution gave him no guidance on the President's relationships with the public. With no one else to consult (he had no cabinet yet) he called in his closest friends in New York—Adams, Alexander Hamilton, John Jay, and James Madison—for advice on public access to the President and the presidential mansion. What he sought, he said, were rules that were appropriate for a republic, eschewing monarchic aloofness on one extreme and over-familiarity on the other. The rules, he said, were less important than the principle—and precedent—he was setting for his successors to the presidency.

"As the first of everything *in our situation* will serve to establish a precedent," he explained to Madison, "it is devoutly wished on my part that these precedents be fixed on true principles."[15] It was the first of dozens of precedents he would set for his successors that would make him father of the American presidency as well as father of his country.

Already smarting from comparisons of his inauguration to a coronation, he argued that the President's house had been bought (or in his case rented) and paid for with public monies. As such, he concluded, it belonged to the public, and, on May 26, 1789, he declared the presidential mansion open to the public—which it remains to this day. He had yet to decide when, however, and how often. In the end, it would be Martha Washington who would take the lead in answering such questions by bringing order to the presidential mansion and comfort to both its residents and visitors.

Three weeks after Washington's inauguration, Martha set off for New York in the family coach with her two grandchildren, ten-year-old Nelly Custis and eight-year-old Washy. The same clanging church bells, massive parades, cheering crowds, and eleven-gun salutes that had greeted her husband welcomed her along the route north. Baltimore staged a display of fireworks followed by an endless "serenade" that lasted until 2 a.m.

Two days later, two cavalry units met her carriage in Chester, Pennsylvania, to escort her into Philadelphia. Once the bells, cheers, and gunfire faded, Martha dashed to the most fashionable stores to buy a panoply of clothes for herself, Nelly, and Washy. After leaving Philadelphia, Martha and the children rode to Elizabeth Town, New Jersey, where the same decorated barge that had carried her husband to New York awaited— with the President on board to surprise his wife and escort her across the waters to Manhattan. The governor waited as they landed in Manhattan and led the entire Washington family on parade up Broadway.

"Dear little Washy seemed lost in a maze at the great parade," Martha wrote to her niece Fanny back at Mount Vernon.

> The Governor of the state met me as soon as we landed and led me up to the house. I thank God the President is very well . . . the house he is in is a very good one and is handsomely furnished all new for the

General. . . . I have not had one half hour to myself since the day of my arrival. My first care was to get the children to a good school. . . . My hair is set and dressed every day. You would think me a good deal in the fashion if you could but see me.[16]

Once settled in the mansion, she helped the President decide on "a line of conduct which combined public advantage with private convenience," limiting visitors to one hour, two days a week. He would receive guests—men only—on Tuesdays from three to four and Martha would host a tea party on Friday evenings for both men and women eager to "see the President" or "pay their respects." Limited only by the requirement that they be "respectably dressed," all were welcome, without invitations.

His decision to open his doors to the public was more than astonishing in the eighteenth-century world of absolute monarchs, whose fears of assassination kept them hidden from public view behind fortified castle walls. Elected unanimously by the people of his country, George Washington had no such fears, and he welcomed Americans of all social classes to his house—with no guards standing by.

"To draw such a line for the conduct of the President as will please *every* body, I know is impossible," he explained to Madison.

The true medium I conceive must lie in pursuing such a course as will allow him time for all his official duties of his station. This should be the primary object. The next, to avoid as much as may be, the charge of superciliousness and seclusion from information by too much reserve and too great a withdrawal of himself from company on the one hand and the inconveniences as well as reduction of respectability by too free an intercourse and too much familiarity on the other.[17]

Even thirty-five years later, a French official visiting the presidential mansion would express astonishment that, unlike European palaces, the gates were "defended by neither guards, ushers, nor insolent valets. A single servant opened the door, and we were then introduced into the reception room." Equally astonishing was the President's dress—"without decorations, without all those puerile ornaments which so many fools wear in the antechambers of European palaces."[18]

Initially, Washington decided against all entertaining, but relented in favor of a weekly dinner with members of Congress. On other days, however, dinner was to be a private affair for his own family and members of his "presidential family" such as his secretary or other close advisers. To limit demands on his time, he decided against accepting any invitations, although he reserved the right to attend theater (his passion) and drive into the country to visit farms (another passion)—and he could not resist attending a ball that the French minister hosted in his honor.

Too accustomed to entertaining at Mount Vernon, however, the Washingtons did not wait long to invite friends to dinner. Although the first guests apprized the offerings as "the least showy dinner that I ever saw," by summer's end both Washingtons had tired of republican simplicity. As Martha ordered many of the same foods and wines she had served at Mount Vernon, she drew such comments as: "It was a great dinner . . . the best of the kind I ever was at."[19]

When word of Martha's lavish dinners reached the public, however, one newspaper complained that "in a few years, we shall have all the paraphernalia yet wanting to give the superb finish to the grandeur of our AMERICAN COURT! The purity of republican principle seems to be daily losing ground . . . we are on the eve of another revolution."[20]

Although the press reports infuriated the Washingtons, Martha determined to set precedents for her successors—as the President was doing for his—by imposing her personality on capital social affairs and dispelling suspicions that she and her husband had monarchical ambitions.

"She received me with great ease and politeness," wrote Abigail Adams of the First Lady after their first encounter. "She is plain in her dress, but that plainness is the best of every article. . . . Her hair is white, her teeth beautiful, her person rather short than otherwise. . . . Her manners are modest and unassuming, dignified and feminine, not the tincture of hauteur about her."[21]

Evidently pleased by each other's unpretentiousness, the First and Second Ladies took to each other immediately. "Mrs. Washington," Abigail wrote in her second report on Martha, "is one of those unassuming characters which create love and esteem. A most becoming pleasantness sits upon her countenance and an unaffected deportment which renders her the object of veneration and respect. With all these feelings and sensations I found myself much more deeply impressed than I ever did before their Majesties of Britain."[22]

In embracing the title "Mr. President" and designating the presidential mansion as the "People's House," Washington defined the relationship of the nation's elected officials as servants rather than rulers of the people who had elected them. His self-characterization as a public "servant" rather than a public "ruler" put a different light on each assumption of power he would make during his eight years in office.

When the flow of people through the presidential mansion began to ebb, Washington faced mounds of correspondence to answer. Some letters congratulated him on his accession to the presidency, but, as often as not, they pleaded for and sometimes demanded jobs in his administration or contracts to provide him and the government with goods and services. Hundreds of applications—and supplications—came from relatives and friends who believed their ties to the President, by blood or otherwise, were reason enough to warrant his hiring them.

In fact, Congress had yet to create any cabinet departments or even a judiciary, leaving the President unable to make any appointments other than a few personal aides and no government to run.

Left with nothing to do, the President rejoiced at first at the prospect of a few hours of leisure after the frenzied activities of the inauguration and post-inauguration period. He took several solitary horseback rides and spent happy hours with Martha and the children. But as his hours of inactivity stretched into days, and the days into weeks, he realized how few responsibilities he had and how powerless he was in what was the highest elective office in the land. He was used to constant activity, exercising authority, and now faced four years languishing in a post he had reluctantly accepted out of a sense of patriotic duty.

"I can declare," Washington wrote to his friend, former French consul Hector St. John de Crèvecoeur,

> that no prospects however flattering, no personal advantage however great, no desire of fame however easily it might be acquired, could induce me to quit the private walks of life at my age and in my situation. But if by any exertions or services of mine my country can be benefitted, I shall feel more amply compensated for the sacrifices which I make.[23]

For the moment, however, the presidency offered him no opportunities to make such exertions. He had come to New York to govern a nation in turmoil that desperately needed governing, only to find that the Constitution he had championed actually prevented him from doing the job he had come to do.

Adding to his frustration and fury was the comedy of manners still under way in Congress, where members seemed more concerned with pomp and ceremony than the plague of crises disrupting American life. Settlers in the West were pleading for help against attacks by both Indians and renegade British troops. Thousands of former Continental Army soldiers remained unpaid for their service, while European nations that had loaned Congress funds to fight the Revolutionary War were demanding repayment. With Congress unable or unwilling to respond, Washington drew up plans to throw off constitutional restraints on his powers and act to defend the nation against impending disaster.

# CHAPTER FOUR

❧❦❧

# *"Do You Advise and Consent?"*

Under the Confederation of American States, the single-chamber Confederation Congress had served as both executive and legislative branches of government, and the Secretary of War, Secretary for Foreign Affairs, and three-man Board of Treasury remained responsible to Congress, there being no President.

Although the new Constitution let the President nominate executive department heads "by and with the advice and consent of the Senate," Washington had been unable to do so when he took office, because the Congress had yet to pass the legislation to create cabinet departments. The President had no choice, therefore, but to deal with the existing department heads that Congress had appointed. With no constitutional authority over them, however, it was delicate business, and he searched for the right diplomatic niceties to address them and win their cooperation.

With his desk cleared of mail—and the rest of the mansion cleared of visitors—Washington wrote to Secretary for Foreign Affairs John Jay: "In the present unsettled state of the Executive Departments, I do not conceive it expedient to call upon you officially, yet I have supposed that some informal communications from the Office of Secretary for Foreign Affairs might neither be improper nor unprofitable.

For finding myself at this moment less occupied with the duties of my office . . . I am desirous of employing myself in obtaining an acquaintance with the real situation of the several great departments. . . . For this purpose, I wish to receive in writing . . . a clear account of the department at the head of which you have been. . . . As I am now at leisure to inspect such papers and documents . . . I have thought it fit to address this notification to you accordingly.[1]

With all-too-many ambitious eyes besides his own ogling top-level appointments in the Washington administration, Jay immediately complied with the President's request, as did other department heads. At the time, Secretary Jay and Secretary of War Henry Knox were negotiating a free-trade agreement with Georgia's Creek Indians aimed at diverting their trade from Spanish outposts in Florida to American trade posts to the north in Georgia. Relations with Indian nations fell under foreign affairs at the time, and both Knox and Washington realized that the President's constitutional treaty-making powers were subject to the "advice and consent of the Senate." Accordingly, they appeared before the Senate in what turned into a seriocomic performance and provoked Washington's first major redesign of the new American government and assumption of powers not granted to him by the Constitution.

After the doorkeeper announced the arrival of the President and Secretary Knox "to obtain the Senate's advice and consent," Washington's face reddened with "an aspect of stern displeasure" as he walked down the aisle—like a schoolboy in class—to hand John Adams a copy of Knox's negotiation proposals. Adams, who deeply respected the President, was equally red-faced. The upside-down protocol of Vice President Adams's constitutional role as President of the Senate, however, had put the President of the United States in a subordinate position within the Senate chamber . . .

. . . and General George Washington subordinated himself to no one!

*Secretary of War Henry Knox had become one of George Washington's closest friends during the Revolutionary War, in which Knox was a major general in command of the artillery.* (LIBRARY OF CONGRESS)

As Washington fumed, Adams mumbled the first of seven sections in the Knox-Washington proposal, then paused to ask the Senate the only question suggested by the Constitution:

"Do you advise and consent?"

Puzzled senators shrugged their collective shoulders and looked at each other for guidance. None had ever heard the question before. None knew exactly what it meant or how to respond. "Carriages were driving past and made such a noise" that Pennsylvania Senator William Maclay asked Adams to repeat what he had said.

"I could tell it was something about Indians," Maclay recalled, "but was not master of one sentence. Signs were made to the doorkeeper to shut down the sashes."

As other Senators shouted for Adams to reread the paper more audibly, the Vice President shot an embarrassed glance at Washington, then reread the passage from the first section in the Knox-Washington proposal. He spoke in a louder, clearer voice—again concluding with the question lifted from the Constitution: "Do you advise and consent?"

"There was a dead pause," according to Senator Maclay, who finally "rose reluctantly" to point out that "the business is new to the Senate." Robert Morris, the other Senator from Pennsylvania, agreed and suggested "that the queries be submitted to a committee"—which provoked a lengthy debate on the meaning of "advise and consent" and "the mode of doing business by committee."[2]

Adams finally halted the debate with angry raps of his gavel and read the second section of the policy proposal—with the same results . . . then the third. . . . He ended each with the same, inane question:

"Do you advise and consent?"

. . . and received the same inglorious results.

With each postponement, Washington grew more annoyed—until his annoyance erupted into uncontrollable fury, and, according to Maclay, he "started up in a violent fret."

"This defeats every purpose of my coming here!" the President roared. He then "went on that he had brought the Superintendent at War with him to give every necessary information . . . and yet he was delayed and could not go on with the matter." Although Washington "cooled by degrees," he eventually stood and marched out of the hall "with sullen dignity," and "a discontented air," as 300-pound Henry Knox waddled behind breathlessly.[3]

Knox adored Washington—had been his closest friend and aide during the entire Revolutionary War. Born in Boston and, like Washington, orphaned at twelve, Knox quit school and went to work for a bookseller until he was twenty-one, when he opened his own bookstore and studied every book on its shelves, including tomes on engineering. When the war began, he closed the shop to join the Revolution and became so remarkable an artillery specialist that he earned a commission as a colonel and eventually major general as commander of the artillery.

With the British army occupying Boston, Knox led a corps of volunteers through snowstorms to Fort Ticonderoga, New York, in a heroic effort to recover fifty-nine heavy artillery pieces. After dragging forty-three cannon and sixteen mortars over frozen ponds and through huge snow drifts back to Boston, Knox and his men positioned the pieces on the heights surrounding the city. With Patriot cannon looming above, the British had little choice but to evacuate the city or face slaughter under a barrage of Patriot shells. On March 17, 1776, the British army set sail from Boston harbor with nearly 1,200 loyalists aboard, bound for Halifax, Nova Scotia.

Knox's heroic role in the capture of Boston spawned a close friendship with Washington that would endure the rest of their lives. Knox served in every campaign with Washington—Trenton, Valley Forge, Monmouth, Yorktown—and as he followed Washington in and out of the Senate chamber, he was as upset as Washington over the treatment accorded the President.

As commander in chief of the Continental Army for more than eight years, Washington expected unquestioned obedience by subordinates—without debate. Now chief executive of his nation, he had subjected himself to the humiliation of subordinating himself to his own Vice President to try to obtain Senate approval of a policy he believed essential to national security. The Senate was evidently as embarrassed as he, and it formed a committee to determine "the mode of communication between the President and the Senate on Treaties and Nominations."

"How," the committeemen asked, "are the President and Vice President to be arranged when the President enters the chamber?" "Would the Vice President be disposed to give up the chair? If not, ought the President of the United States be placed in an awkward situation when there?"[4]

Washington solved the problem himself, resolving to remove certain executive functions from the legislature's control. Washington reasoned that while the Constitution subjected approval of the final treaty to Senate *advice and consent*, it specifically assigned the *treaty making* itself—that is, the initiation, negotiations, and drawing of final terms of a treaty—to the President alone. He applied the same principle to executive appointments. "He"—that is, the President—"shall nominate and . . . shall appoint ambassadors, other public ministers and consuls . . . and all other officers of the United States." Congress could approve or reject presidential nominees and appointments, but had no visible role in their initial selection.

"It could be no pleasing thing I conceive," Washington scolded the Senate, "for the President to . . . hear the propriety of his nominations questioned. . . . As the President has a right to nominate without assigning his reasons, so has the Senate a right to dissent without giving theirs."[5]

In explaining his decision to the Senate, he noted that the framers of the Constitution had set the phrase "by and with the advice and consent of the Senate" within *commas*—not once, but twice—thus making it clearly secondary and parenthetical to the President's express powers to make treaties and appointments. "When these powers are exercised," he declared, "the Senate . . . is evidently only a council to the President, however its concurrence may be to his acts."[6]

Although Washington conceded the need for "oral communications . . . in all matters respecting treaties," he refused ever again to appear personally before the Senate without the presence of the rest of Congress, saying it put "the President of the United States . . . in an awkward situation" of being subordinate to the vice president who is ex officio President of the Senate. Washington's decision stripped the Senate of any pretensions to eminence over the presidency, ensuring that no president would ever again submit to Senate interrogation. In the future, the President would appear in the Capitol at only joint sessions of Congress, with the President designating "not only the *time*, but the *place* and manner of consultation."[7] By limiting the "advice-and-consent" rule, Washington's pronouncement set a precedent for all future presidents and, indeed, raised the first pillar of power of the presidential edifice: the power to set foreign policy.

On January 8, 1790, President George Washington delivered the nation's first State of the Union message to Congress and cited "providing for the common defense" as the most urgent issue facing the nation. "To be prepared for war," he declared, "is one of the most effectual means of preserving peace.

> A free people ought not only to be armed but disciplined, to which end a uniform and well digested plan is requisite, and their safety and interest require that they should promote such manufactures as tend to render them independent . . . for essential . . . military supplies.[8]

Although defense and foreign affairs dominated his talk, he also called for establishment of a national postal service and post roads as a means of "facilitating the intercourse between the distant parts of our country." In an even more radical—and surprising—departure from critical issues, Washington asked Congress to provide aid "to seminaries of learning already established . . . [and] the institution of a national university.

> Knowledge is in every country the surest basis of public happiness. To the security of a free constitution, it contributes . . . by teaching the people themselves to know and to value their own rights . . . to distinguish between oppression and the necessary exercise of lawful authority . . . to discriminate the spirit of liberty from that of licentiousness, cherishing the first, avoiding the last, and uniting . . . temperate encroachments with an inviolable respect to the laws.[9]

Congress responded quickly to his defense proposals with "An Act for Regulating the Military Establishment of the United States." Called the "Troops Act," it gave the House powers to order states to draft troops in an emergency. The Senate proposed stretching the House bill to give the President powers to order states to call up militia in a federal emergency.

Senator William Maclay of Pennsylvania was outraged, predicting, "Give [Secretary of War] Knox his army and he will soon have a war on his hands. Indeed, I am clearly of opinion that he is aiming at this even now. . . . The Constitution certainly never contemplated a standing army in time of peace."[10] Yielding to Maclay's concerns, Congress rejected giving the President power to call up troops. It also rejected a Knox proposal for establishing camps to effect universal military training of all white, adult males.

---

Congress did not get around to establishing executive departments until late summer—the Department of Foreign Affairs (renamed "State" two months later), on July 27; Department of War, August 7; and the Department of Treasury, August 28. The departments immediately became centers of controversy when the Senate sought to retain control over department heads by having them serve indefinitely unless removed for cause by congressional impeachment. In effect, department heads would serve independently of the President, beholden only to Congress.

"It will nurse faction," Federalist Representative Fisher Ames of Massachusetts warned the Congress.

> It will . . . shelter fools. Sir, it is infusing poison into the Constitution . . . it is tempting the Senate with forbidden fruit. It ought not to be possible for a branch of the legislature even to hope for a share of the executive power, for they may be tempted to increase it.[11]

Opponents of presidential power fired back, declaring, "The power of creating offices is given to the legislature. Under this general grant, the legislature have it under their supreme decision to determine the whole organization, to affix its tenure, and declare the control."[12]

Federalist Ames again leaped to the President's defense, with a barrage of references to the Constitution:

> The executive powers are delegated to the president. The only bond between him and those he employs is the confidence he has in their integrity and talents. When that confidence ceases, the principal ought to have the power to remove those whom he can no longer trust with safety.[13]

But Antifederalists refused to cede until Virginia's James Madison, Washington's principal ally in the House, lured the needed swing votes in Washington's favor. He did so with a stark warning that failure to subject department heads to presidential authority would leave the presidency a ceremonial post and allow the secretaries of State, War, and Treasury—all of them appointees, rather than elected officials—to form a powerful triumvirate with all but unchecked powers over the nation's revenues, foreign affairs, and military.

Senate Federalists were less united than in the House, however, and Virginia Senator William Grayson, a staunch Antifederalist and close political ally of Patrick Henry, warned his colleagues that "the matter predicted by Mr. Henry is now coming to pass: consolidation of the new government. And the first attempt will be to destroy the Senate, as they are the representatives of the state legislatures."[14]

Washington again responded with a "violent fret," then met privately with the Vice President and demanded full control of every executive department, including the right to dismiss department heads without cause. If Congress refused to relegate full control over executive functions to the President, he hinted he might resign.

Although the House voted for the President's right to remove department heads without Senate consent, the Senate vote resulted in a tie. For the first time, Vice President Adams was now able to assume a role in

*Representative James Madison had been George Washington's*
*closest ally in the House of Representatives until Washington*
*sought to assume powers not granted by the Constitution.*
(LIBRARY OF CONGRESS)

shaping the new American government and cast the deciding vote. He
voted in favor of the President—*his* President. In effect, Adams made a
public show of respect that he believed every citizen owed the President
of the United States—including members of the U.S. Senate.

"The essence of a free government consists in an effectual control of
rivalries," he explained. "The executive and the legislative powers are
natural rivals; and if each has not an effectual control over the other,
the weaker will ever be the lamb in the paws of the wolf. The nation
which will not adopt an equilibrium of power must adopt a despotism.
There is no other alternative. Rivalries must be controlled or they will
throw things into confusion."[15]

Adams's vote not only forced the Senate to cede authority over the executive branch of government to the President, it transferred far-reaching extra-constitutional powers to the President. In effect, it altered the first sentence of Article II, Section 1 of the Constitution from . . .

*The executive power shall be vested in a president of the United States of America.*

. . . to mean . . .

**All** *executive powers shall be vested* **solely** *in a president of the United States of America.*

It was a formidable change that allowed Washington to raise a second pillar of presidential power—the power over executive appointments—and further establish the executive as a *separate* branch of government. Although his successors would have to shore them up occasionally, President Washington had now raised two of seven pillars of presidential power during his first year in office—control over foreign affairs and control over executive appointments and the executive branch of government.

"Congress have by law vested him with powers not delegated by the Constitution, which I suppose they would have entrusted to no other man," complained North Carolina's Antifederalist Representative John Steele.[16]

Washington's triumph actually streamlined government operations. By transferring executive functions from Congress, he lessened the risk of endless debates—in and out of committee—over decisions that could adversely affect national security. With executive functions centralized in the executive branch, a single individual—the President—now had powers to react immediately to security threats with rapid-fire, unilateral decisions.

Nor did the transfer of executive functions weaken the power of either branch to restrict extra-constitutional activities by the other. The

President retained veto powers to check excessive legislative zeal in Congress, while the House and Senate retained their respective powers to restrain excessive executive zeal. The House retained control over appropriations to fund executive operations, and the Senate could reject presidential appointments and foreign treaties. Both houses, together, retained power to override presidential vetoes and, in an extreme case, remove the President from office "on impeachment for, and conviction of, treason, bribery, or other high crimes and misdemeanors." Ironically, the pillars of power Washington was erecting to strengthen the executive branch were also strengthening the legislative and judicial branches and, indeed, the entire federal government.

"The national government is organized . . . to the satisfaction of all parties," Washington concluded with pride in a letter to his friend Gouverneur Morris, who was in Paris on personal business. "The opposition to it is either no more or hides its head."[17]

After only four months in office, Washington had succeeded in reshaping the presidency into an institution that differed substantially from its description in the Constitution. He had opened the doors of the presidential mansion to the public and made the presidency a public institution. By seizing control of executive departments from Congress, he converted the executive into a powerful separate branch of government. By acceding to Washington's demands, Congress, in turn, avoided the embarrassing burlesque of trying to make decisions by committee—a process that had plagued the Confederation Congress.

In 1777, for example, a series of Revolutionary War defeats convinced Congress to transfer supreme command of the army from Washington to a five-man Board of War. The collective deliberations of the board produced a disastrous scheme for Major General Lafayette to lead an invasion of Canada towards winter's end—just as spring floods and melting ice and snow promised to make the army's march all but impossible. When Lafayette arrived in Albany, New York, to lead the invasion, however, he found only a handful of troops, no arms or ammunition or other provisions, and no one in command. The board resigned, and Congress not only restored Washington as commander in chief, it gave him dictatorial powers to direct the military as he saw fit.

Curiously enough, some historians insist that governing a nation was "beyond Washington's ken"[18]—convinced, perhaps, by Thomas Jefferson's disingenuous appraisal years later that Washington's "talents were not above mediocrity, possessing neither copiousness of ideas, nor fluency of words. His time was employed in action chiefly, reading little, and that only in agriculture and English history."[19] Jefferson himself, however, had not fired a shot during the Revolutionary War. After pledging his life, his fortune, and sacred honor, he had fled to the safety of his aerie at Monticello, in the hills of central Virginia, far from the fields of battle. Despite a tenuous exoneration by the Virginia House of Delegates, he still faced accusations of incompetence as governor of Virginia in 1781 for disregarding Washington's instruction to prepare militarily for the British invasion of Virginia and allowing British troops to burn Richmond to the ground.

In fact, Washington had proved himself a remarkably skilled administrator during the war, coordinating the recruitment, training, arming, feeding, clothing, housing, and transport of as many as 25,000 men. He devised a military strategy that permitted an untrained army of underfed, ill-clothed, ill-equipped citizen-soldiers to defeat the world's most powerful, best-equipped, and best-trained professional army and mercenary force. In addition to devising and directing military strategy, Washington directed the army's political and diplomatic strategy, coordinating military activities with the nation's Congress, with thirteen state governors, with a huge French army and naval force, and with French diplomats.

Far from finding presidential functions beyond his ken, Washington was probably the most well prepared executive ever to assume the presidency in American history, having transformed a relatively small tobacco plantation into a diversified agro-industrial enterprise stretching across 20,000 acres, producing tons of tobacco and grains. It included a fishery, meat-processing plant, textile and weaving plants, distillery, gristmill, smithy, brick-making kiln, a cargo-carrying schooner, and endless fields of grain, tobacco, fruits, and vegetables.

Nor had he expanded his plantation haphazardly. In adding a grist-mill, he converted his wheat crops into flour instead of selling them to a miller, thus capturing the profits of both miller and grower. Similarly, the distillery added the profits of the processor to those of the grower, while the smithy and kiln allowed him to profit from the manufacture of horseshoes, tools, and bricks for his own farm by supplying neigh-boring farms. A consummate practitioner of synergistic production and distribution, he bought his schooner to cut shipping costs of his exports to southern and West Indian markets and of imports to Mount Vernon. A lithe participant in the export-import trade, he bought tens of thou-sands of pounds worth of goods each year in Britain and the West Indies. Even in his fields, he recognized that tobacco devoured soil nu-trients in about four years. As a result, he developed a six-year crop ro-tation scheme that continually rejuvenated his fields while producing bumper crops of barley, corn, potatoes, peas, turnips, and clover—as well as tobacco.

In addition to his agricultural success, he was one of America's most successful investors and land developers, acquiring more than 100,000 acres, reselling and leasing properties to settlers across Virginia, Mary-land, Pennsylvania, New York, and the Ohio Valley. Combined with his years in the Virginia House of Burgesses as a legislator and as com-mander in chief of the Continental Army, his success developing and operating his Mount Vernon enterprise made him America's most expe-rienced executive in both business and government.

Knowing that he was the sole elected official who represented the entire nation, he sought to ensure as broad a geographic representation as possible in his cabinet and generate a national consensus for presi-dential decisions. It would prove unworkable and, indeed, one of the President's poorest decisions.

Washington began building his cabinet by retaining his longtime intimate Henry Knox of Massachusetts as Secretary of War. The appointment provoked no accusations of favoritism because Knox was already on the job as holdover Secretary of War from the Confederation Congress.

Washington wanted to appoint Philadelphia's Robert Morris as Secretary of Treasury. Morris had been Secretary of Finance under the Confederation and earned the sobriquet "financier of the Revolution" until Congress replaced him with a three-man Treasury Board. Morris, however, declined, and Washington turned to the young lawyer Alexander Hamilton, whom he also trusted implicitly.

Twenty-three years younger than Washington, Hamilton had been a daring, courageous officer in the Revolutionary War—and one of Washington's most trusted aides-de-camp. After the war, Hamilton studied law and married into a politically powerful family that gave him strong ties to the New York business and banking communities. After founding the Bank of New York he rose to leadership in state politics and the Constitutional Convention. A passionate advocate of the Constitution, Hamilton wrote fifty-one of the eighty-five brilliant essays of the *Federalist*, which made so compelling an argument for ratification.

Washington tried to retain New York's John Jay as head of foreign affairs. Author of five *Federalist* essays, Jay revered the President but had no inclination to serve as a mere extension of Washington's overarching persona and declined, setting his eye instead on the U.S. Supreme Court, where he would be free to act independently.

Washington's second choice for Secretary of State was the second most important figure in America's minuscule "foreign service"—his fellow Virginian Thomas Jefferson. Eleven years younger than Washington, Jefferson was serving the last of five years as America's minister plenipotentiary in Paris and had served five years with Washington in the Virginia House of Burgesses beginning in 1768. Like Washington, Jefferson had supported Henry's famous "liberty-or-death" resolutions to take up arms against British rule but failed to serve in the war. Although Jefferson had been a lukewarm supporter of ratification, Washington fully anticipated his becoming a compliant aide, given the President's vast experience in foreign affairs as commander in chief of the Continental Army liaising with French Army and Navy leaders, as well as French diplomats.

In appointing his first department heads, Washington was not, therefore, seeking any instruction in their respective fields of knowledge, nor did he intend ceding them any of his executive authority. He expected them to serve as conduits, funneling reports on conditions in their spheres of responsibility, along with proposals for executive action and suggestions for legislation that Washington could propose to Congress.

Washington made it clear to his department heads that they would function not as ministers in a British cabinet or as an executive council with veto powers as in the former colonial governments. They were to be his executive assistants to gather information and make recommendations but accept his decisions and implement his directives. He intended keeping all executive powers in his own hands.

As Jefferson later complained, every letter addressed to a department head "was communicated to the President." Department heads had "the trouble of making up, once a day, a packet of all their communications for the perusal of the President.

> If an answer was requisite, the secretary of the department communicated the letter and his proposed answer to the President. Sometimes he returned them with an informal note, suggesting an alteration or a query. If a doubt of any importance arose, he reserved it for conference. By this means, he was always in accurate possession of all facts and proceedings in every part of the Union and to whatever department they related; he formed a central point for the different branches . . . and met himself the due responsibility for whatever was done.[20]

In addition to the three executive departments, Congress established two executive *offices*: The *office* of attorney general was a consultative post, with a lawyer retained to advise the President on the Constitution and the law. As first established, it had no law enforcement powers, although the Constitution gave the President vague authority to "take care that the laws be faithfully executed." The other *office*—the postmaster general—was a temporary position to establish post offices and post roads. Post offices were private franchises, which gave the postmaster general no permanent executive responsibilities.

Washington picked Virginia Governor Edmund Randolph—another former military aide and longtime friend—to be attorney general and Samuel Osgood of Massachusetts as postmaster general. A former member of the Continental Congress and then appointed to the three-man Board of Treasury, Osgood had opposed ratification of the Constitution, but he proved a gracious friend on Washington's arrival in New York, offering his beautifully furnished home as a temporary presidential residence.

The creation of executive departments created job openings in each, and applicants again inundated Washington's desk with pleas for work. From the first, however, President Washington fixed on establishing a precedent for all succeeding presidents by abjuring nepotism and discountenancing personal or blood ties in selecting candidates. In making his appointments, he considered only previous experience and success of the candidates, occasionally skewing his considerations only to effect broad geographic representation.

To his beloved nephew Bushrod Washington, then an accomplished twenty-seven-year-old attorney who had asked for a post as U.S. district attorney for Virginia, the President replied, "However deserving you may be . . . your standing at the bar would not justify my nomination of you . . . in preference of some of the oldest and most esteemed General Court lawyers."

Although Bushrod would later win appointment (deservedly) to the U.S. Supreme Court under the Adams administration, Washington told his nephew that political enemies would examine every appointment to

expose "partiality for friends and relatives. . . . My conduct in nominations . . . must be exceedingly circumspect and proof against just criticism,
for the eyes of Argus are upon me, and no slip will pass unnoticed."[21]

Apart from relatives, a wide range of unqualified applicants appealed
to the President. Their number seemed infinite.

"We are two unfortunate German Officers who were in His Brittan-
ick [sic] Majesty's Service in America during the late unhappy war,"
wrote two of the more brazen applicants, "and having married American sisters . . . we retired with a small capital sufficient to have settled in
an easy situation . . . but after the most indefatigable industry, we were
reduced to such extremities as obliged us to return [to New York] in
hopes of assistance."[22]

Appalled by their gall, Washington kept his answer short and curt:

> The distresses of my fellow creatures are never known to me without
> giving pain, and happy should I be could I relieve the wants and neces-
> sities of every one; but, Gentlemen, that is out of my power, and there
> are thousands of my own countrymen whose misfortune should cer-
> tainly claim my first attention; but even here I am unable to gratify my
> feelings, for I receive no emolument from my public services, and my
> private fortune would be totally inadequate to the numerous applica-
> tions which are made to me for assistance.[23]

Other applicants—the sick and crippled detritus of the Revolution,
along with the poor and hungry—drew more sympathetic responses.

"I have lost my husband, I have only one son to depend on," wrote
the distraught widow of Brigadier General David Wooster, whose home
British troops had plundered. She said her son had "never been able to
recover from the war and at present is entirely out of business with a
large family to support. I know he has petitioned your Excellency for a
post under the new Constitution . . . and must entreat of your Excellency to become a father to him, and relieve him in some measure from

his troubles. Forgive a mother's feelings whose future happiness depends on that of her son."[24]

Clearly moved—indeed, often overwhelmed—by such letters, Washington tried to separate his emotions from his obligations as President. It was fortunate he had been a soldier, with eyes front, unable to see the horrors along the side of the road as he marched to battle.

"Madam," he replied to Mary Wooster,

> I have duly received your affecting letter. Sympathizing with you as I do in the great misfortunes which have befallen your family in consequence of the war, my feelings as an individual would forcibly prompt me to do everything in my power to repair those misfortunes. But as a public man, I must be allowed to decide upon all points of my duty without consulting my private inclinations and wishes. I must be permitted . . . to nominate such persons alone to offices as, in my judgment, shall be the best qualified.[25]

Distraught over having to reject and reject and reject, he expressed his emotions to former Massachusetts Governor James Bowdoin, a political ally who had crushed Shays's rebellion in his state two years earlier. "No part of my duty," Washington told Bowdoin, "will be more delicate, and, in many instances more unpleasing, than that of nominating or appointing persons to offices.

> It will often happen that there will be several candidates for the same office, whose pretensions, abilities, and integrity may be nearly equal. . . . I shall, however . . . have entered upon my administration unconfined by a single engagement, uninfluenced by any ties of blood or friendship, and with the best intentions and fullest determination to nominate those persons only who . . . were the most deserving and who would probably execute their several functions to the interest and credit of the American Union.[26]

One by one, Washington filled every post and replied to every job applicant—among them former General Benjamin Lincoln, a hero of the Revolution who had led the force that crushed Shays's Rebellion in Massachusetts in 1787. Like many applicants, he believed his earlier service to the nation had earned him a permanent—and perhaps lucrative—role in the new government, and he had a sad tale to support his need for a federal appointment.

"When I left public life," Benjamin Lincoln lamented to his former commander in chief, "I had not the least idea of ever returning to it again.

> I then supposed . . . I should be able to give bread to my family in the evening of life. But painful to relate . . . I am stripped of those means of support upon which I had leaned with too much confidence . . . the consequence of which is that I must as a farmer, at this late hour of life, begin the world anew or offer myself as a candidate for some office in the new government.[27]

Even Robert R. Livingston, who, as chancellor of New York had administered the oath of office to Washington, asked for a job—much to Washington's embarrassment. The President tried his best not to hurt Livingston's feelings:

> To you, Sir, and others who know me, I believe it is unnecessary for me to say that when I accepted this important trust . . . I gave up every idea of personal gratification that I did not think was compatible with the public good. . . . I have, therefore . . . resolved whenever I am called upon to nominate persons . . . that I shall do it with a sole view to the public good. . . . The delicacy with which your letter was written did not require me to be this explicit . . . but the desire which I have that those persons whose good opinion I value should know the principles on which I mean to act . . . has led me to this full declaration.[28]

Infuriated by Washington's rejection, Livingston abandoned his Federalist allegiance and began opposing every legislative initiative of the Washington administration.

As the President filled executive posts, Congress tried fulfilling two more constitutional imperatives—establishment of a judiciary and restoration of national solvency. It also faced the political imperative of drawing up a bill of rights for the states to amend the Constitution.

With Virginia's James Madison taking command, the House dealt with national finances first, enacting a tariff law that imposed duties of 7 to 8 percent on a wide range of imports, including tea and molasses— the very duties that Parliament had imposed in 1773 and provoked the Boston Tea Party. Congressmen from New England—the biggest importer of both commodities—howled at Madison's proposals, but Madison reminded them that Americans had not objected to the British molasses and tea taxes themselves, but to their imposition by a legislative body in which Americans were unrepresented. "It was the principle upon which that tax was laid," he insisted, "that made them unpopular under the British government."[29]

In addition to imposing import duties, Congress passed a tonnage bill that exacted duties based on cargo capacity of ships entering American ports. Ships built and owned by Americans paid the least; ships built and owned by foreigners the most.

A third revenue act to end smuggling and ensure "collection of revenue" authorized creation of a Revenue Marine as part of Hamilton's Department of Treasury. Later called the Revenue Cutter Service, it would become the U.S. Coast Guard in 1915.

A fourth revenue act gave the federal government ownership of all lighthouses, beacons, and buoys. Infuriated, the Antifederalist minority called the act unconstitutional and a blatant usurpation of power, but they and the leaders of every coastal state could only watch helplessly as the federal government expanded its grip over the rights and properties of the states.

"The practice of crying out 'this is unconstitutional,'" Federalist Congressman Fisher Ames mocked the southerners, "is a vice that has grown inveterate by indulgence, and those cry out most frequently who were opposed to its adoption."[30]

With few federal laws on the books, Congress delayed creating the judiciary in favor of addressing the nationwide outcry for a bill of rights. Five states were ready to secede over the issue, and powerful political leaders such as Virginia's Patrick Henry and New York Governor George Clinton threatened to call for a second constitutional convention to replace the existing document if Madison failed to fulfill his election campaign pledge to win passage of a bill of rights in the First Congress.

After considering almost one hundred proposed amendments for such a bill, Madison reduced them to seventeen, and on September 25, Congress passed twelve, and President Washington sent them to the states for ratification. Of these, the states approved ten, which became part of the Constitution on December 15, 1791.

Two weeks after agreeing to the amendments, Congress fulfilled the last of its constitutional obligations by creating a federal judiciary with a Supreme Court, a circuit-court system (now the federal courts of appeal), and fifteen federal district courts—one in each state, plus one each in the districts of Maine and Kentucky. As a sop to the Senate for his victory in the battle over control of executive departments, Washington agreed to consult senators on judicial appointments and forego making nominations to which they objected. The precedent of "senatorial courtesy" that he established continues to this day.

To serve on the nation's first Supreme Court, he appointed two members each from the northern, middle, and southern circuits: John Jay of New York and William Cushing of Massachusetts from the North; James Wilson of Pennsylvania and Virginia's John Blair from the middle states; and North Carolina's James Iredell and South Carolina's John Rutledge from the South, with Jay named Chief Justice. In addition to judges, Washington appointed a U.S. district attorney and a federal marshal for each state.

Passage of the Federal Judiciary Act completed the congressional task of establishing a functioning government, and, with the autumn harvest beckoning many members back to their farms and plantations, Congress was ready to adjourn at the end of September 1789. James Madison, however, insisted that his colleagues address one last matter: Like Congress itself, the executive and judiciary branches had no money. The American government was deeply in debt and effectively bankrupt.

With rare unanimity, Congress ordered Treasury Secretary Hamilton to report on the extent of the national debt, the debts of each state, the methods in place—if any—for servicing those and future debts. With that, Congress estimated forthcoming government expenses and agreed on three budgets—$639,000 for 1789, slightly more than $541,000 for 1790, and nearly $741,000 for 1791, with a special $10,000 added to the President's budget to meet emergency expenses. Congress then adjourned for the rest of the year. Although it had approved a budget, it had appropriated no funds and left the government without liquid funds.

With no revenues expected from import duties until the resumption of the shipping season the following spring, Washington had to seize more powers not granted by the Constitution: He sent Treasury Secretary Hamilton to borrow money from private banks against future government revenues, thus assuming at least temporary control over government borrowing and spending for the first time. With his close ties to the banking community, Hamilton obtained a $50,000 loan from the Bank of New York, which he had helped found, and another $50,000 from the Bank of North America at a time when no other bank and almost no government in the world would lend the American government a penny.

With cash in the Treasury to meet day-to-day expenses, Hamilton began fulfilling his congressional mandate to determine how much the

*Secretary of the Treasury Alexander Hamilton
borrowed aspects of the British government's
financial system to help George Washington devise
a financial system to wipe out American
government debts and lead the nation to prosperity.*
(LIBRARY OF CONGRESS)

federal government and each of the states owed domestic and foreign creditors. He knew he would have to act quickly and decisively to stave off national disaster. Indeed, powerful nations were contemplating serious trade boycotts if Congress did not repay its foreign debts. Meanwhile, thousands of angry Americans who had fought in the Revolutionary War and remained unpaid for their service prepared to march on the federal capital. Unless Washington solved the government's fiscal crisis, the veterans were prepared to plunge the nation into civil war.

CHAPTER FIVE

*The Shell Game*

With the framework of government in place, Washington set about dispelling popular fears that the Constitution had simply replaced the British monarchy with a homegrown equivalent. Although eleven of thirteen states had ratified the Constitution before his election, Washington realized that a majority of the people did not meet property qualifications necessary to vote. Indeed, most of those who did not vote in the four most populated states—Virginia, Pennsylvania, Massachusetts, and New York—had opposed ratification.

Fearing disunion and anarchy, Washington sought to promote unity among the citizenry in peace as he had among the soldiery during the Revolution—by mingling with them as no contemporary monarch had ever dared or deigned. "It would be advantageous to the interests of the Union," he explained to Vice President Adams, "for the President to make a tour of the United States . . . to become better acquainted with their principal characters and internal circumstances, as well as to be more accessible to numbers of well-informed persons."[1]

He told Treasury Secretary Hamilton that, as the only government official elected to represent the entire nation, it was important "to acquire knowledge of the face of the country, the growth and agriculture . . . and the temper and disposition of the inhabitants towards the new government."[2] Instead of a mythical figure in formal portraits, he would transform himself into a living "people's president," walking their streets and country lanes, showing his face in their taverns, slogging over muddy fields to appraise their soil and crops, admiring their farmyards and kitchen gardens. Although he detested it, he would let them touch him, shake his hand, and such—and set still another precedent for his successors to the American presidency.

With the First Congress in recess, therefore, Washington set out on Thursday, October 15, 1789, on a festive and triumphant twenty-nine-day journey through Connecticut, Massachusetts, Maine, and New Hampshire, visiting Revolutionary War sites, farms, and a variety of industrial facilities—sawmills, gristmills, textile and silk-making facilities, glassworks, and shipyards. "Manufactury . . . seemed to be going on with spirit," he exulted in his diary. "The farms . . . are small, not averaging more than 100 acres. They are worked chiefly by oxen."[3]

Thousands cheered as he approached each stop, with officials falling over each other to greet him and veterans fighting their way to the front of crowds to salute him. The President adopted a strict rule against lodging in private homes, even refusing an invitation of Governor John Hancock to sleep at magnificent Hancock House on the crest of Beacon Hill in Boston. Public accommodations, Washington insisted, left him "unembarrassed by engagements, and by a uniform adherence to it, I shall avoid giving umbrage to any by declining all such invitations."[4]

His decision to sleep in taverns and inns endeared him all the more to the public, as did his habit of stopping at almost every farm of consequence along his journey to talk knowledgeably with the owner and scoop up handfuls of soil or grain with his huge, rough hands for a closer look and a careful whiff.

Although most city dwellers were unaware of his achievements at Mount Vernon, most farmers recognized him as one of the nation's—and perhaps the world's—leading agriculturalists—indeed, a renowned scientist in his field. A pioneer in crop rotation, his experiments in soil fertilization had been published in scholarly journals in Britain and France (anonymously, to avoid prejudicing readers), and he was a pioneer of and authority in the hybridizing and grafting of fruits and vegetables. He exchanged hundreds of cuttings and seeds with leading agriculturalists in France and England and produced the nation's first dwarf fruit trees and Virginia wine grapes, planting each new species himself in his small experimental garden behind the mansion at Mount Vernon.

With insatiable curiosity, he stopped at every farm of any consequence on his travels. In Stamford, Connecticut, he found "all the farmers busily employed in gathering, grinding, and expressing the juice of their apples, the crop of which they say is rather above mediocrity. The average crop of wheat . . . is about 15 bushels to the acre from their fallow land. The destructive evidence of British cruelty are yet visible . . . as there are the chimneys of many burnt houses standing in them yet."[5]

Each of the cities he visited staged parades, speeches, and public dinners in his honor, but what touched him most were the cheering crowds, often in tears of joy at the sight of the world's greatest military hero—the "Father of Our Country"—presenting himself before and among his countrymen—not as their king empowered by God, but as their president, empowered by them—*We the people.*

---

When Washington returned to New York, Hamilton showed the President a draft of his report on government finances. After digging through more than a decade of federal and state spending records, Hamilton calculated that the newborn U.S. government had inherited foreign debts of just over $11.7 million—about $2 million to Dutch banks and the rest to the French government. Domestic debts totaled just over $42.4 million, including back pay to Revolutionary War veterans, debts to wartime suppliers, unpaid interest, outstanding bonds, and outstanding currency, whose real value had plunged to about two and one-half cents for every dollar of face value. Called "continentals," the basic unit of

American currency had collapsed and provoked the expression, "not worth a continental." Few American creditors and no foreigners would accept American currency or government certificates in payment of debts; the drop in foreign trade plunged the nation into an economic depression, with surpluses of virtually every commodity accumulating in port-side warehouses along the Atlantic coast.

In addition to federal government debts, the states collectively owed about $25 million—$21.5 million of it from the Revolutionary War. Arguing that the Revolution had been a national enterprise, Hamilton proposed that the national government assume all state war debts, thus putting states on a sound financial footing and tying them more tightly to federal controls—in effect, uniting them economically. High state property taxes, Hamilton argued, lay behind much of the unrest in the farmlands—especially in areas with small farms that yielded their owners only a subsistence living. By assuming state debts, the federal government would allow states to reduce property taxes—and the resulting political, social, and economic turmoil.

"The cause in which the expenses of the war was incurred was a common cause," Washington agreed. "The states in Congress declared it so at the beginning and pledged themselves to stand by each other. If then some states were harder pressed than others . . . it is but reasonable . . . that an allowance ought to be made them."[6]

To cover costs of assuming state debts, Hamilton suggested a new 25 percent federal tax on liquor distillers. A "whiskey tax," he reasoned, would not only win support from anti-liquor church-goers and physicians, it would be largely hidden in the price of the finished product— much like import duties.

Although the whiskey tax would help cover costs of assumption, it would do nothing to ease the burden of the huge federal government debt from the war. To that end, Hamilton proposed a plan devised by an English financier early in the century to bail the British government out of bankruptcy. Although nothing short of financial flim-flam, the scheme remains the basis of financial and monetary policy of the United

States and every other western government to this day—as well as all fifty American state governments.

A group of private British banks implemented the scheme after a series of seventeenth- and early eighteenth-century wars had left the English government so deeply in debt that its "paper"—i.e., its bonds and currency—was worthless, along with its credit. British banks, however, saw a way to profit from government debt by pooling some of their resources to form a new bank—the Bank of England—and buy worthless government bonds at next to nothing. In doing so, they not only consolidated government debt in friendly British banking hands, their collective purchases sent market prices for government bonds soaring. Suddenly, the once-worthless bonds had value.

Meanwhile, the British government set up a "sinking fund," or reserve, that it pledged to fill with tax revenues to retire the public debt— i.e., the bonds that the Bank of England had been buying. Although the British government had no cash at the time, Britain remained the world's most important trading nation and collected hundreds of millions of pounds a year from import duties. After years of spending its revenues to support the nation's huge military establishment and the king's lavish way of life, the government's pledge to sequester revenues to retire outstanding debt sent values of government bonds still higher, and the Bank of England reaped a fortune "on paper." The government had no intention of reducing its spending or retiring the debt, of course, but the *news* that it would do both was enough to stabilize the market for its bonds and allow the Bank of England to sell at face value some of the bonds it had bought at next to nothing.

As the Bank of England amassed cash from the sale of once-worthless government paper, the British government could now borrow from the Bank of England without affecting its credit standing overseas. In this way, the Bank of England converted the government's huge annual deficits and crushing debt from *liabilities* into valuable *assets*.

Although the government continued spending recklessly on foreign military adventures and the king continued his personal profligacy, the

Bank of England now controlled the market for government debt, and the promise that the government would repay its debt—false though it was—sustained prices of outstanding government paper at or about 100 percent of face value. The Bank of England helped sustain market values by buying whenever investors sold and selling whenever investors bought.

With the Bank of England always ready to convert bonds into cash at or near face value, bonds became a basis for granting public and private credit. Not only could bond owners use them as collateral, so could the government. Whenever the government needed to spend more money than it earned, it simply floated more bonds, which the Bank of England funneled into the market. Eventually, the Bank of England began printing bank notes (paper money) which it backed with government bonds—which, in turn, were backed by "the full faith and credit" of the government—which, in fact, was bankrupt.

As Hamilton and Washington rocked with laughter and disbelief at the audacity of the Bank of England scheme, Hamilton took advantage of Washington's good mood to propose a similar, albeit more ethical, scheme for solving America's government financial problems. Hamilton knew that, above all else, his plan would have to be ethical for Washington even to listen, let alone consider.

As things stood, the American government had virtually no specie—gold, silver, and so forth—to pay its debts, and no credit to borrow even enough to meet current expenses. Market values of outstanding government debt certificates, promissory notes, and paper money had plunged to near zero. To restore government credit, Hamilton suggested calling in all outstanding government paper at *face* value—regardless of actual market values—and paying for it with a combination of new government paper *and* options to buy government lands in the western wilderness at substantial discounts. The new paper would carry a lower face value than the paper it replaced, but would make up the difference with discounted options for "real" estate of unquestioned value.

The property component would establish faith in the government's ability to repay the new certificates, because the government owned millions of acres of land in the western wilderness, and, in an agrarian nation, land was far more valuable than money. Paper currency could be spent only once; its value was finite, and, once spent, it was gone. The value of land, on the other hand, seemed infinite, yielding endless renewable wealth in crops, timber, pelts, furs, and minerals, year after year—over and above the intrinsic value of the land itself. Americans could live off the land indefinitely and trade the commodities it produced; they could do next to nothing with paper money and only guess its value as they approached the market to buy goods.

To further public faith in the new securities and the government's financial strength, Hamilton proposed establishing a "sinking fund," or reserve account, into which he would deposit a fixed percentage of government revenues each year to ensure repayment of government debts. In addition, he suggested creating a Bank of the United States—like the Bank of England—as the government's own bank, buying and selling government bonds and providing ready cash when government spending exceeded revenues. If the economy boomed, as Hamilton hoped it would, government income would not only cover current expenses but pay interest on the national debt, retire the debt itself, and put federal government finances on a sound foundation, thus calming the nation's financial markets and stimulating foreign trade.

Washington endorsed every element of Hamilton's scheme but the establishment of a national bank, which he feared was unconstitutional. Attorney General Edmund Randolph agreed: "In every aspect . . . under which the Attorney General can view the act so far as it incorporates the bank, he is bound to declare it his opinion to be against its constitutionality." The Constitution, he said bluntly, did not give Congress "the power of creating corporations."[7]

When Congress reconvened, Washington sent Hamilton to deliver his detailed report, with all his proposals except for the national bank.

Few congressmen understood a word of what he said. Some simply closed their ears to the scheme because of its British origins and their deep-seated hatred of all things British—good or bad. Others, annoyed at their own ignorance as much as Hamilton's erudition, howled insults at him, calling him a puppet of moneyed interests—with some justification. Through his marriage, he had established close familial ties to New York's most prominent banking family. A North Carolina newspaper suggested that bankers were behind the scheme. "Were the paper nobility [a euphemism for bankers] to gain control of the certificates of southern states, one section of America would be paying taxes to support a favored class in another."[8]

During fifteen years of Revolutionary War and Confederation, the government had paid soldiers, farmers, craftsmen, and other citizens with government I.O.U.'s, which they, in turn, had resold to bankers, merchants, and speculators for whatever they could get—seldom more than 50 percent of face value and sometimes less than 10 percent. Hamilton's proposal to recall paper at *face* value promised untold riches for those who had exploited soldiers and others struggling to survive. Although somewhere between 25 percent and 40 percent of government securities were still in the hands of original holders, a handful of speculators had accumulated the rest. One Boston money broker had accumulated almost one-fifth of all outstanding U.S. debt certificates—almost $6 million at face value—for a three-man Dutch syndicate.

Before Hamilton could even respond, delegates from the South assailed him for proposing that they help northern states repay their war debts. Virginia and most southern states had already repaid most of their own war debts and were irate at the prospects of being taxed to help repay debts of other states with less responsible fiscal policies.

"Why should Virginians be taxed—unconstitutionally at that—to help discharge the obligations of Connecticut or Massachusetts?" asked the bold-type columns of the *Virginia Independent Chronicle* of Richmond.[9]

Even Federalists from Hamilton's own party denounced him. Virginia Congressman James Madison, a Washington loyalist who had joined Hamilton in writing *The Federalist* essays and championed ratification of the Constitution, abandoned his old political ally and reviled assumption as unconstitutional. Virginia Governor Henry "Light-Horse Harry" Lee, the heroic wartime general and close friend of Washington, raged that disunion would be preferable to domination and economic exploitation by "an insolent northern majority."[10]

Washington fired back, calling Hamilton's critics "enemies of government" who, he said, were always "more active than its friends and always upon the watch to give it a stroke. . . . If they tell the truth, it is not the whole truth; by which means one side only of the picture appears; whereas if both sides were exhibited it might and probably would assume a different form in the opinion of just and candid men."[11]

Although most northern Federalists rallied behind Hamilton, they included among their number a vocal group of northern Quakers who injected slavery into the debate, demanding an end to the slave trade and emancipation of American slaves. Infuriated southerners of all political leanings—Federalists and Antifederalists alike—retaliated by rejecting Hamilton's assumption scheme. As northern and southern delegates assailed each other, talk of disunion began to dominate delegate conversations in the hallways of Federal Hall and nearby taverns.

"People seem almost ripe for a national division of North and South," Massachusetts Representative Benjamin Goodhue reported, while Vice President John Adams lamented that "old friends both in Virginia and Massachusetts hold not in horror as much as I do a division of this continent into two or three nations and have not an equal dread of civil war."[12]

Connecticut's lieutenant governor Oliver Wolcott, a staunch Federalist and supporter of Hamilton's assumption plan, wrote to his son, an auditor at the U.S. Treasury, that Congress should first "take care of the . . . white people of this country [before] they amuse themselves with the other people. The African trade is a scandalous one, but let us take care of ourselves first."[13]

The vicious struggle over assumption took its toll on the President, and, in early May, he left for a five-day vacation on Long Island, where he developed a cold that deteriorated into pneumonia by the time he returned to New York. Four doctors came to treat him. Six days into the illness, his breathing grew labored, and, according to Secretary of State Thomas Jefferson, "he was thought by the physicians to be dying."[14] As word spread to the public, "a universal gloom" spread "throughout the country."[15] Infuriated by the pessimism of the doctors, Martha took charge of the sickroom and applied home remedies that had always cured her grandchildren. She had lost one husband and two children; she was not going to lose this man, whom she adored more than any other living person.

Whatever it was that she did, it worked. "A copious sweat came on," Jefferson reported, "his articulation became distinct, and in the course of two hours it was evident he had gone through a favorable crisis."[16] As Washington's color improved, his fever diminished, and, the next day, Martha pronounced her husband out of danger.

"The severe illness which attacked the President . . . absorbed every other consideration, in my care and anxiety for him," Martha wrote to a friend.

> During the President's sickness . . . he seemed less concerned himself as to the event than perhaps any other person in the United States. Happily he is now perfectly recovered and I am restored to my ordinary state of tranquility, and usually good flow of spirits. If Congress should have a recess this summer . . . I hope to go home to Mount Vernon for a few months: and from that expectation I already derive much comfort. Especially as, I believe, the exercise, relaxation and amusement to be expected from such a journey, will tend very much to confirm the President's health. This is also the opinion of all his Physicians.[17]

Most members of Congress were as elated as Martha over the President's recovery, and Treasury Secretary Hamilton redoubled his efforts to win congressional passage of his assumption scheme. Needing only about three votes to win passage, he turned to his fellow cabinet member, Secretary of State Jefferson, for help. A consummate gourmet and longtime mentor to Madison, Jefferson arranged for a quiet dinner with fine food and wines for Hamilton, Madison, and himself. With a bit of prodding from Jefferson, Hamilton agreed to rally enough northern votes to situate the new federal capital city on the Potomac River in Madison's home state of Virginia in exchange for Madison's switching his own vote and rounding up enough additional southern votes to pass the assumption measure. Madison agreed.

On July 10, the House voted 32 to 29 to designate a ten-mile-square area along the Potomac in Virginia as the new federal capital and charged President Washington with defining the exact boundaries. Two weeks later, Madison switched his vote on assumption and convinced two other southern Federalists to do the same, and Hamilton's bold scheme became law on August 4, 1790.

Now the northerners cried out in protest, with the loudest shouts emanating from Philadelphians, who had hoped to make their city the national capital. One Philadelphian assailed what he called "the corrupt bargain" between Madison and Hamilton, while another warned, "Might not America's most valuable rights be someday similarly traded away." A "Citizen of America" denounced the new location as "wild and savage."[18]

Ignoring critics, Washington grew so elated with Hamilton's success in Congress that he decided to visit Rhode Island, which had ratified the Constitution on May 29 and joined the Union. He had purposely avoided visiting the tiny state during his trip to New England the previous year, but now wanted to welcome it as the thirteenth state. He, Jefferson, and other friends of note boarded a comfortable packet for a pleasant two-day cruise eastward through the calm waters of Long Island

Sound to Narragansett Bay. Putting in at Newport first, Washington surprised some members of his party by insisting on a visit to America's oldest Jewish congregation. Founded in 1658 by fifteen Jewish families, Yeshuat Israel (now Touro Synagogue) welcomed the visibly aging Washington with a biblical allusion and a prayer that "when, like Joshua, full of days and full of honor, you are gathered to your fathers, may you be admitted into the heavenly paradise to partake of the water of life and the tree of immortality."[19]

Visibly moved, Washington publicly embraced an element of the Bill of Rights for the first time, declaring, "It is now no more that toleration is spoken of as if it was by the indulgence of one class of people that another enjoyed the exercise of their inherent natural rights. . . . I am pleased with your favorable opinion of my administration and fervent wishes for my felicity. May the Children of the Stock of Abraham who dwell in this land continue to . . . sit in safety under his own vine and fig tree, and there shall be none to make him afraid."[20]

After two days in Newport, the President and his party sailed to Providence for the usual parades, speeches, and banquets, before sailing back to New York to pack his papers and his and his family's personal effects. The government was moving from New York to Philadelphia, where it would sit for ten years, until the new federal city on the Potomac River was ready to receive it.

After completing the move, Washington and his family set off for Mount Vernon for the first time in seventeen months, satisfied—indeed, elated—that his government "under one federal head," as he had put it in 1783,[21] was now in place and functioning. After only slightly more than a year in office, he had, in effect, reconfigured the Constitution to give him and his successors to the presidency full authority over executive departments and determination of foreign policy. Not only had he stripped Congress of executive functions, his appointees were under constraints to carry out his policies—not their own or those of Congress. Unlike the British prime minister and his cabinet, who were responsible to the majority party in Parliament, President Washington's department heads were responsible to him, and he was responsible only to the American people—regardless of who controlled Congress.

After only slightly more than a year in office, however, Washington still lacked the law-enforcement arm he needed to execute laws as required under the Constitution, but he was an experienced enough politician to await the appropriate opportunity to acquire that power. Despite resistance by Congress, he had already expanded his constitutional authority far beyond that envisioned by the framers, and he knew better than to try to assume too much power too quickly in a land that had only recently overthrown an absolute monarch.

"In a government which depends so much in its first stage on public opinion," Washington exulted as he rode home to Mount Vernon for the 1790 summer recess, "the current of public sentiment runs with us, and all things hitherto seem to succeed according to our wishes. In the meantime, population increases, land is cleared, commerce extended, manufactures introduced, and heaven smiles upon us with favorable seasons and abundant crops."[22]

Unfortunately, heaven was about to stop smiling.

# CHAPTER SIX

❦

## *Alive with Wrath*

With a pack of his beloved hounds bounding ahead, Washington resumed his exhilarating morning rides across his 20,000-acre plantation at Mount Vernon in the summer of 1790. He always returned to the mansion for dinner, where Martha had gathered their grandchildren, step-children, adopted children, nieces, nephews, brothers and sisters, and a broad assortment of relatives and friends at the table for the huge, joyful mid-day meal. Both Martha and George Washington adored children, and, aside from their two grandchildren "Washy" and Nelly," they had also "adopted" and raised as their own Martha's niece Fanny, whose mother had died, and the three children—two boys and a girl— of George's late brother Samuel. Indeed, George was putting Samuel's two boys through the University of Pennsylvania and planned to send Martha's grandson George Washington Parke Custis ("Washy") to Princeton.

It was not long, however, before political discontent over assumption began to cloud Virginia's political skies and temper the joyous atmosphere at Mount Vernon. Led by former Governor Patrick Henry, the outspoken foe of the Constitution, Virginia's Assembly protested that it found "no clause in the Constitution authorizing Congress to assume the debts of the states." Hamilton responded by warning Washington, "This is the first symptom of a spirit which must either be killed or will kill the Constitution."[1]

Although Congress had clearly assumed for itself or ceded to the President powers not granted by the Constitution, assumption was now the law of the land, and Henry and his Virginians had little choice but to conform or secede from the Union. As he had after ratification, Henry stirred the political pot to a boil, only to desist and urge his followers to remain in the Union and continue struggling "in a constitutional way" against expansion of the federal government.[2]

Emboldened by his victory, Hamilton asked Congress to empower the Treasury to establish the sinking fund for accumulating revenues to retire the national debt and to enact the tax on imported and domestic liquors and on domestic stills. As he knew it would, his tax proposal won immediate support from scientists and certain church groups, which favored "heavy duties upon all distilled spirits . . . to restrain their intemperate use in our country." Comparing spirits consumption to a plague, Hamilton said he saw "no just cause why the more certain and extensive ravages of spirits upon human life should not be guarded with corresponding vigilance and exertions."[3] Congress agreed and passed the taxes over the objections of southern and western delegates.

Hamilton was wise enough a politician to await the approach of the festive Christmas season of 1790 before proposing creation of the Bank of the United States. A cofounder of the Bank of New York, Hamilton knew other bankers too well to trust them with direct control of government funds. He wanted to establish a government-owned bank where, at day's end, he himself could count the government's money. With the Constitution already fraying at the edges, Washington remained skeptical, and he submitted Hamilton's proposal to his cabinet and to his ally in Congress, James Madison. All agreed that a bill creating a government bank was unconstitutional. Jefferson cited the Tenth Amendment: "I consider that 'all powers not delegated to the U.S. by the Constitution . . . are reserved to the states.' The incorporation of a bank . . . has not, in my opinion, been delegated to the U.S. by the Constitution."[4]

And James Madison not only echoed Jefferson's opinion, he went so far as to prepare a veto message for the President in case Congress passed the measure. Having heard all the arguments against the bill, Washington waited to hear from Hamilton, who responded with a 13,000-word earful of arguments for establishing the bank. The Treasury Secretary knew his old army commander better, perhaps, than anyone outside the President's immediate family. As a wartime aide, he had become one of Washington's legendary "three sons" during the Revolutionary War, with Lafayette and South Carolina's John Laurens.

Unable to have children of his own and disappointed by the failure of his stepson John Parke Custis to enlist in the war, Washington had all but adopted Hamilton, Lafayette, and Laurens. Only approaching twenty when they volunteered to fight without pay—as, indeed, Washington had done—they proved themselves as dedicated to the founding of the new nation and as fearless in battle as Washington himself, fulfilling the commander in chief's fantasies of the heroic soldier-sons he never had.

For Hamilton and Lafayette—both orphaned as youngsters (again like Washington)—Washington became the father they never had, mentoring them in the arts of war, leadership, diplomacy, and the principles of republican government. As his closest aides, they ate with him, slept near him, and became an integral part of his life. All three had fought heroically in key battles throughout the war, and all three led the fearsome bayonet charge that breached the perimeter of British defenses in the American triumph at Yorktown.

To Washington's deep despair, Laurens was killed in action at the end of the war, and Lafayette returned home to France. Only Hamilton remained at his side now—a supremely successful lawyer, banker, and political leader—a man who knew the workings of Washington's mind as well as Washington himself.

Convinced (like Washington by then) that the Constitution had been written on "frail fabric,"[5] Hamilton humiliated Attorney General Randolph and Secretary of State Jefferson by shredding each of their arguments and providing an almost irrefutable military-style argument in favor of his own proposal: Article One, Section 8 of the Constitution, he reminded them, gave Congress "the power of collecting taxes . . . borrowing money . . . regulating trade between the states, and . . . raising, supporting, and maintaining fleets and armies." It also gave Congress power "to make all laws which shall be necessary and proper for carrying into execution the foregoing powers." It was, therefore, "clearly" constitutional for the government to make "all needful rules and regulations concerning the *property* of the United States." The money the government dispensed was U.S. *property*, which the government had an obligation to protect in an appropriate repository—a bank. "A bank," he declared, "relates to the collection of taxes . . . facilitates the means of paying . . . by creating a convenient . . . medium in which they are to be paid."[6]

Hamilton then focused on what he knew had been Washington's worst nightmare as commander in chief during the Revolution—the inability of Congress to raise money to supply the army and pay its men. Few in government had forgotten Washington's desperate plea for his men at Valley Forge at Christmas 1777:

> *It is not easy to give you a just and accurate idea of the sufferings of the troops. On the 23rd [of December], I had in camp not less than 2,898 men unfit for duty by reason of their being bare foot and otherwise naked. . . . I can not but hope that every measure will be pursued . . . to keep them supplied from time to time. No pains, no efforts can be too great for this purpose. The articles of shoes, stockings, blankets demand the most particular attention.[7]*

Reminding Washington of his plight during the Revolution, Hamilton declared, "A bank is . . . an essential instrument in the obtaining of loans to government. A nation is threatened with a war. Large sums are wanted on a sudden to make the requisite preparations. Taxes are laid . . . but it requires time to obtain the benefit of them. If there be a bank, the supply can at once be had."[8]

Hamilton's argument convinced his chief, who, in turn, bullied recalcitrant congressional leaders into passing the bill. President Washington signed it into law on February 25, 1791, and, to the surprise of Federalists as well as Antifederalists—indeed, to Washington himself—American and European financiers and industrialists snapped up $8 million of the bank's capital stock of $10 million, with the President subscribing to the remaining $2 million for the U.S. government.

The bank was to establish branches across the United States and have an exclusive federal charter to issue notes and bills. With taxes on imported and domestic spirits expected to yield nearly $1 million a year, the U.S. government and its creditors envisioned quick and early repayment of Revolutionary War debts.

Despite the opposition it had engendered, assumption proved to be an enormous political and economic triumph for Washington and Hamilton, who together now raised another pillar of power in the presidential edifice: the power over the public purse. With two other pillars of power in place—foreign affairs and executive appointments—power over the public purse gave the President, after less than two years in office, wide latitude to borrow and spend without congressional approval.

"The astonishing rapidity with which the . . . bank was filled," Washington exulted to his aide David Humphreys, "gives an unexampled proof of the resources of our countrymen and their confidence in public measures. On the first day of opening the subscription, the whole number of shares (20,000) were taken up in one hour, and application made for upwards of 4000 shares more were granted. . . . Our public credit stands on ground which three years ago would have been considered madness to have foretold."[9]

A predecessor of the Federal Reserve Bank, Hamilton's Bank of the United States restored public confidence in the faith and credit of the new

U.S. government and set off a wave of unprecedented national prosperity. As revenues flowed into the Treasury, the federal government began paying off its debts with interest; the weather cooperated and produced record crops for farmers and furs and pelts for trappers; American craftsmen flourished and American goods appeared in markets around the world. "The country appears to be in a very improving state," Washington concluded, "and industry and frugality are becoming much more fashionable than they have hitherto been. Tranquility reigns among the people."[10]

Although many historians credit Hamilton for the entire scheme—and he did envision and implement it—it was Washington who studied and researched it before approving it and sending it to Congress. Even Hamilton admitted that Washington's influence *alone* won its passage. Congress would never have approved it on Hamilton's word alone; indeed, the U.S. Senate took pains to credit the President for his economic program.

"The benefits which flow from a restoration of public and private confidence," it declared in a rare, specially prepared address, personally delivered and read aloud to the President by John Adams at the presidential residence, "are conspicuous and important. . . . We observe, Sir, the constancy and activity of your zeal for the public good. The example will promote our efforts to promote the happiness of our country."[11]

Hamilton's swift, effective distortion of constitutional intent and his efficient seizure of powers over the national purse left Jefferson all but an ornament in Washington's cabinet. Shaken by his fall to irrelevancy, Jefferson grew convinced that executive assumption of extra-constitutional powers threatened the nation with tyranny. He resolved to unseat Hamilton and, if necessary, destroy him.

His resolve presaged the organization of the nation's first political parties, with him and Hamilton as titular leaders—each with opposite views on the role of the federal government in American political life. Coaxing James Madison to join him on a "botanical" excursion to Lake Champlain, in upstate New York, Jefferson recruited the diminutive Virginian for his new party with a promise of the most important post in a future Jefferson administration—that of Secretary of State. For Jefferson, Madison became nothing less than "a pillar of support."[12] On the way to Lake Champlain, Jefferson and Madison lured New York's powerful, five-time Antifederalist governor, George Clinton, into their political camp, which they now began calling the Democratic-Republican Party.

Jefferson had both political and emotional motives for opposing Hamilton. Politically, he believed Hamilton's Bank of the United States was an unconstitutional government intrusion in business. He also feared the bank concentrated too much power over government finances in the hands of the executive and, combined with executive powers over the military, it opened the way for reestablishing monarchy. As Patrick Henry had raged in his battle against ratification, "the sword and the purse" were the two greatest powers of government and "the junction of these in the same hands is . . . despotism."[13]

Apart from political motives, Jefferson had deep-seated emotional motives for plotting against Hamilton—stemming largely from the humiliations Jefferson had suffered in almost every cabinet-level confrontation with the glib New York lawyer. Hamilton was a street fighter. Orphaned and often forced to survive on his wits as a child, he had developed a quick tongue that made him a far more effective courtroom lawyer than the soft-spoken Jefferson, a Virginia gentleman who grew up coddled by slaves on his father's tobacco plantation.

Hamilton's astonishing heroism as an officer in the Revolutionary War further embarrassed and embittered Jefferson. While Hamilton charged into enemy lines at Trenton, Monmouth, and Yorktown, gentleman Tom Jefferson sat by the fire in his southern mansion without firing a shot. An admitted failure as a wartime governor of his state, Jefferson still smarted from taunts of cowardice, while Hamilton collected accolades for his wartime heroism. Consumed with envy, Jefferson responded by vowing to destroy the low-born hero from New York.

Although Jefferson and Hamilton managed to work together in the early days of the administration, each had radically different visions of the presidential structure they were helping Washington build. Hamilton mistrusted the intelligence of the ordinary citizen and his ability to govern; he believed in a strong, national government led by a highly educated elite under a powerful chief executive—conforming in many ways to Plato's *Republic*.

Jefferson, on the other hand, distrusted government—especially a centralized national government—and held a naive belief akin to Rousseau's in the goodness of man and his ability to govern himself free of government intrusion in his life. Although Hamilton (and, indeed, Washington) reviled anarchy as an inevitable result of Jeffersonian society, Jefferson exalted anarchy as "proof that the people have liberty. . . . I hold it that a little rebellion now and then is a good thing. . . . The tree of liberty must be refreshed from time to time with the blood of patriots and tyrants."[14]

The great—and still-unexplained—irony of the political divisions between the two men are the irrational fantasies that generated some of those divisions. Jefferson accused Hamilton of being a monarchist when, in fact, Hamilton had been the primary author of *The Federalist* essays that rallied support for republican government under the very Constitution that Jefferson now embraced. Hamilton, moreover, had never owned slaves and had led the fight to free slaves in New York State. An active member of the New York Manumission Society, he had publicly stated his belief in the equality of blacks and whites and called slavery "repugnant to humanity . . . inconsistent with the liberality and justice which should distinguish a free and enlightened people."[15]

In contrast, Jefferson owned about two hundred slaves, believed they were inferior to whites, and, like many southern planters, he pretended to embrace populism while condemning Hamilton and northern Federalists as aristocrats.

Clearly envious of Hamilton's evident influence with Washington, Jefferson initiated the feud by either inventing or embellishing the fable of Hamilton having toasted British King George III at a New York dinner. Never one to let facts stand in the way of his conclusions, Jefferson simply scoffed at Hamilton's authorship of two-thirds of the *Federalist* essays and his critical role in winning manumission of slaves in New York and that state's ratification of the Constitution.

As Washington's first term neared its end, raw ambition turned Hamilton and Jefferson into all-but-crazed adversaries. Each took advantage of divisions in Congress between northern Federalists and southern states' rights advocates to nourish the embryos of America's two-party political system. With Washington expressing weariness with the burdens of office, both Hamilton and Jefferson lusted to succeed him. Jefferson and Madison fostered formation of "Democratic Clubs" by former Antifederalists in major cities to promote Jefferson's candidacy, while Jefferson worked to undermine Hamilton's influence on Washington.

"The Department of Treasury," Jefferson warned the President, "possesses already such an influence as to swallow up the whole executive power, and future presidents . . . will not be able to make head against this department."[16] Jefferson went on to accuse Hamilton of preparing "a change from the present republican form of government to that of a monarchy."[17]

To build his political party, Jefferson needed financial backers, a publicity machine, and a large constituency of loyal voters. Always quicker than Jefferson, Hamilton already had all three, tapping wealthy New York bankers for financial support and votes and corralling political workers from the nearly five hundred customs officials, tax collectors, and Treasury Department employees who depended on him for employment.

For publicity, Hamilton, John Jay, and New York Senator Rufus King pooled $2,500 for New York printer John Fenno to found the *Gazette of the United States* to promote popular support of Federalism. Hamilton ensured the newspaper's financial support with Treasury Department paid–notices. In addition to the *Gazette of the United States*, Hamilton had editorial support from the Federalist *Massachusetts Centinel, Providence*

*Gazette, New York Packet, Pennsylvania Packet*, and *Charleston Evening Gazette*. As John Adams later put it, Hamilton was "in a delirium of ambition . . . had fixed his eyes on the highest station in America, and he hated every man, young or old who stood in his way or could in any manner eclipse his laurels or rival his pretensions."[18]

Jefferson had little to counter Hamilton's political juggernaut. His staff at the State Department was minimal, although he and Madison hoped the Democratic Clubs would be able to organize a large enough bloc of supporters to counter Hamilton's banker friends and Treasury bureaucrats. He could count on press support from only three newspapers, however—Boston's *American Herald*, the *New York Journal*, and Philadelphia's *Freeman's Journal*.

To further disseminate his views and promote his candidacy, he called on the failed poet/journalist Philip Freneau to establish and edit a new periodical, the *National Gazette*. He fed Freneau some financial support by giving him a sinecure as a translator at the State Department, with no obligation even to set foot in the department, let alone translate documents. With printing costs covered by an Antifederalist New York printer, Freneau wrote vicious editorials attacking Hamilton as the dishonest leader of a monarchist conspiracy "bottomed on corruption,"[19] while proclaiming Jefferson a "Colossus of Liberty." Hamilton countered with editorials in the *Gazette of the United States* under the pseudonym "Catullus," one of ancient Rome's great lyric poets.

"Mr. Jefferson has hitherto been distinguished as the quiet, modest, retiring philosopher—as the plain, simple, unambitious republican," Catullus wrote unpoetically. Jefferson's pose, Catullus contended, was but an "artful disguise—like Caesar *coyly refusing* the proffered diadem . . . but tenaciously grasping the substance of imperial domination."[20]

The two newspapers attacked each other, exposing their political backers. A letter in Fenno's *Gazette of the United States* asked whether Freneau's State Department salary from Jefferson "is paid him for *translations* or for *publications*, the design of which is to vilify those to whom the voice of the people has committed the administration of our public affairs?"[21]

Unlike Hamilton's backers, many Jefferson supporters were poor back-country farmers. Hamilton, however, was the "friend to order and good government" for America's wealthiest voters—bankers, merchants, and owners of great land holdings. The wealthiest Americans supported a strong central government that would use force, if necessary, to crush farmer tax revolts, maintain law and order, and put government finances on a sound foundation.[22]

Unaware of—or unwilling to see—the growing split in his cabinet, Washington set off in a joyous mood in the spring of 1791 on the second part of his quest to tour the United States, determined to have "the same effect to the Southward as it did to the Eastward" in 1789.

"Something of a soothing nature is much wanted in the southern states," declared Tobias Lear, Washington's secretary and closest personal aide. "The additional duty on distilled spirits and the Bank of the U.S. are said . . . to be extremely disagreeable there. But it is to be hoped that the presence of our Chief Magistrate will . . . dispel the gloom of discontent"[23]

Unfortunately, Washington was aging rapidly, and, racked by arthritic pains, he made the political error of departing in a large, new, comfortable, cream-colored carriage that had just arrived from England. Pulled by four magnificent cream-colored Belgian draft horses, the ornate "chariot," as he called it, seemed more of an emperor's equipage than that of a popularly elected official in a self-governing republic. His route took him through Maryland, eastern Virginia, the Carolinas, and Georgia, where obsequious federal appointees assured him that the South was "favorable towards the central government" and that the people gave "their full assent to the measures adopted by it."[24] The President concluded that southerners everywhere were "happy, contented, and satisfied with the government under which they were placed." Where the case was otherwise, it was not difficult to trace the cause to some demagogue or speculating character.

"The country appears in a very improving state," he wrote to David Humphreys, a presidential aide who had remained behind in the capital.

Tranquility reigns among the people, and with it that disposition towards the general government which is likely to preserve it. They begin to feel the good effects of equal laws and equal protection. The farmer finds a ready market for his produce, and the merchant calculates with more certainty on his payments.[25]

Jefferson was less sanguine, however. "There is a vast mass of discontent gathered in the South and how and when it will break God knows."[26]

## CHAPTER SEVEN

# Tar and Taxes

"What was it that caused the Revolution if it was not this?" wrote an angry Democrat-Republican about Hamilton's "whiskey tax " in Philadelphia's *National Gazette*.

The tax had gone into effect on March 3, 1791, and affected nearly all Americans, with particularly harsh effects in western Pennsylvania, where farmers owned about one quarter of America's whiskey stills. Indeed, whiskey had become fundamental to frontier economics.

After the Spanish barred American navigation on the Mississippi River, the absence of roads over the rugged Appalachian Mountains left western farmers with no means of transporting grain in bulk to market. By distilling it into whiskey, however, they were able to carry the fruit of their labor in kegs and jugs by packhorse or mule over narrow mountain trails to eastern towns. Nearly every farmer west of the Appalachians put in a still, but Hamilton's tax now threatened to shut most of them down. Based on still *capacity* rather than production or sales, it touched *every* farmer whether he made whiskey to sell or drink himself—or if, for whatever reason, he shut down his still for a while and made no whiskey at all.

For most farmers, therefore, the whiskey tax was nothing less than legalized government theft that would bankrupt them and let eastern bankers foreclose on their farms and reap the profits from reselling the lands.

Western farmers were not alone in opposing the whiskey tax, however. A majority of Americans opposed it to some degree. Whiskey was the most widely consumed beverage in America—for medicinal purposes as well as pleasure—and it had evolved into a form of cash in small towns and rural areas, with a far more stable value than the crudely printed paper currencies that banks turned out. In a barter economy, buyers and sellers everywhere routinely traded "white lightning," as they called their colorless whiskey, in various-sized jugs for dry goods and other provisions.

As with Britain's 1765 stamp tax, opposition to the whiskey tax began at popular meetings, where citizens channeled their outrage by forming "action committees" to seek redress within the constitutional system. When state governments failed to respond, protesters turned to Congress. Faced with under-representation in that body, back-country farmers petitioned for the right to carve out new states on the frontier. As independent states, they would gain equal representation in the U.S. Senate and louder voices in the House with which to seek repeal of the hated tax. Maine sought separation from Massachusetts, Kentucky from Virginia, and western Pennsylvania demanded independence as the new state of Westsylvania, much as the State of Franklin (later Tennessee) had done in western North Carolina in 1784.

"No country or people can be either rich, flourishing, happy or free," came the cry from the West, "whilst annexed to or dependent on any province, whose seat of government is . . . four or five hundred miles distant, and separated by a vast, extensive and almost impassable tract of mountains, by nature itself formed and pointed out as a boundary."[1]

Backed by moneyed interests in the East, President Washington and Congress responded with outrage, accusing secessionist leaders of irresponsibility, disloyalty, even treason. Washington predicted that if "the daring and factious spirit which has arisen" were not subdued, "we may bid adieu to all government in this country, except mob government from whence nothing but anarchy and confusion can ensue."[2]

Some of Washington's outrage was personal as well as political. Over the years, he and many other absentee landowners with properties in the West had grown exasperated with what they deemed lawless tenant farmers, not to mention squatters, who consistently failed to pay rent. Although Washington hired a local agent to collect rents in his western Pennsylvania holdings, the farmers simply bribed the agent with whiskey and, by 1792, Washington despaired of ever collecting a penny. After putting his lands up for sale, he summarily fired his agent: "The continual disappointments I meet with in the receipt of my rents under your collection in the counties of Fayette and Washington," wrote the President, "lays me under the painful necessity of placing the business in other hands."[3]

Infuriated by Washington's hostility towards state separatists, secessionist leaders in Vermont and Maine turned to Canada and Britain for protection. "The locality of Vermont, as well as the disposition of its inhabitants," wrote Ethan Allen's brother Levi in a petition to the governor general of Canada, "renders its connection with Canada the most natural as well as the most advantageous of any."[4]

In the West, British agents contacted secessionist leaders in Kentucky, Ohio, and western Pennsylvania—only to find themselves bidding against Spanish agents who promised rights of free navigation on the Mississippi River and free trade in New Orleans if they declared independence from the United States and "put themselves under the protection of Spain."[5]

Canada's Governor John Graves Simcoe, whose troops had encouraged Indian raids against American settlers in the West, wrote to the British foreign minister for support. He said he believed American government failure to protect the frontier against Indian raids and win free Mississippi River navigation rights from Spain had left Kentuckians ready to secede. He urged offering Kentuckians access to the St. Lawrence for their grain—to "make the state of Kentucky look up to . . . [Britain] for union and alliance. . . . They must experience great disadvantages if they continue an American state."[6]

When, therefore, the first whiskey-tax collectors arrived near Pittsburgh, in September 1791, farmers were ready to fight for independence from the government of President George Washington, the once-revered commander of these very rebels. Newspapers reflected their views, assailing Washington, Congress, and the army—much as they had assailed King George III, Parliament, and the Redcoats two decades earlier.

The *Pittsburgh Gazette* called the whiskey tax "obnoxious to the interest of the people" by reintroducing "the laws of Great Britain and of countries where liberty, property, and even the morals of the people are sported with." The newspaper charged that the tax discriminated against one domestic manufacture, one region of the country, and against citizens of the "laborious and poorer class."[7]

On September 6, sixteen farmers kidnaped tax collector Robert Johnson, cut off his hair, tarred and feathered him, and left him in the woods near Pittsburgh to die. A federal district court issued arrest warrants for the attackers, but the marshal was so terrified he sent a simple-minded cattle drover to serve the papers. The rebels pounced on the poor man, whipped him, tarred and feathered him, and left him tied in the woods, where he lay in agony for five hours before being rescued.

A month later, the attacks grew more vicious, with one gang assaulting a young school teacher they believed had applied for a job as tax collector. They waited until nightfall, pulled him from his bed, dragged him to a blacksmith shop and branded him with hot irons before rolling him in tar and feathers and throwing him into the street shrieking and writhing in pain.

In scenes reminiscent of the Stamp Act protests of 1765 in the East, rebel torches set skies aglow across the West; night after night, mobs marched over the land, blasting stills of farmers who paid the tax, setting fire to homes of government sympathizers, and tarring and feathering tax collectors and anyone suspected of harboring a tax collector. Hamilton urged Washington to crush the protesters:

> My present conviction is that it is indispensable . . . to exert the full force of the law against the offenders. . . . If this is not done, the spirit of disobedience will naturally extend, and the authority of the government will be prostrate. Moderation enough has been shown; 'tis time to assume a different tone.[8]

As it turned out, the early onset of winter sent most "whiskey boys" back to their homes without the need for Washington to intervene. But the whiskey protest was not the only violent conflict facing the President in the West at the end of 1791. Even as Pennsylvania farmers were attacking federal tax collectors, Indian tribes in the Northwest Territory had formed a confederation and sent an army to wipe out American settlements south of the Great Lakes, between the Ohio and Mississippi Rivers.

Although Britain had ceded the territory to the United States in the 1783 treaty that ended the Revolution, the British government left troops there to harass the new American government and try to provoke its collapse. While British warships seized American ships off eastern shores in the Atlantic, British troops supplied Indian tribes with arms and ammunition to attack American settlers in the West.

In November 1791, after a tribal army in Ohio crushed an American force under Territorial Governor Arthur St. Clair, Washington lost his patience. Ignoring constitutional restraints, he ordered Secretary of War Knox to send St. Clair with a force of 2,000 men to "seek the enemy . . . and strike them with great severity"—in effect assuming for himself the constitutional prerogative of Congress to declare war.[9]

Inexperienced in battlefield command, St. Clair led his troops to disaster. "I have now the painful task," he reported to Secretary Knox on November 9, 1791, "to give you an account of as warm and as unfortunate an action as almost any that has been fought, in which every corps was engaged and worsted."

As his troops slept, he said, the Indians freed or killed all the horses in the encampment, then showered it with bullets and slaughtered more than 900 Americans, including 40 officers. "The camp and the artillery were abandoned," St. Clair related, "for not a horse was left alive to have drawn it off.

> But the most disgraceful part of the business is that the greatest part of the men threw away their arms and accouterments. . . . I found the road strewed with them for many miles, but was not able to remedy it, for having had all my horses killed and being mounted upon one that could not be pricked out of a walk, I could not get forward myself, and the orders sent forward either to halt or to prevent the men from parting with their arms were unattended to.[10]

St. Clair's was the worst defeat at the hands of Indians since Braddock's loss near Fort Duquesne (now Pittsburgh) in the summer of 1755, when Washington himself had barely escaped death in a similar Indian ambush. Just as he had converted Braddock's defeat into personal triumph by leading survivors to safety, Washington converted St. Clair's defeat into a political advantage.

With unprecedented openness for a head of state, he marched into Congress to "communicate to you the information received from Major General St. Clair of the misfortune which has befallen the troops under his command. Although the national loss is considerable . . . yet it may be repaired without great difficulty, excepting as to the brave men who have fallen."[11]

His startling announcement after only three years in office contrasted sharply with European monarchs who routinely concealed bad news from constituents. In presenting Congress—and the American people—with the truth about St. Clair's defeat, Washington not only set a precedent for "open government" in the United States, he used the bad news to provoke Congress into avenging the American loss by passing the Militia Act. The act gave Washington extra-constitutional powers to draft state militia into a federal force to fulfill Section 3, Article II of the Constitution, which instructed the President to "take care that the laws be faithfully executed."

The measure extended the President's powers beyond simple law enforcement to include suppression of domestic insurrections, repelling invasions by foreign troops, and coping with a variety of other threats to national security. Although the Militia Act initially required consent of a federal judge, Congress later removed that restriction, giving the President all-but-unfettered powers "to raise . . . armies" and call up militia without a declaration of war by Congress. The act raised another pillar of power—the fourth in the increasingly large and mighty presidential edifice: the power to lead the nation to war without the immediate consent of Congress or the people. To no avail, the advocates of states' rights reiterated the ominous warning of Patrick Henry: "The junction of . . . the sword and the purse . . . in the same hands is despotism."[12]

After only three years in office, the politically wily Washington had transformed the office of the president from that of an impotent figurehead to one that commanded almost as much power as the British king he had overthrown with his victory at Yorktown.

With four pillars of presidential power firmly in place—executive appointments, foreign affairs, finance, and military—Washington sought to establish presidential authority as a stabilizing rather than a repressive force. In doing so, he addressed the concerns of Patrick Henry and Antifederalists that future presidents would convert their powers over sword and purse into tyrannical rule. He decided on a two-fold strategy of preparing for war but making peace and accommodation the major thrust of governmental policy. In other words, he would explore every road to peace before going to war—again, a precedent for successors in the use of military power. To implement his policy, he ordered Secretary of War Knox to recruit the retired Revolutionary War hero Major General "Mad" Anthony Wayne to travel west and raise an army of 5,000 sharpshooters. At the same time, he ordered Knox to draw up a peace proposal to the Indians to try to avert war.

"Brothers," Washington declared in the peace overture:

> The President of the United States entertains the opinion that the war which exists is founded in error and mistake on your parts: That you believe that the United States want to deprive you of your lands and drive you out of the country. Be assured this is not so. On the contrary . . . we should be greatly gratified with the opportunity of imparting to you all the blessings of civilized life, of teaching you to cultivate the earth and raise corn; to raise oxen, sheep, and other domestic animals; to build comfortable houses and to educate your children so as ever to dwell upon the land.
>
> Brothers: The President of the United States requests you . . . to reflect how it will be for your interest to be at peace with the United States . . . than to continue a war which . . . must in the end prove ruinous. . . . Reflect upon the consequences . . . Repair to Philadelphia . . . and there make a peace. . . . If your tribes can prove that you have a right to any lands comprehended by the said treaties and have not been compensated therefor, you shall receive full satisfaction.[13]

After Knox dispatched infantry Captain Alexander Trueman with the President's message, he learned to his dismay that Wayne, by then a not-too-successful rice grower in Georgia, had refused his commission, saying that the peace overture would undermine his credibility. "I cannot . . . think of committing my military character (which is dearer to me than life) to the fortuitous events of a war—which I can not direct," Wayne complained. If Trueman's peace overture met with success, he argued, "the glory and honor will belong to another." All out war, on the other hand, could lead to disaster, in which case "I must share in the disgrace."[14]

Washington was not surprised by Wayne's refusal. The President had often characterized Wayne as "brave, and nothing else . . . more active and enterprising than judicious and cautious"—a man who was very apt to "run his head against a wall where success was both impossible and useless."[15] Wayne was, however, Washington's most experienced battlefield commander, and, when a band of Indians ambushed and killed Trueman before he could deliver his peace overture, Washington again reached out to Wayne, and Wayne relented.

In the spring of 1791, the "Mad" major general began the long ride west to Ohio to raise an army without the consent of Congress and confront the Indians. The outcome would determine the fates of thousands of settlers, the Washington administration, and the Union itself. If Wayne failed, the evident inability of the federal government to protect western settlers would almost certainly provoke secession by the western territory and union with Canada under the protection of British troops.

When the House of Representatives learned of Wayne's plans, critics jumped to their feet in protest. "We are preparing to squander away money by millions, and no one, except those who are in the secrets of the cabinet knows for what reason." Wayne issued a retort, defending the war as justified by the Indians and asserting that "a vigorous and effectual exertion" would "bring the matter to a final issue."[16]

———

As Wayne rode west to settle the nation's Indian problems, Washington began looking to younger leaders to take the reins of government. With less than a year left until the end of his term, Washington wanted nothing more than to retire. He believed he had done his job. Sixty years old, without teeth, racked by arthritic pains in his joints, he found the simple act of feeding himself at the table set his mouth ablaze with pain. He longed—indeed, he began planning—to retire to his beautiful and beloved Mount Vernon "under the shadow of my own vine and my own fig tree, free from . . . the busy scenes of public life."[17] Only the threat of disunion, he said, could keep him in Philadelphia, and all but dismissing the possibility of such a threat, he asked James Madison to write a farewell address to Congress. Martha was ecstatic.

In mid-May 1792, he left the capital for a short visit to his plantation, where he rejoiced over his healthy-looking crops. "The harvest . . . promises to be abundant," he exulted to a friend, "particularly wheat." He said his crops appeared "much more flattering than I had known them for many years past, and the country generally exhibited the face of plenty."[18]

Clearly delighted to be home and focusing on his first love—farming—he looked forward to what he had told James Madison was "the fulfillment of my fondest and most ardent wishes to spend the remainder of my days (which I cannot expect will be many) in ease and tranquility."[19]

Besides his gift as an agricultural scientist, Washington was also a consummate inventor, and he turned to improving the efficiency of his farming operations by developing new tools and farm structures. He designed a radically new threshing barn that remains "a milestone in American farm architecture," according to modern authorities.[20] The two-story barn was a sixteen-sided, virtually round structure with second-story floor boards spaced one and one-half inches apart. Threshers had always separated the grain from the chaff outdoors, either by hand with flails or by treading, with horses stamping loose the grain with their hooves. Washington's barn eliminated two costly drawbacks of outdoor threshing—exposure to wet weather and theft.

He built the barn near an embankment to allow horses to enter the second-floor threshing room by an earthen ramp. As they walked in circles, stomping the stalks, the grain dropped through the cracks between floor boards to the ground floor, where workers shoveled it to the center for cleaning and packing into barrels and bags for shipment to Washington's gristmill. At the end of the day, iron bars on the window and "a good lock . . . upon the lower door" prevented theft at night.[21]

Elated by the efficiency of his new threshing barn, he declared, "Nothing short of conviction that my dereliction of the chair of government . . . would involve the country in serious disputes regarding the chief magistrate . . . could, in any wise, induce me to relinquish the determination I have formed [to retire]."[22]

Unfortunately, when Washington returned to Philadelphia a few weeks later, he found that the feud between Jefferson and Hamilton had expanded beyond the cabinet room into the press and provoked serious public disputes over the expanding powers of the federal government. When the two men ran out of barbs to fire at each other's politics, they attacked each other's characters. In one pseudonymously written article, Jefferson charged that Hamilton's mother had never received a divorce from her first husband and was living in a common-law relationship with her second husband, rendering Alexander and her other son illegitimate. To further tar Hamilton, Jefferson's *Gazette of the United States* noted the high incidence of mixed-race illegitimate children in the West Indies— an indirect smear of which Hamilton could never cleanse himself.

As their feuding intensified, Hamilton's newspaper accused Jefferson of subverting "the principles of good government" by fostering disorder and opposition to taxes to promote his candidacy for the presidency. Hamilton called Jefferson a danger "to the union, peace, and happiness of the country" and defended himself, asserting that far from being a monarchist, "I am affectionately attached to the republican theory. I desire above all things to see the quality of political rights, exclusive of all hereditary distinction."[23]

When Jefferson tried to discredit Hamilton in the privacy of Washington's office, the President would have none of it and rebuked Jefferson for imagining a monarchist plot. He then endorsed the Hamilton fiscal program as his own and ordered Jefferson to support administration policies or quit.

> I believe it will be difficult, if not impracticable to manage the reins of government or to keep the parts of it together . . . if . . . after measures are decided on, one pulls this way and another that, before the utility of the thing is fairly tried. It must inevitably be torn asunder, and, in my

opinion, the fairest prospect of happiness and prosperity that ever was presented to man will be lost—perhaps forever![24]

Washington thought he might be able to end the feuding by bringing his various department heads together regularly for joint meetings, and, in doing so, he originated the concept of the President's "cabinet." Although he did not use the term because of its British origins, he found gathering department heads together for regular conferences more practical than contacting each of them separately to learn their opinions. His cabinet meetings established a routine that his successors in office have maintained to this day.

Privately, Jefferson dismissed Washington's rebuke, telling friends, "His mind has been so long used to unlimited applause that it could not brook contradiction or even advice offered unasked." Unable or unwilling to believe that Washington had fully understood Hamilton's fiscal program, Jefferson denigrated the President: "I have long thought . . . it was best for the republican interest to soothe him by flattering where they could approve the measures and to be silent when they disapprove."[25]

To counter Jefferson's lies about a monarchist plot, Hamilton attacked Jefferson as corrupt for paying Freneau as a translator in the State Department: "Is it possible," Hamilton asked, "that Mr. Jefferson, the head of a principal department of the government, can be the patron of a paper, the evident object of which is to decry the government and its measures?"[26]

As the feud intensified, Washington realized he could no longer ignore it. Fearing the cabinet split would undermine the presidential structure he was building, he sent an emotional appeal to his longtime protégé Hamilton:

Differences in political opinions are . . . unavoidable . . . but it is to be regretted, exceedingly, that subjects cannot be discussed with temper on the one hand, or decisions submitted to without having the motives which led to them, improperly implicated on the other: and this regret borders on chagrin when we find that men of abilities—zealous patriots—having the same *general* objects in view, and same upright intentions to prosecute them, will not exercise more charity in deciding on the opinions, and actions of one another.[27]

When Madison told Jefferson of Washington's request that he write a farewell address, Jefferson rushed to the presidential mansion. Reiterating the widespread discontent in the South with Hamilton's fiscal policies, Jefferson insisted that only the President's remaining in office could avoid disunion. "The confidence of the whole union is centered on you," he warned. "Your being at the helm will be more than an answer to every argument which can be used to alarm and lead the people in any quarter into violence or secession. North and South will hang together if they have you to hang on."[28]

After rejecting Jefferson's warning as an exaggeration, Washington left Philadelphia with his wife and family in July 1792 for what would be their longest sojourn at Mount Vernon since his accession to the presidency. Although the flow of mail did not cease, Washington's responses did.

"The President is buried in solitude in Mount Vernon," Secretary of War Knox explained. Alexander Hamilton, however, succeeded in disturbing the President's solitude with a written warning that refusal to serve a second term would be "the greatest evil that could befall this country" and would be "critically hazardous to your own reputation." Playing on his former commander's weaknesses, Hamilton insisted that "the clear path to be pursued by you will be again to obey the voice of your country . . . to . . . sacrifice your tranquility and happiness to the public good."[29]

Hamilton's letter infuriated Washington. He responded by assailing both Hamilton and Jefferson for creating the very political divisions they now said required his presence to heal. "My earnest wish," he wrote to Jefferson, "is that instead of wounding suspicions and irritable charges, there may be liberal allowances, mutual forbearance, and temporizing yielding *on all sides*. Without them . . . the wheels of government will clog—our enemies will triumph and . . . accomplish the ruin of the goodly fabric we have been erecting."[30]

Three days later, he admonished Hamilton with a profusion of mixed metaphors that always muddied his writing when he was angry . . . or furious . . . or, as now, steaming:

> How unfortunate would it be if a fabric so goodly erected . . . should from diversity of sentiments or internal obstructions to some of the acts of government . . . be harrowing our vitals in such a manner as to have brought us to the verge of dissolution. Melancholy thought! . . . My earnest wish is that balsam may be poured into *all* wounds which have been given to prevent them from gangrening and from the fatal consequences which the community may sustain if it is withheld. The friends of the Union must wish this. Those who are not, but wish to see it rended [*sic*], will be disappointed.[31]

Despite Washington's refusal to announce for a second term, the Electoral College cast 132 of 135 votes for him as President on December 3, 1792, with three abstentions. Although the Electoral College evidenced no opposition to Washington, opposition to his government was growing across the land—over taxes, continuing Indian attacks, British depredations against American shipping, and impressment of American sailors into the Royal Navy. The chorus of complaints was growing louder each day, and the presidential structure Washington had built so carefully over the previous four years began trembling ominously.

On February 22, 1793, the national celebration of Washington's sixty-first birth night[32] evoked the first concerted series of attacks on his character, with the *National Gazette* calling the festivities a "monarchical farce." Ignoring the attacks, Washington decided that, with the nation still far from united, his obligation to his country was to continue in office. On March 4, 1793, much to Martha Washington's distress, he took the oath of office for the second time. By then, however, rioters had replaced celebrants in the streets and threatened to engulf the nation in civil war.

## CHAPTER EIGHT

# The French Plot

By early 1793, events overseas had so intensified the Jefferson-Hamilton feud that it threatened to explode into a nationwide conflict that would pit Americans against each other. In France, extremists had taken control of the three-year-old revolution, overturned the monarchy, and discarded the constitution. An outgrowth of French participation in the American Revolution, the French Revolution had started at the Palace of Versailles in the spring of 1789, where the Estates General, a French assembly representing clergy, aristocracy, and bourgeois, tempered Louis XVI's absolute monarchy with a constitution that made him share power with an elected national assembly.

Spurring the change were the economic consequences of the king's military adventure in support of the American Revolution. Although French involvement ensured American victory over France's ancient Anglo-Saxon enemy, it left France bankrupt—without achieving the king's goals of recapturing Canada and replacing Britain as America's primary trade partner. Although Americans emerged from the Revolution emotionally embracing all things French, they continued buying more goods from the hated British than they bought from France. American merchants were simply too accustomed to dealing in a language and

*French king Louis XVI ceded his divine right to rule France in 1789, when he put his name to the first constitution in French history—a document that mirrored the Declaration of Independence.* (Réunion des Musées Nationaux)

currency they understood, and British merchants extended long-term, open-ended, revolving credit that French merchants were unable or un-willing to provide.

The resulting breakdown of the French economic fabric produced a parallel effect on the social fabric. Tens of thousands of French officers, soldiers, and sailors returned from America to France having witnessed individual liberties for the first time and bearing testimony to their benefits. As British statesman Edmund Burke put it, "They imbibed a love of freedom nearly incompatible with royalty. It seemed a grand stroke of policy to reduce the power and humble the pride of a great and haughty monarch."[1]

With the help of America's then-minister to France, Thomas Jefferson, Lafayette had drawn up a preamble to the French Constitution, which he called "The Declaration of the Rights of Man and the Citizen." Paraphrasing England's John Locke, America's Declaration of Independence, and Rousseau's *Le Contrat Social*, it asserted that "all men are created equal" and "born with certain inalienable rights, including life, liberty, property and the pursuit of happiness." A few provocative phrases from Rabelais, Abbé Raynal, and Voltaire added icing to the constitutional cake and bulked it up into a massive confection that anyone would find tasty without actually swallowing, let alone digesting.

Americans rejoiced over the document's resemblance to their own Declaration of Independence and the evident contagion of American ideals in Europe. Even Washington hailed the French Revolution as part of a new era of liberty that was dawning over the western world. "It is with real pleasure, Sir," Washington wrote to the president of the French National Assembly, "that I embrace the opportunity . . . of testifying through you to the National Assembly the sincere, cordial and earnest wish that . . . the enjoyment and exercise of the essential rights of man shall perpetuate the freedom and happiness of the People of France." The new constitution, Washington asserted, "promised the blessings of liberty to the French nation."[2]

From the first, however, the French constitution meant different things to different classes of Frenchmen. Lafayette and the enlightened young knights who had fought in America envisioned their new constitution as the basis of an American-style French republic, with a constitutional monarch in the role of president. The royal family and the "old dukes," however, saw it as heresy that blasphemed the king's divine right to absolute rule. God, after all, had designated the French king "His Most Christian Majesty"; no piece of paper—no constitution—could change that.

*Lafayette, a hero of the American Revolution, led the initial phase of the French Revolution, which replaced absolute monarchic rule with a constitutional monarchy. With the help of his friend, American ambassador Thomas Jefferson, Lafayette wrote the preamble to the French Constitution, which he called "The Declaration of the Rights of Man and the Citizen."* (RÉUNION DES MUSÉES NATIONAUX)

To ordinary French people, however, centuries of deprivation under autocratic rule gave the new constitution still another meaning. Never having experienced self-rule in either their religious or civil lives, they interpreted rights to life, liberty, and the pursuit of happiness as—above all else—the right to assuage the hunger gnawing at their innards. They stormed out of their neighborhoods in Paris to find food and vent their fury at those who had deprived them of it—butchers and bakers at first,

*Storming of the Bastille. Unused to individual liberties, desperately hungry Parisians saw liberty as a license to assault their enemies and those whom they held responsible for their economic woes. On July 14, 1789, they stormed the dreaded Bastille prison.* (RÉUNION DES MUSÉES NATIONAUX)

then the hated symbol of authority whose monstrous shadow seemed to block every ray of sunlight from the working-class slums of eastern Paris: the Bastille prison.

Although troops slaughtered the first attackers, they broke ranks as they recognized their own fathers, brothers, and neighbors in the mob. The soldiers turned against their officers, spun their cannons about, and aimed at the prison walls to blast open a passageway for the mob. On July 14, 1789, rioters seized the prison governor, dragged him to a lamppost, and to the cheers and jeers of thousands, hung him by the wrists and, as he wriggled and shrieked, they disemboweled him.

"Then it is a full-blown riot?" asked the king when told of the violence.

"No, Sire," his aide replied. "It is a full-blown revolution."[3]

The following morning at eleven, the rotund little king waddled into the National Assembly and displayed his signature on Lafayette's "Declaration of the Rights of Man" and the new constitution, ending thirteen centuries of absolute monarchy in France. Although assembly members cheered and shouted *"Vive le roi,"* their cheers came too late. Widespread drought had combined with national bankruptcy to produce famine; as starvation and unemployment spread, mob frenzy engulfed the nation; rioters raged through cities, towns, villages, and countryside, looting and burning manors, chateaux, and any other structure that smacked of aristocratic plenty. No foreign armies would ever wreak as much havoc on French monuments and historic structures as the French themselves during the French Revolution.

Thomas Jefferson, who witnessed the storming of the Bastille just before his return to America, called the French Revolution "an illumination of the human mind," and predicted it would assure the French "a good deal of liberty."[4] Dismissing violence as an unfortunate consequence of social progress, Jefferson asserted, "If the happiness of the mass of the people can be secured at the expense of a little tempest now and then, or even a little blood, it will be a precious purchase. *Malo libertum periculosum quam quietam servitutem.* [I prefer dangerous liberty to quiet servitude.]"[5]

In contrast to Jefferson's indifference to the increasing violence in France, the carnage appalled Washington, Hamilton, and other American leaders. Washington warned that "little irritation would be necessary to blow up the spark of discontent into a flame that might not easily be quenched."[6] Hamilton condemned radical leaders of the French Revolution as "assassins reeking with the blood of murdered fellow citizens."[7] Vice President Adams said the French revolutionaries "make murder itself as indifferent as shooting a plover."[8]

As the French Revolution grew bloodier, Jefferson returned to America to assume his post as the nation's first Secretary of State. "Each of us . . . thought well of the other as a man," Jefferson recalled his first encounter with Hamilton, "but as politicians it was impossible for two men to be of

*The execution of Louis XVI on the guillotine in Paris in January 1793 transformed President George Washington from a supporter to an arch-antagonist of the French Revolution—and, indeed, of all permanent alliances between the United States and foreign nations.* (RÉUNION DES MUSÉES NATIONAUX)

more opposite principles."[9] The differences in their principles widened after the execution of French King Louis XVI in January 1793. "LOUIS CAPET [the king's family name] HAS LOST HIS CAPUT," scoffed the headline in the Jefferson-backed *National Gazette*, while Jefferson himself sent Lafayette a disingenuous note of consolation: "We are not expected to be transported from despotism to liberty in a feather bed."[10]

Treasury Secretary Alexander Hamilton responded to the execution with disgust—especially the "horrid and disgusting scenes" of schoolboys licking the king's blood and an executioner selling knots of the king's blood-encrusted curls.

Washington was too appalled by events in France to comment on the death of Louis XVI, but he turned noticeably cold towards Jefferson and kept a bust of the French king displayed prominently in his office—for all to see as they entered and left.

On February 1, 1793, France declared war on Britain, Holland, and Spain. Under the Franco-American treaty of alliance of the American Revolutionary War, each nation had pledged to come to the aid of the other in the event of attack by foreign enemies, and France now demanded that the United States join her at war against Britain. In addition, the French government called for immediate repayment of three million livres, or nearly $555,000 of the $10 million that France had loaned the American government during the Revolutionary War.

"The liberty of the whole earth depends on the success of the French Revolution," Jefferson exulted, as he urged Washington to support the French. "Nothing should be spared on our part to attach France to us. Failure to do so would gratify the combination of kings with the spectacle of the only two republics on earth destroying each other."[11]

Outraged by Jefferson's embrace of French revolutionaries "wading through seas of blood," Hamilton argued against American participation as self-destructive. Britain, he insisted, remained America's most important trading partner, buying the majority of her exports, producing the majority of her imports, and yielding most of the government's revenues through import duties. To war beside France against Britain, Hamilton asserted, was not only economically suicidal, it was morally indefensible.

"When I contemplate the horrid . . . massacres," he raged, "when I perceive passion, tumult, and violence usurping reason and cool deliberation, I acknowledge that I am glad to believe there is no real resemblance between what was the cause of America and what is the cause of France."[12] Hamilton urged Washington to strengthen ties to Britain, arguing that the treaty with France was a *defensive* alliance in the event of attack on either nation by a third nation. Britain had not attacked France; France had been the aggressor, declaring war on England when England had been at peace.

Washington agreed with Hamilton that France had embarked on an offensive, not a defensive war, and that the treaty did not apply. He also agreed on the economic good sense of seeking a rapprochement with

*Secretary of State Thomas Jefferson was so enamored with the French Revolution that he seemed unable at times to distinguish between the interests of the United States and those of France. President Washington ultimately demanded his resignation.*
(LIBRARY OF CONGRESS)

England. With the United States all but defenseless (there was no navy and Wayne was still trying to raise a small army in the West) the President knew he could not risk war with England—or any other nation, for that matter. The powerful British navy could easily blockade American ports and shut coastal trade, while the British military in Canada could combine with Spanish forces in Florida and Louisiana to sweep across the West and divide it up between them.

More than annoyed by the continuing feud between Jefferson and Hamilton over foreign affairs, Washington recognized his error in having appointed department heads without ensuring uniformity in their political thinking. Government by consensus was proving impossible, and, to prevent further turmoil in his cabinet, he took full control of foreign policy himself, limiting the Secretary of State's authority to execution rather than determination of policy decisions.

"It behooves the government of this country," the President warned Jefferson, "to use every means in its power to prevent the citizens . . . from embroiling us with either of these powers [England or France] by endeavoring to maintain a strict neutrality. I therefore require that you will . . . [take] such measures as shall be deemed most likely to effect this desirable purpose . . . without delay."[13]

For once, Jefferson put ideology aside and bowed to the realities of his nation's perilous military posture, agreeing with the President and Hamilton that it was "necessary in my opinion that we take every justifiable measure for preserving our neutrality."[14]

Just as Jefferson and Hamilton seemed to rally behind the President and a single policy to keep the nation out of the spreading European conflict, the editors of the newspapers Jefferson and Hamilton had helped found suddenly lurched out of control in their lust for profits. Fenno's Hamiltonian *Gazette of the United States* condemned French atheism, anarchy, and mass slaughter; Freneau's Jeffersonian *National Gazette* replied by reminding readers how France had ensured American victory over British tyranny in the struggle for liberty and independence.

As groups gathered outside newspaper offices to read the papers—or hear them read by the more literate of their number—the war divided the American people. Half sided passionately with their ancestral motherland, while the other half demanded—just as passionately— that the American government support her Revolutionary War ally against America's former oppressor.

As profits from newspaper sales poured into their pockets, Fenno and Freneau fanned the flames of war, with Fenno urging the nation to break ties with France, while Freneau assailed Anglophiles as monarchists and traitors. What began as street-corner debates deteriorated into brawls that spread down alleys and avenues in major cities and exploded into rioting. All but forgotten in the national mayhem, President George Washington pleaded for national unity, saying it would be "unwise in the extreme . . . to involve ourselves in the contests of European nations."[15] The newspapers all but ignored his pleas.

In an effort to calm the presses and the nation, Washington proposed issuing a formal proclamation of neutrality—only to rekindle the flames of discord in his cabinet. Jefferson argued that the Constitution gave the President no powers to issue proclamations. Moreover, it clearly assigned to Congress the power to declare war and, he insisted, a declaration of neutrality was, in effect, a declaration that the nation would not go to war. Any declaration of neutrality, therefore, fell within the purview of congressional, not presidential, powers.

Jefferson's argument annoyed the President, and Hamilton shot back, saying that the President's powers stretched well beyond strict constitutional restraints. For one thing, Congress was not in session and the President was constitutionally bound to "take care that the laws be faithfully executed." Moreover, the Militia Act had already given the President powers to issue proclamations for troop call-ups and, by extension, any other legal purpose to defend national interests—including a neutrality proclamation. Hamilton scoffed at Jefferson's semantics over the term "neutrality" and suggested that the President simply eliminate the word in his final document. Although their pledges to the President bound both Jefferson and Hamilton to secrecy on all cabinet discussions, both men now despised each other so much that they put aside all pretenses of decorum and began publishing anonymously signed newspaper articles attacking each other.

Before Washington could decide on the final language of his proclamation, Citizen Edmond-Charles-Edouard Genet, the French Republic's new minister plenipotentiary (ambassador) to the United States, arrived in Charleston, South Carolina, with two sets of instructions from the French revolutionary government. Genet had sailed from France on the

*Edmond Genet, the first French minister plenipotentiary of the French revolutionary government, arrived in America with secret orders to overthrow the government of George Washington.*
(Réunion des Musées Nationaux)

30th anniversary of the Treaty of Paris that had sealed England's victory over France in the Seven Years War and stripped France of its colonies around the world. The largest of these had been New France—*La Nouvelle France*—which included all of Canada and the vast Louisiana Territory stretching from the Appalachian Mountains to the Rocky Mountains and from Hudson Bay across the Great Lakes to the Gulf of Mexico.

On arriving in Charleston, Genet's official instructions ordered him to seek *passive* American cooperation under the Franco-American treaties of 1778 for mutual defense. In effect, he was to convince Washington to let France bring captured ships and cargoes into American ports for auction and refitting. He was also to coax the American government into paying enough of its war debts to allow him to purchase badly needed American foodstuffs to ease the famine in France.

Genet, however, also carried a second set of secret instructions that were far different. These ordered him to raise *three* armies—the *Armée du Canada* to seize Canada from Britain, and the *Armée du Mississippi* and *Armée des Florides* to "liberate" Louisiana, the rich Mexican silver mines, and the Floridas from Spain. He was also to organize and launch a fleet of privateers to prey on British shipping. If Washington's government refused to cooperate, he was to exploit the Jeffersonian pro-French ferment in America to foment revolution, topple the American government, and convert the United States into a French puppet state. Once under French control, the United States would become part of a French-dominated American federation of Canada, Florida, Louisiana, and the French West Indies.

Nor was that the limit of French ambitions. "Your mission," Genet's secret instructions declared,

> is to assist in every way the extension of the Kingdom of Liberty [i.e., France] . . . the emancipation of Spanish America . . . the deliverance of our ancient brothers of Louisiana from the tyrannical yoke of Spain . . . the addition of the beautiful star of Canada to the American constellation, and prepare the uprising of the Spanish colonies in South America.[16]

In addition to territorial conquest, he was to offer Congress a new treaty "in which the two nations should amalgamate their commercial and political interests and establish an intimate concert, which would promote the extension of the Empire of Liberty . . . and mutual nationalization of French and American citizens." His instructions assured him the support of Secretary of State Jefferson, who had, without the knowledge of Congress, suggested mutual naturalization and union of France and the United States when he was American minister to France in 1785.[17]

By the time Genet arrived in America, Jeffersonian newspapers had whipped Francophilia into mass hysteria that engulfed daily life in Boston, New York, Philadelphia, Charleston, and other cities. Reinventing themselves as revolutionary egalitarians, Jeffersonian republicans addressed each other as "Citizen" and "Citess" (for women) and shot angry stares or insults at those who used "monarchist" forms of address such as "Mister," "Sir," or "Madam." The title "Reverend" was "not only anti-republican, but blasphemous," according to the *New-York Journal*, which hailed the outlawing of the Catholic Church in France. Charging the church with "striving to keep the people in ignorance," it called for overthrow of the Pope.[18]

The editor of the *Boston Gazette* asserted that "every friend of the Rights of Man in America will constantly feel an *attachment* for their French *brethren*. . . . France is contending the cause of both EUROPE and AMERICA, and GOD grant her success."[19]

When, therefore, Genet landed in Charleston, pier-side crowds gave him a thunderous welcome. Instead of sailing on a conventional ship to the national capital in Philadelphia to present his credentials to the chief of state—the normal protocol for arriving diplomats—Genet had scoffed at diplomatic niceties and commandeered a warship to Charleston. He arranged for a group of French agents to sail in advance and organize a warm welcome for him.

In fact, the entire South seemed in the grip of Francophilia and Anglophobia—much of it residual antagonism for the Washington-Hamilton assumption scheme, the 25 percent federal tax on stills and whiskey, and a treaty with the Creeks that blocked white settlements on Indian lands in the western Carolinas and western Georgia. Charleston, therefore, not only embraced Genet's arrival, Governor William Moultrie all but reasserted South Carolina's sovereignty as an independent state and promised Genet, "The cause of France is our own."[20]

Waving the French banner of worldwide revolution, Genet assailed President Washington and called his Federalist supporters monarchists seeking to restore ties to England.

"In the United States," the Frenchman cried out, "men still exist who can say, 'Here a ferocious Englishman slaughtered my father; there my wife tore her bleeding daughter from the hands of an unbridled Englishman,' and those same men can say, 'Here a brave Frenchman died fighting for American liberty; here French naval and military power humbled the might of Britain.'"[21]

As the crowd roared its approval, Charleston adopted Genet's cause as its own. Governor Moultrie ignored federal law and the Constitution by helping Genet commission four privateers that set out to sea to attack British shipping off the American coast. The promise of plunder lured hundreds of American volunteer seamen, and in the ensuing months they brought dozens of British vessels into American ports for French consuls to sell or refit with cannons to expand Genet's fleet of privateers. To Charleston's delight, Genet was doing what Washington had refused to do: waging war on Britain.

Building on his base in Charleston, Genet organized a network of agents to raise an army of Americans for a French war in North America against England and Spain and to recapture Canada, Louisiana, and the rest of the North American empire France had lost in 1763.[22] Within weeks after Genet's arrival, French agents had organized nearly forty so-called "Democratic Societies" across the United States, merging some into Democratic Clubs that Jefferson's supporters had formed to support his presidential ambitions.

With 250 blank military and naval commissions for qualified officers to lead the assaults, Genet promised Indian fighter Elijah Clarke a commission as a French major general—and $10,000 cash—to lead American volunteers into Spanish Florida. Southern frontiersmen had suffered more than a decade of savage Indian and Spanish raids and went "recruiting-mad for the French service."[23]

In Georgia, frontier farmers overran territory the United States had ceded to the Creek Indians and called for secession from the United States and establishment of either an independent state or a French protectorate.

Genet commissioned Revolutionary War hero George Rogers Clark as a French major general to command a "Legion of Revolution and Independence of the Mississippi" to free the Mississippi Valley from Spain. It was Clark who had led the war in the West during the Revolutionary War, sweeping through Illinois, Ohio, Indiana, and Kentucky. Widespread secessionist sentiment allowed Clark to recruit more than 2,000 Kentuckians by promising them 1,000-acre land grants in conquered Spanish territory.

Some 4,000 other Kentuckians signed "intents" to enlist once the fighting began. Clark told Genet that once he received commissions for his officers and money for boats, guns, and ammunition, his army would be ready to seize control of the Mississippi River Valley and form a new, independent nation incorporating all the lands west of the Appalachians.

By April 18, 1793, Genet's plans were complete. "I have prepared the revolution of New Orleans and Canada," he wrote to the French foreign minister in Paris. "I have destroyed the maritime commerce of the English in these waters."[24] He said he planned to rally the American people to force Washington to support him with additional troops, weapons, and funds—or resign in favor of the Francophile Jefferson.

With his privateers marauding British ships along the coast, Genet left Charleston for Philadelphia in a coach and four on what metamorphosed into a triumphal procession, with Jefferson's Democratic Clubs heralding Genet's approach as a Second Coming. Church bells tolled his arrival in each town, cannons boomed, French flags flapped in the wind in what he called "a succession of civic festivals." By the time he reached Richmond, Virginia, news of his activities had plunged the national capital of Philadelphia into crisis and widened the already bitter divisions in the cabinet.

Washington was irate, fearing that Genet's activities would provoke Britain into declaring war on the United States. Jefferson tried calming the President, arguing that if Genet's military schemes succeeded they would give the United States sovereignty over Spanish Florida, while a

French flag over Louisiana would restore American navigation rights on the Mississippi River.

Hamilton scoffed at Jefferson, and Washington, siding with his Treasury Secretary, all but dismissed his Secretary of State, threw off all constitutional restraints, and issued a formal proclamation with the force of law, albeit without the word "neutrality." On April 22, he declared the United States *at peace*—with Britain, France, and all other combatants, and he said the nation would engage in "conduct friendly and impartial toward the belligerent powers." Washington enjoined all Americans "from all acts and proceedings inconsistent with the duties of a friendly nation toward those at war," including "any hostilities on the seas," and he barred American ships from carrying "any of those articles deemed contraband by the modern usage of nations."[25]

The proclamation was one of the most important acts of Washington's presidency, raising a fifth pillar of presidential power and, in effect, reinforcing three others—the powers over foreign policy, national defense, and finance. The Constitution, of course, gave the President no power to issue a proclamation of war or peace—or anything else, for that matter, despite Hamilton's assertions to the contrary. In doing so, he again assumed a power that the Constitution had specifically reserved to the legislature. A presidential proclamation was, in effect, nothing less than a new law, and, like the power over the purse and the military, the Constitution had reserved the right to legislate to Congress, not the President.

At the time he issued it, however, Washington had no way to enforce his proclamation. America had no navy, and "Mad" Anthony Wayne was still trying to assemble a minuscule army to fight Indians in the West. In effect, Washington had no federal police force to ensure public observance of the law. Although he called on state governors to help enforce his proclamation, all he could do himself was order Treasury Secretary Hamilton to alert the Treasury's five hundred customs agents and tax collectors to watch for contraband shipments destined for belligerent nations.

Although it did not take hold immediately, Washington's Neutrality Proclamation established a new principle of international law as well as American constitutional law—namely, the concept of neutrality and the rights of nonparticipating neutral nations in wartime. Although rules abounded governing relations between warring nations, the world had ignored the rights of neutrals until George Washington raised the issue. (A year later, he would issue the American Neutrality Code of 1794.)[26]

With no navy to enforce Washington's order on the high seas, however, Antifederalist governors intent on weakening presidential powers reasserted claims of state sovereignty. One by one, they opened their harbors and allowed Genet's ships to sail in and out at will with captured British cargo vessels. Luring hundreds of unemployed shipbuilders back to work to refit them as warships, Genet soon had a fleet of more than eighty vessels to patrol American coastal waters and capture British ships and cargoes.

To taunt the President and further expose presidential impotence, Genet bought boldfaced newspaper advertisements calling on "Friends of France" to ignore Washington's Neutrality Proclamation and enlist in the French service to fight the British.

"Does not patriotism call upon us to assist France?" asked his advertisements. "As Sons of Freedom, would it not become our character to lend some assistance to a nation combating to secure their liberty?"[27]

Washington countered Genet's attempt to recruit Americans by ordering Attorney General Edmund Randolph to arrest any American seamen serving on French privateers when they stepped ashore. Sheriff's deputies did exactly that, arresting two American seamen when they disembarked in Philadelphia from the *Citizen Genet*, a privateer the French minister had modestly renamed for himself. Genet wrote an angry letter to Jefferson: "The crime of which they are accused, which my mind cannot conceive and my pen reluctantly records, is serving France, defending with her children the common and glorious cause of liberty."[28]

Charged with conspiring to attack the property and citizens of nations at peace with the United States, one of the men went to trial before the Federal Circuit Court of Philadelphia, with Genet paying for his defense. Although the judges (including two U.S. Supreme Court associate justices) ordered a jury verdict of guilty, Genet bribed jurors to ensure the opposite. Cheering members of Genet's Jacobin Democratic Society led the sailor from the courthouse back to his ship to reenlist before attending a dinner that Genet sponsored that evening to celebrate the young man's triumph over the federal government.

A second jury later found the second sailor innocent, with the defense attorney charging that the President's Neutrality Proclamation was unconstitutional and without the force of law. Instead of rallying Americans around their own flag, Washington's proclamation—and his prosecution of two ordinary sailors—further divided the nation and left him looking helpless to control the nation's course.

Ecstatic over his legal victories, Genet exulted to his foreign minister in Paris that Washington "interferes with my programs in a thousand ways and obliges me to urge the convocation of Congress, the majority of which . . . will be decidedly in my favor."[29] Genet ordered Democratic Societies to foment revolution nationwide and overthrow Washington.

Still smarting from the whiskey tax, many Americans were all too eager to respond, and, apart from Americans, increasing numbers of immigrants were roiling America's political waters. Some 50,000 Irish immigrants needed less than a thimble of whiskey to spill out of taverns to protest British persecution in Ireland, while thousands of penniless refugees from Acadia, Canada, whom the British had brutally expelled from their homeland at the end of the French and Indian War, were also ready to march to war against their persecutors.

There were, however, many other Americans who retained deep emotional and familial connections to what had been their motherland only a decade earlier and many of them longed to strengthen political ties to Britain.

Newspaper editors on both sides of the political fence did everything they could to sell more newspapers by inciting both sides. They appealed to Anglophiles—charging the French with "contending for plunder and empire"—and to Francophiles—charging the British with inciting Indian raids against settlers in the West, failing to evacuate western frontier posts, and impressing American sailors into the British navy. Some charged Britain with planning to reclaim their former American colonies.

But it was Genet who wreaked the most havoc.

As Washington sat in the presidential mansion furious over his lack of power to respond, Genet's fleet of privateers captured more than eighty British merchant vessels—many inside American territorial waters—and sailed them into American ports to be sold by French consuls. Almost every day saw French consuls selling captured ships and cargoes at pier side, while Hamilton's American customs officials looked on helplessly. Genet ordered Jacobin clubs in each port to offer free rum on the quays to ensure riotous welcomes for every privateer and menace any American official who even breathed a protest. To the cheers of thousands, one French privateer sailed into Boston harbor with a banner flying from its mast listing eleven prominent Bostonians as "aristocrats" and "enemies of France."

Genet made a show of personal defiance of Washington's Neutrality Proclamation when his own flagship, *l'Embuscade*, captured a British vessel in Delaware Bay—well within American territorial waters—and sailed up to Philadelphia with the British boat in tow, its flag flying upside down. Not only was Washington's presidency collapsing, so was the Union.

When Genet himself arrived overland in the outskirts of Philadelphia, five hundred coaches with ardent Francophiles waited to escort him into the city. Thousands rushed into the streets to cheer and march—and discard all pretenses of neutrality or loyalty to the President. An estimated 5,000 supporters rallied outside Genet's hotel window that evening and set off endless demonstrations that raged through the night into the next day—and the next—and the next.

John Adams described "the terrorism excited by Genet in 1793, when 10,000 people in the streets of Philadelphia, day after day, threatened to drag Washington out of his house and effect a revolution in the government or compel it to declare war in favor of the French Revolution and against England." Adams said he "judged it prudent and necessary to order chests of arms from the war office" to protect his house.[30] Washington feared for the safety of his wife and grandchildren and considered sending them home to Mount Vernon.

Making matters worse was the sudden arrival of the French fleet from the Antilles. Genet ordered gangways lowered and sent French seamen to join the Jacobin mobs in the crowded streets.

"The town is one continuous scene of riot," the British consul wrote in panic to his foreign minister in London. "The French seamen range the streets by night and by day, armed with cutlasses and commit the most daring outrages. Genet seems ready to raise the tricolor and proclaim himself proconsul. President Washington is unable to enforce any measures in opposition."[31]

As pro-French mobs formed on street corners demanding Washington's head, Genet sent the President an ultimatum "in the name of France" to call Congress into special session to choose between neutrality and war. Genet warned Washington that if he refused to declare war against Britain, Genet would "appeal to the people . . . the decisions of the President. . . . I have acquired the esteem and the good wishes of all republican Americans by tightening the bonds of fraternity between them and ourselves," Genet ranted. He predicted that Americans would "rally from all sides" to support him and "demonstrate with cries of joy . . . that the democrats of America realize perfectly that their future is ultimately bound with France."[32]

Washington's presidential edifice was tottering. With no law enforcement arm at his disposal, his other pillars of power seemed ready to fall, along with the American republic.

CHAPTER NINE

*"The President Was Much Inflamed"*

Genet took full advantage of the turmoil in Philadelphia by converting eight more American ships into French privateers in local dockyards. The alterations put hundreds of grateful shipfitters to work, while the promise of plunder from English and Spanish ships brought throngs of rowdy American seamen and would-be seamen to dockside.

After Britain threatened to declare war on the United States for the French attacks, Washington issued a set of "Rules Governing Belligerents," which prohibited Genet and other foreigners from recruiting Americans for foreign wars and outfitting privateers on American territory. The President instructed Jefferson to notify Genet that his grants of military commissions infringed on U.S. sovereignty and that he was to remove his ships from American waters.

By then, however, Jefferson had expressed such open support for Genet that he was caught in a political vise. Declaring Genet a friend of the United States, Jefferson assured Washington and anyone else who would listen that "it is impossible for anything to be more affectionate, more magnanimous, than the purport of his mission."[1]

Although Jefferson minimized the dangers of pro-French riots on the waterfront as "the old spirit of 1776 rekindling,"[2] Washington recognized

Genet's ships for what they were—an occupying force that Genet was using to dictate American policy. He called an emergency session of the cabinet and exploded with anger. Was Genet "to set the acts of this government at defiance with impunity?" he thundered. "What must the world think of such conduct, and of the government . . . submitting to it? We are an independent nation. We will not be dictated to by the politics of any nation under heaven."[3]

Washington accused Jefferson's Democratic Clubs of planning "nothing short of the subversion of the government of these states, even at the expense of plunging this country in the horrors of a disastrous war."[4] Washington now expressed open opposition to the French Revolution. All his closest French friends from America's Revolutionary War, including Lafayette, were aristocrats. Indeed, almost all the heroic French officers of the American Revolution were aristocrats, and the members of America's own officer corps, including Washington, were largely the equivalent of a landed aristocracy. He had no difficulty imagining a bloodbath in America if Francophile street mobs gained control of political power. Although American mobs had been ruthless in their use of tar and feathers during tax protests, they had stopped short of outright butchery. French mobs routinely disemboweled their victims alive before hacking off their heads and other body parts to plant on pikes for display in street parades.

Jefferson made the mistake of bringing Freneau's pro-French newspaper to a cabinet meeting. Its headline accused Washington of "monarchical ambitions" and illustrated the article that followed with a cartoon showing Washington's crowned head beneath a guillotine blade.

Washington snapped—-erupting with an angry outburst that few had ever witnessed in public off the battlefield.

> The President was much inflamed. [He] got into one of those passions when he cannot command himself; ran much on the personal abuse bestowed upon him; defied any man . . . to produce one single act . . .

which was not done from the purest motive . . . that by God he had rather be . . . on his farm than to be made emperor of the world.

Jefferson said the President then shouted that if anyone tried to introduce monarchy in America, "no man would set his face against it more . . . that there was more danger of anarchy being introduced . . . the president was evidently sore and warm."[5]

In fact, the President was more than "sore and warm." He was irate and all but irrational. Beset by personal problems, he had reached the end of his patience and ability to deal objectively with the overwhelming number of crises he now faced. Earlier in the year, the French Revolutionary Government had declared Lafayette, the soldier-son Washington adored, an enemy of the Revolution. Forced to flee the country, he had only just crossed the French border when Austrian troops seized him and threw him into prison for complicity in having started the French Revolution. Washington had ordered Secretary of State Jefferson to order American ministers in London, Amsterdam, and Paris to remonstrate on behalf of Lafayette and to provide funds for his wife and children.

To add to Washington's woes, his favorite nephew George Augustine Washington had died of tuberculosis. Young Washington had fought gallantly in the Revolution before marrying Martha Washington's niece Fanny, and his death left Fanny a still-young widow with three infant children. The Washingtons had raised Fanny as their own since the death of her mother, Martha's sister, when Fanny was twelve, and had, without success, cared for her ailing husband for many months at Mount Vernon.

"My dear Fanny," the grieving President wrote. "It is unnecessary to describe the sorrow with which I was afflicted at the news of his death. . . .

To express sorrow with the force I feel it would answer no other purpose than to revive in your breast the poignancy of anguish which, by this time, is abated. The object of this present letter is to convey to your

mind the warmest assurances of my love, friendship, and disposition to
serve you. These also I profess to have . . . for your children. I know not
what plans you have contemplated . . . the one that strikes me most favorably . . . is to return to Mount Vernon. You can go to no place where
you will be more welcome—nor to any where you can live at less
expense or trouble . . . which would ease you of that anxiety which the
care of so large a family would involve you in.

And he signed it with "love to the children—and with affectionate
sentiments" to her.[6] Shortly thereafter, Fanny and her three children
moved into the mansion at Mount Vernon, adding three more children
to the five the Washingtons were already raising at the plantation—at
the age of sixty-one. It was little wonder that Washington snapped from
the strain when Jefferson showed him a cartoon disparaging the President and showing him on the guillotine about to lose his head.

---

In a near-treasonous action that he hid from the President, Jefferson
gave Genet's confederate André Michaux, a French botanist, a letter of
introduction to Governor Isaac Shelby of Kentucky, implying approval
of Genet's efforts to raise an army in the West. All but accused of disloyalty for his support of Genet, Jefferson offered his resignation, but
the President raged at his Secretary of State, demanding that he remain
in office until the end of the year and fulfill his oath of office by trans-
mitting the presidential order for Genet to remove his warships.

Although furious at Washington's order, Genet suddenly found
himself unable to dispute it. He had arrived with only 60,000 livres, or
slightly more than $10,000—far from enough to raise an entire army.
The French foreign ministry had assured him that Jefferson would fund
his expeditions with American government arms, cannons, and cash.
Jefferson, however, adroitly side-stepped his entanglement by passing
along the Frenchman's requests to Secretary of War Henry Knox and, of

all people, Treasury Secretary Hamilton. Knox replied angrily that he would not lend Genet so much as a pistol, while Hamilton reacted with equal furor.

When Jefferson refused to intercede, Genet charged the Secretary of State with duplicity and expanded his direct appeals to the American people. He ordered leaders of his Democratic Societies to change their mission from promoting Franco-American friendship to promoting revolution and union with France. Like Jacobins in France, they had already infiltrated the press and local political establishments; at a signal from Genet, they could fill the streets with shrieking mobs and frighten newspaper readers with menacing headlines.

"The freedom of this country," claimed New York's *Columbian Gazetteer*, "is not secure until that of France is placed beyond the reach of accident."[7] The *Baltimore Daily Repository* warned that if Europe's monarchs defeated France, "the craving appetite of despotism will be satisfied with nothing less than American vassalage in some form or another." Philadelphia's *General Advertiser* insisted that "the salvation of America depends on our alliance with France."[8]

Genet waxed ecstatic in his report to the Foreign Ministry in Paris: "Composed of the patriots of '76 and the most respectable citizens," he wrote, "the Democratic Societies have formed as if by magic from one end of the continent to the other, and set down as a foundation for their association these powerful words: Liberty, Equality, Rights of Man, Country, France, Republic. . . . The American people voluntarily constitute themselves France's advocate."[9]

Reports in the Hamiltonian press that Jefferson was in the pay of the French government convinced Washington that Jefferson was too torn between his allegiance to the French Revolution and his obligations to serve the United States. Without warning Jefferson, Washington told his cabinet (including a surprised Jefferson) that he had acted independently of the Secretary of State and demanded Genet's recall by the French government. He then asked for opinions on whether to ban Democratic Societies, which numbered well over forty. Hamilton charged that their members were paid by Genet and the French Government to provoke anti-government sentiment. Knox agreed, but Washington argued that outlawing the societies would only incite defenders of the Bill of Rights. He decided, instead, to rely on the imminent recall of Genet and Jefferson's departure from government to quiet them. He would soon receive help from an unexpected source.

Abandoning hope for cooperation from the American government, Genet ordered the French fleet to sail to New York for repairs and resupply before dividing into three squadrons for assaults on Canada, Florida, and Louisiana. Before it arrived, however, the British frigate *Boston* had sailed into New York waters from Halifax to combat French depredations on British cargo ships. When the captain saw the French fleet on the horizon, he quickly disguised his ship as a French frigate—*La Concorde*—and raised the French tricolor. As the French fleet sailed into port, he signaled an invitation to the captain and officers of Genet's flagship *l'Embuscade* to dine and share a rare brandy. The French captain all but leaped into a dinghy with his men, who rowed across the bay and delivered themselves into British hands—and irons.

As New York's Tories doubled over in laughter, Francophiles rioted in the streets demanding revenge. Within days, the British captain obliged, offering to wager custody of his French captives on the results of a one-on-one naval duel between the British and French frigates off the coast of Long Branch, New Jersey. As word of the impending duel spread, life in New York came to a standstill; thousands fought their way onto every imaginable means of transport to travel to the Jersey shore to watch the historic encounter. Some waged sums they could ill afford on the outcome.

As crowds thickened, arguments and fights sent tents tumbling and small boats overturning. Rioting threatened to engulf the beaches until the echo of shots over the water drew the crowd's attention toward the two combatants. With the signal to begin, cannons on the two ships launched a fearsome two-hour barrage that filled the air with spectacular displays of smoke and flame; hailstorms of cannonballs, nails, broken glass, and other shrapnel damaged both ships, littering their decks with dead and wounded sailors. Then the British captain fell—fatally—and the *Boston* abandoned the battle and sailed away, with *l'Embuscade* in pursuit.

Five hours later, *l'Embuscade* returned with the French captain and his mates aboard, and led the rest of the French fleet into New York harbor in triumph. Huge banners streamed from her masthead: "Enemies of equality: Reform or tremble!" read the banner on the foremast. "Freemen, Behold! We are your friends and brothers!" flew from the mainmast. "We are armed for the defence of the Rights of Man!" waved from the mizzen.

As the ships eased into port, more than 5,000 French sailors and marines spilled over the rails to join the city's Jacobins and Francophiles in an endless orgy of drunkenness and violence that all but leveled the waterfront's tumbledown warehouses. Within days, Tories and their families had fled the city, and a week later, on August 7, Genet himself arrived in an adjutant general's uniform prepared to mobilize cheering Americans to unseat the President. The hysterical mobs did nothing to dissuade him, chanting, "Genet to power!" and "Down with Washington!"—and serenading him with revolutionary airs, while cannons and church bells sounded their explosive welcomes.

As pro-French editors welcomed Genet, their cartoonists portrayed the heads of American political leaders dropping from guillotine scaffolds. One cartoonist showed Vice President Adams embracing "a stinking prostitute" with the face of Washington. Another showed Chief Justice John Jay leading royalist plotters in seating "King Washington" on the American throne. And another showed Genet tearing the crown off the President's head.[10]

Washington fumed that he needed a permanent law enforcement arm if he was to maintain order, but the Constitution, in assigning him to execute the laws—"faithfully"—gave him no mechanism for doing so. For the moment he was helpless to prevent Genet from staging a coup d'état.

"The whole of America has risen to acknowledge me," Genet exulted. At thirty years of age, he was ready to raise the French flag over New York, reclaim New France, and restore his nation's glory in the Americas. At a dinner hosted by New York's ardent Antifederalist governor George Clinton, Genet declared that "the cause of France is the cause of mankind." All but swooning at his words was the governor's daughter Cornelia, who had canonized the butchers of the French Revolution and fell instantly in love with Genet.

On the morning of August 15, Genet issued drafts totaling $100,000 to local shipbuilders to repair and refit the fleet. As church bells pealed, he climbed aboard his flagship dressed in full military regalia to issue orders for the assaults on Halifax, St. Augustine, and New Orleans once the repairs were complete. On the quays below, a crowd formed to serenade him:

> *Liberty! Liberty! Be thy name adored forever;*
> *Tyrants beware! Your tott'ring thrones must fall;*
> *Our int'rest links the free together,*
> *And Freedom's sons are Frenchmen all.*[11]

By midday, however, the chant diminished; one by one, the church bells ceased ringing; and as the atmosphere about the ship turned silent, Genet came topside and looked over the rail. The waterfront was deserted; the air still and silent. He disembarked and walked toward the inn where he had been lodging. A servant awaited, his bag packed to leave. Genet demanded an explanation. The answer struck like a dagger:

"Yellow fever, *Monsieur*."

"The coolest and the firmest minds," John Adams recalled later, "have given their opinions that nothing but the yellow fever . . . could have saved the United States from a fatal revolution of government."[12] Had the epidemic arrived a month later, Genet's armies would have invaded Florida, Canada, and Louisiana; he himself would have roused his Jacobin legions in New York, Boston, and Philadelphia and marched into the capital to unseat President Washington.

On August 15, however, the terrible, swift disease sent New Yorkers and Philadelphians—Jacobins and non-Jacobins alike—fleeing by the thousands to the perceived safety of the countryside. Life came to a standstill in both cities. The entire government shut down in Philadelphia, with the Washingtons going home to Mount Vernon. Before the first autumn frosts arrived to kill the offending mosquitoes, the French sailors had mutinied, seized control of Genet's ships, and sailed home to France.

To add to his indignities, Genet ran out of funds and was unable to pay outstanding debts to merchants in Boston, New York, Philadelphia, Charleston, and elsewhere. The drafts for $100,000 he had issued to New York shipbuilders to refit the French fleet were worthless.

On December 31, 1793, Jefferson resigned from office and retired to his plantation in Charlottesville, Virginia, ending the deep division in the cabinet and leaving the President in firm control of administration policies.

To Washington's relief, a new French ambassador, Jean-Antoine-Joseph Fauchet, arrived in Philadelphia a month later. After conforming to strict diplomatic protocol by presenting his credentials to the President, he presented Washington's Secretary of State–designate, Attorney General Edmund Randolph, a French-government warrant for the arrest and execution of Edmond Genet. A guillotine aboard Fauchet's ship stood ready to carry out the sentence. Although Vice President Adams despised Genet, he recoiled at the fate awaiting the young Frenchman. "Poor Genet I fear is undone," Adams wrote to his wife, Abigail. "Bad as his conduct has been, I cannot but pity him. What will become of him, I know not."[13]

Genet pleaded with Randolph not to enforce the warrant, all but sobbing that a former Paris police chief was waiting below deck on

Fauchet's ship, sharpening the guillotine blade to sever his neck. A former Virginia governor and close friend of Washington, Randolph turned to the President for guidance.

"We ought not to wish his punishment," Washington decided, and granted the Frenchman political asylum and the protection of the government he had tried to overthrow.[14] Fearing Fauchet's agents would kidnap him, Genet sneaked out of Philadelphia during the night and found his way to a secluded hideaway on a friend's farm in Bristol, Connecticut, where he temporarily disappeared from public view. Two months later, to the astonishment of New York Federalists, the arrogant Frenchman who tried to overturn the American government reappeared beside New York Governor George Clinton marching in the Independence Day parade on July 4. By the end of August, substantial funds materialized to permit his purchase of a farm in Jamaica, Long Island, where he assumed the title of *cultivateur américain*. In November, he married the governor's daughter, Cornelia Clinton, who had used her dowry to buy the farm, where he became an American citizen and disappeared from public life amidst his vegetables and fruits.[15]

Although the Genet affair had shaken the presidential structure, the Frenchman's flight to Long Island and Jefferson's resignation and retreat to his farm in Charlottesville, Virginia, left Washington's presidency intact. He acted immediately to tighten structural supports and reinforce the foundations of the various pillars of presidential power. Loyalty to the President became Washington's primary consideration in cabinet and other executive appointments, reminding each cabinet member that in swearing "to preserve, protect and defend the Constitution of the United States," they were also swearing to preserve, protect, and defend the President of the United States and his policies.

The President then told them that henceforth they were to provide him with lists of alternative policies to guide his decisions, but after he made his decision, they were all to support that decision or quit. Within the cabinet, he was to be an absolute monarch, and successor presidents who failed to follow his precedent—the so-called "weak presidents"—would do so at their own risk.

Although his new cabinet policy would cost him some of his closest friends and turn a few into enemies, Washington believed that a firm presidential grip on cabinet activities would end the turmoil in and out of government.

# CHAPTER TEN

## *"Venomous Reptiles on Our Shores"*

The departures of Jefferson and Genet all but ended the conflict in Washington's cabinet and on American streets. The ensuing calm gave Washington's Neutrality Proclamation a chance to take hold, while strict enforcement of his Rules Governing Belligerents offered Britain ample proof of America's intent to engage in only peaceful trade. The results—all of them beneficial—were precisely what Washington had hoped for.

As neutral American ships ferried ever-increasing cargoes to France and Britain, American shipbuilders, merchants, craftsmen, and farmers reaped the benefits of prosperity. With the economic boom, dissatisfaction with the federal government and the Washington administration diminished sharply.

But neutrality soon proved a two-edged sword for U.S. foreign relations. Just as the nation was sailing farther into profitable neutral waters, shocking news arrived that the British government had adopted a harsh new policy and ordered its navy to seize virtually *all* ships bound for France and the French West Indies—neutral or not. It then designated *all* goods bound for France as contraband—corn, wheat, flour . . . anything. Ignoring Washington's Neutrality Proclamation, the British government seized at least 250 American vessels in the months that followed.

There were two motives for the new policy: First, the British military hoped to starve the French population into submission. With the French government bankrupt, and so many feudal landowners dead, imprisoned, or in exile, peasants had been incapable of managing farms they had seized during the French Revolution, and, in the continuing drought, famine had engulfed the nation. The British saw famine as an ally that they were not about to allow Americans to subdue with shiploads of corn, wheat, and root vegetables.

A second motive for seizing American ships was to fill the British navy's need for English-speaking sailors. An eighteenth-century equivalent to the modern military draft, impressment was the only way Britain could man its enormous fleet—the world's largest. Low pay and often cruel treatment not only discouraged enlistments but provoked an inordinately high number of desertions when ships put into port. Desertions were especially high in American ports, where British sailors could blend into the local population and flee into a vast wilderness where recapture was all but impossible.

By 1793, the British navy had only about 25,000 men, or 200 men for each of its 115 battleships. To bring manpower to full strength, the British began impressing young Americans foolish enough to wander near the quays at night, while naval vessels stopped every ship they could on the high seas and seized any English-speaking sailors—and male passengers—they found.

Nor were the French of any help. America's erstwhile ally was guilty of even worse atrocities. With their nation bankrupt and racked by famine, French authorities found piracy more profitable than conventional commerce and seized every American ship that sailed into French waters, confiscating its cargo and tossing its crew into prison for ransom.

For the third time in his presidency, Washington was unable to retaliate against outrageous transgressions by foreign powers. Britain remained the most powerful nation in the western world; her fleet could easily blockade America's ports and halt *all* U.S. international trade. Still more threatening was the continuing occupation by British troops of north-western frontier posts within U.S. territory, where they incited Indian raids on American settlers.

In clear violation of the 1783 Treaty of Paris recognizing American independence, Britain had refused to relinquish the posts until the United States fulfilled its treaty obligations to force Americans to pay prewar debts to British merchants and compensate American Tories for properties seized during and after the Revolution. Washington realized that, the Constitution notwithstanding, a President needed powers to raise and deploy the military without congressional consent.

Facing national humiliation or war, Washington's political instincts devised a dual policy that combined bravado with wisdom—bravado, to placate Congress and the public; wisdom, to further what he considered the best interests of the nation. He called on the nation to gear for war, asking Congress to raise an army of 15,000 men and state governors to ready 80,000 militiamen. He also asked Congress to appropriate funds and authorize building six frigates, thus giving birth to the U.S. Navy.[1]

While American war hawks flapped their wings, Washington coaxed the courtly, experienced negotiator Chief Justice John Jay to go to England to seek an understanding and rapprochement with the British government. As one of the negotiators of the 1783 peace treaty with Britain and as Secretary for Foreign Affairs from 1784 to 1789, Jay had made many friends in the English government and knew all the niceties of diplomatic engagement with the English. The choice of Jay, however, reignited antigovernment passions of Antifederalist Francophiles, who claimed the appointment was an unconstitutional amalgamation of judicial and executive branches.

To counter accusations in the press that he was preparing to give the nation back to Britain, Washington appointed Virginia's high-profile Antifederalist Senator James Monroe as minister plenipotentiary to the revolutionary government of France, with the special assignment of broadening Franco-American trade. A political protégé of Thomas Jefferson, Monroe was as outspoken a Francophile as Jefferson. By sending Monroe to Paris while Jay went to England, Washington appeared to be acting even-handedly in dealing with the two warring nations.

As Jay and Monroe sailed off to their separate destinations, Washington coaxed Congress to erase all lingering constitutional objections to the President's Neutrality Proclamation by conceding his right to make unilateral foreign policy decisions without *prior* "advice" by the Senate. On June 6, as Jay arrived in London, Congress did Washington's bidding and went a step farther by passing the Neutrality Act forbidding U.S. citizens to enlist in the service of a foreign nation and banning the refitting of foreign warships in American ports.

Passed as a sop to Britain to strengthen Jay's hand in negotiations, the act gave President Washington's Neutrality Proclamation constitutional legitimacy and reinforced his powers over foreign affairs and national defense. As a gesture of good will, the British Government responded to the Neutrality Act by partially reversing its previous orders banning all American trade with France and the French West Indies. American ships now would be permitted to carry noncontraband goods to the French.

After six months of negotiations, John Jay won three major concessions from Britain: withdrawal of British troops from the Northwest Territory behind the Canadian border; limited resumption of American trade with the British East and West Indies; and establishment of a most-favored-nation relationship between the two nations, with each granting the other preferential tariffs. Both sides agreed to set up a joint commission and use binding arbitration to settle all British claims against Americans for pre-Revolutionary War debts and compensation for British seizures of American ships in the years following the Revolution.

The treaty made no mention of two issues that had long provoked so much American anger towards Britain: impressment of American sailors into the British navy and compensation to southern plantation

*John Jay, the first Chief Justice of the U.S. Supreme Court, negotiated a treaty with Britain that put the two nations on an equal status with most-favored-nation trade advantages for each.* (LIBRARY OF CONGRESS)

owners for the thousands of slaves the British army had carried away during the Revolutionary War. Anger over the slave issue lay behind the fanatical southern support for France and the willingness—indeed, eagerness—of southerners to join France in war against Britain.

Although Jay had hoped to win concessions on both issues, he recognized that Britain had little incentive to yield on either. Aside from her sheer economic and military power, Britain had scored an important naval victory over the French fleet that left British warships in full command of the Atlantic Ocean, with no need to cede privileges to weaker nations. Knowing that, Jay had good reason to be concerned.

Although Jefferson had retired to his aerie in Charlottesville, Virginia, and Genet had buried himself in the vegetable fields of Long Island, New

York, the Democratic Societies they had organized had acquired lives of their own. Depending on the temper of the local citizenry, they continued to demonstrate for local self-rule, universal white male suffrage, and, often, violent overthrow of existing federal and state governments. Anticipating the outrage that his failures on the impressment and slave compensation issues would provoke, Jay coaxed British negotiators to keep treaty terms secret until Washington and the U.S. Senate could ratify it, and he sailed for home on November 19, 1794.*

During the summer of 1794, as Jay's negotiations in Britain reached a climax, a flurry of Democratic Society leaflets promised that the revolutionary government in France would support the farmer tax revolt in western Pennsylvania, giving it an entirely new and frightening complexion.

"France has been called to lead a gigantic revolution and worldwide uprising to liberate the oppressed peoples of the world," declared Jacques Pierre Brissot de Warville, a mediocre journalist-turned-pamphleteer who envisioned himself a prophet and clawed his way to leadership among French revolutionaries. "All Europe will be Gallicized, communized, and Jacobinized," he barked as he called on the French to revive the centuries-old Crusader tradition of enrichment from conquest and plunder.[2]

Faced with loss of their properties for nonpayment of the whiskey tax, farmers in far-off Mingo Creek outside Pittsburgh were more than eager to accommodate Brissot's ambitions. Goaded by the fiery young lawyer David Bradford, they formed a new Democratic Society to Gallicize, communize, and Jacobinize western Pennsylvania.

A Maryland newcomer who had failed in his chosen profession, Bradford had sought to make a name for himself in politics. The secessionist movement gave him the opportunity to assume the role of an American Maximilien Robespierre—the leader of the French Revolu-

---

*Impressment would continue for another decade and become one of the basic risks of going to sea for a generation of American men—until Britain's 1815 victory in the Napoleonic Wars ended her need to maintain a large navy.

tion who had also proved incompetent at the bar. "We are ready for a state of revolution and the guillotine of France," Bradford harangued the Mingo Creek Democratic Society. "We are ready to inflict punishment on the miscreants that enervate and disgrace our government."[3]

Washington responded by openly denouncing whiskey-tax protests as "the first *formidable* fruit of the Democratic Societies." He accused the societies of sowing "the seeds of jealousy and distrust among people of the government."[4] He attacked the clubs as "the most diabolical attempt to destroy the best fabric of human government and happiness that has ever been presented for the acceptance of mankind." Washington, blamed Genet for having "brought the eggs of these venomous reptiles to our shores,"[5] but he lacked power to prevent the eggs from hatching.

The whiskey-tax protests reached a climax of sorts at dawn, on July 16, 1794, when a mob of several hundred rode up to the elegant mansion of Revolutionary War hero Colonel John Neville, a staunch supporter of the federal government and supervisor for tax collections in western Pennsylvania. Eyes aflame at the prospect of watching the violent consequences of his fiery oratory, Bradford spurred his horse to the front of the mob and demanded that Neville resign his post and surrender all official government papers relating to the whiskey tax.

While his wife and little granddaughter lay on the floor, Neville challenged the farmers, ordering them to "stand off" and firing a warning shot above their heads. They answered with a barrage of rifle fire that shattered windows but left the occupants unhurt. Neville sounded a signal horn to arouse his slaves, who rallied around their master and returned fire, killing one attacker, wounding four others, and forcing the rest into the cover of nearby woods. Neville sent a servant to ask help from the militia at Fort Fayette near Pittsburgh, but only seventeen soldiers arrived that evening, and six deserted before morning.

By then, the mob had swelled to nearly eight hundred, with Bradford screaming for blood. Neville responded with more gunfire that claimed the life of a popular militiaman who had fought in the Revolutionary War. By evening, Neville and his slaves ran out of ammunition and fled as the mob overran the mansion. Enraged by the deaths of comrades, the mob made quick work of the interior, smashing fine furniture, pictures, china, and glassware and setting the structure on fire—but not before appropriating silverware, jewelry, cash, and a cellar full of liquor. Exhilarated by the warmth of stolen whiskey and soaring flames, the rebels shot Neville's horses and burned his outbuildings and slave quarters. To climax their orgy, they set fire to a huge store of grain, pouring kegs of whiskey on the flames and on each other while dancing about in savage frenzy.

As the flames diminished, Bradford cried out for more vengeance, and those not too drunk to mount their horses rode off across the fields towards the lodgings of U.S. Marshal David Lenox. They dragged him from his bed to hang him until he swore he would resign and never again serve papers on tax evaders. Both Lenox and Neville fled the area. The remaining tax collectors either followed or publicly resigned their commissions.

The state's supervisor for tax collection complained to Secretary of Treasury Alexander Hamilton that the flow of tax revenues had all but stopped in Fayette, Greene, Washington, and Westmoreland counties—an area of westernmost Pennsylvania with about 77,000 people and some 5,000 stills. Hamilton received comparable reports from Kentucky, Georgia, and the Carolinas.

After burning down Colonel Neville's house, Bradford and his Jacobins sent word across the farmlands for opponents of the whiskey tax to meet on Braddock's Field, eight miles outside Pittsburgh, armed and ready to march on the city to burn it down. Bradford had now given up all pretense of being a simple tax protester, as he galloped across the countryside, organizing mobs and ordering them to attack anyone of wealth—no matter how slight. They burned and pillaged large farms, manufacturers, millers, and even the properties of shopkeepers with no sympathies for or connections with the federal government or its whiskey tax.

*Braddock's Field near Pittsburgh, Pennsylvania, where General Edward Braddock led British troops into an ambush by French troops and Indian warriors that left 977 of his 1,459 British troops dead or wounded. Only the heroics of Colonel George Washington managed to save the survivors and lead them through the wilderness to safety. In August 1794, it was the site for the climax of the Whiskey Rebellion.* (LIBRARY OF CONGRESS)

To Bradford's gathering rabble, the ordinary little city of Pittsburgh had become a symbol of plenty, and they were as determined as mobs in Paris to destroy every last symbol of wealth they could find. On August 1, more than 5,000 angry farmers and frontiersmen converged on the appointed meeting ground with muskets, rifles, and enough whiskey for an army twice its size. Bradford had chosen the site carefully—a macabre landscape, still littered with skull fragments and bones of General Edward Braddock's British troops, whom the French and Indians had slaughtered forty years earlier, in July 1755. Ironically, it was there that then-twenty-three-year-old lieutenant colonel George Washington had first gained fame for his battlefield heroics.

As David Bradford rode across the bone fragments of Washington's fallen comrades, the ambitious lawyer was intent on gaining his own share of national fame. A witness described his arrival on the scene:

> Mounted on a superb horse in splendid trappings, arrayed in full martial uniform, with plumes floating in the air and sword drawn, he rode over the grounds, gave orders to the military and harangued the multitude. Never was mortal man more flattered than was David Bradford on Braddock's Field. Every thing depended on his will. The insurgents adored him, and those who hated him paid him the most servile homage in order to be able to control and manage him.[6]

Bradford roused the crowd with cries for secession and independence. "This is not all I want," he shouted, as if calling across the horizon to the President himself. "It is not the whiskey tax only that must go down; your district and associate judges must go down; your high offices and salaries. A great deal more is to be done; I am but beginning yet."[7]

Ironically, only a few days before lawyer Bradford seized control of the Whiskey Rebellion and proclaimed his ambitions to America, Maximilien Robespierre, the French lawyer who had set off the butchery of the French Revolution, had climbed to his death on the Paris guillotine that he had used to slaughter thousands of innocents who dared oppose his leadership.

Pittsburgers spent the night in panic, packing their most precious belongings and preparing to flee the city. "In the morning," recalled Brigadier General John Wilkins, Sr., who led the small militia at Fort Fayette, "the greatest confusion prevailed amongst the people, all sorts of labor and business ceased, all the men preparing to march, the women in tears, some leaving town, some hiding property, and some so shocked as not to know what to do."[8]

With only 250 troops to defend the fort and the city, the militia commander decided on a bold maneuver: Rather than waiting for the rebels to attack and possibly burn the troops alive in the fort, he would

*The Whiskey Rebellion saw upwards of 5,000 tax protesters gather on Braddock's Field near Pittsburgh, prepared to march on the capital in Philadelphia to topple the Washington administration. In the center of the crowd, a tax collector stands tarred and feathered as a stark warning to other tax collectors.* (LIBRARY OF CONGRESS)

ride out with his men and attack insurgents while they milled about drunk and disorganized on Braddock's Field.

As the small band of troops arrived within sight of the rebels, a group of unarmed men incongruously dressed in prim, trim business suits rode up to stop the advance. At their head were Henry Bracken-ridge and Albert Gallatin, two of Pittsburgh's most prominent citizens, who warned that a militia attack would only enrage and provoke the mob to storm Pittsburgh, burn the city, and massacre its inhabitants—including militiamen. Though Brackenridge and Gallatin were both foreign born, they commanded the respect of the entire Pittsburgh community, including the militia commander.

Thirty-six-year-old Brackenridge had come from Scotland to York, Pennsylvania, as a boy. At fourteen, he went to study theology at Prince-ton College, where he befriended James Madison, tutored Henry (later, "Light-Horse Harry") Lee, and roomed with William Bradford (un-related to David Bradford), who had replaced Edmund Randolph as U.S. Attorney General when Randolph became Secretary of State. Brackenridge had served as a chaplain in Washington's army during the Revolutionary War, then went to law school before moving west to

*Henry Brackenridge, a prominent western lawyer and state assemblyman, jumped into the mob of whiskey rebels on Braddock's Field to try to negotiate a compromise that would end their protests and avoid a bloody confrontation with the state militia and federal troops.* (LIBRARY OF CONGRESS)

Pittsburgh to begin life as a frontier lawyer and enter politics. After helping found Pittsburgh Academy (now University of Pittsburgh), he won election to the Assembly and devoted himself to improving the West: A champion of better roads, he had also worked to recover Mississippi River navigation rights from Spain and had fought to repeal the whiskey tax, earning region-wide recognition as the frontiersman's friend and building a lucrative law practice.

Albert Gallatin had been born in Geneva, Switzerland, in 1761 and, after succumbing to the spell of Jean-Jacques Rousseau's writings, fled his homeland at nineteen and landed in Massachusetts. He served in the Continental Army until the end of the war and traveled to Fayette County in western Pennsylvania, where he set up one of the first glass factories in the West. A bitter opponent of the Constitution and champion of state sovereignty, he became the darling of western farmers, who elected him to the state legislature and then the U.S. Senate, where

*Albert Gallatin, the Swiss-born U.S. Senator from
Pennsylvania, opposed the whiskey tax, but joined
with Henry Brackenridge in trying to negotiate a
peaceful settlement of the Whiskey Rebellion.*
(LIBRARY OF CONGRESS)

he faced expulsion from his party in February 1794, for his unyielding
opposition to the whiskey tax.

By birth and breeding both Brackenridge and Gallatin feared and
detested violence. Although both opposed the whiskey tax, they believed strongly in constitutional forms of protest and had no sympathy
for the "unthinking, uncalculated rebellion" of Bradford and his Braddock's Field rabble. Brackenridge called the mob "ignorant and emotional . . . easily led astray by demagogues. It is the duty of men of sense
and respectability to enact the role of sympathetic guardians and to fur-
nish leadership by the exercise of tact and moderation and, when necessary, procrastination and mild deceit."[9]

Determined to save their city, Gallatin, Brackenridge and other civic
leaders decided to face rebel leaders, and they pleaded with the commander of the Fort Fayette militia to allow them to negotiate before he
attacked. He agreed, and the unarmed civic leaders—still in their comic

Sunday-meeting garb—rode to the rebel camp and disappeared into the howling horde.

News of the Pittsburgh uprising had already spread across the frontier. Anti-tax riots erupted in Northumberland and Carlisle, Pennsylvania; in Morgantown, Martinsburg, and Winchester, Virginia; then in Maryland—in Middletown and Frederick, where rioters erected liberty poles, burned American flags at the foot of the pillories, and raised their own flags of independence. After state militia marched into Hagerstown to quell rioters, the militiamen turned against their officers and local magistrates and joined tax protesters.

For Washington, it was one crisis too many. The time had come to raise a sixth pillar of presidential power: law enforcement. He ordered federal troops to march in and seize the town to restore law and order. Although ringleaders fled, Washington's troops hunted them down and imprisoned them.

In Philadelphia, Attorney General William Bradford declared the Braddock's Field demonstration part of "a plan for weakening and perhaps overthrowing the general government." Secretary of War Knox urged the President to send "a superabundant force" to crush the rebels. Alexander Hamilton called the uprising nothing short of treason and seconded Knox: "Whenever the government appears in arms, it ought to appear like a *Hercules* and inspire respect by the display of strength."[10]

Washington agreed: "If the laws are to be so trampled upon with impunity, and a minority, a small one too, is to dictate to the majority, there is an end put, at one stroke, to republican government."[11]

Washington's angry tone set off heated debates. State officials, including Pennsylvania Governor Thomas Mifflin, vigorously opposed military action. "Should an attempt be made to suppress these people," warned an aide just back from Pittsburgh, "I am afraid the question will not be whether you will march to Pittsburgh, but whether they will march to Philadelphia."[12]

Washington sided with Knox and Hamilton, but tempered their demands by agreeing to offer the rebels a chance for amnesty before ordering the attack—much as he had sent Captain Trueman with an offer of peace to the Indians in the West. He said he would send a commission of federal and state officials to western Pennsylvania to urge insurgents to disperse and return to their homes peacefully or face the military might of the U.S. Army. Invoking the Militia Act, he then scrawled his name across a proclamation and ordered Treasury Secretary Hamilton to raise an army of 13,000 in case the westerners refused to yield.

After vowing to lead the army himself, the aging president dismissed the gathering, and, despite considerable pain from an accident on his horse the previous week, called for a tailor to replicate the uniform he had worn as commander in chief in the Revolutionary War. With Indian warriors fanning out across the West, and American secessionists threatening to overthrow his government and dissolve the Union, sixty-two-year-old Washington prepared to mount up, as he had two decades earlier in '75, and go to war to save the nation.

## CHAPTER ELEVEN

# The Madman and the Indians

As whiskey rebels prepared to annihilate Pittsburgh, some 2,000 Indian warriors had massed behind a huge barricade of entangled fallen trees, or "timbers," 250 miles to the west in northern Ohio, where they prepared to annihilate General "Mad" Anthony Wayne's approaching force of 1,000 frontiersmen. Unaware that Britain had signed the Jay Treaty and withdrawn her troops from the surrounding territory, the Indians expected British reinforcements to appear and help them turn the confrontation into a slaughter rich with American scalps and other trophies.

Although he had been unable to comply with Washington's orders to recruit 5,000 men, the intrepid Wayne refused to back away from conflict—especially after the ruthless slaughter of Captain Trueman, Washington's peace emissary. Though rash and often unpredictable, Wayne was always careful to study his enemy before military confrontations, and, as he traveled into Ohio, he learned of the local Indian custom of fasting on the eve of battle. Rather than charging into battle as he usually did, he ordered his men to set up camp about ten miles away and simply wait . . .

. . . and wait.

*General "Mad" Anthony Wayne engineered the victory over Indian warriors at the Battle of Fallen Timbers and went on to expel the Indians from the Ohio Territory and present-day Indiana. After capturing one of the Indian forts, he renamed it Fort Wayne.* (LIBRARY OF CONGRESS)

After three days of fasting, hunger goaded more than one-fourth of the Indian warriors to abandon their makeshift fort among the timbers to search for food. It was the moment Wayne had awaited. He ordered his troops to attack.

Two hours later, the Battle of Fallen Timbers ended, with surviving Indian warriors in full flight—their bodies enfeebled by hunger, their faith in white men shattered by the British failure to come to their aid.

Wayne's men set out in pursuit along the Maumee River into present-day Indiana. Burning Indian villages on the way, the Americans laid waste to the Miami Indian heartland until they reached the junction of the Maumee and two other rivers, where, as a show of dominance, Wayne claimed the Indian fort as his own, and, displaying the conceit that Washington so disliked about him, renamed it Fort Wayne.

Although Washington had ordered Wayne's expedition, he nonetheless recognized the long-term futility of continual war with the tribes and called on Congress to enact new laws for "securing their lands to them, restraining states or individuals from purchasing their lands, and forbidding unauthorized dealings with them. If Congress expects to live in peace with the neighboring Indians and to avoid the expenses and horrors of continual hostilities," Washington warned, "such a measure will be found indispensably necessary; for unless adequate penalties are provided that will check the spirit of speculation in lands . . . this country will be constantly embroiled with . . . Indians."[1]

As a temporary calm settled across Ohio and Indiana, western Pennsylvania remained aboil, as Brackenridge, Gallatin, and their band of "respectable" city gentlemen in suits and ties plunged into an angry mob of drunken farmers, field hands, hunters, trappers, and adventurers on Braddock's Field outside Pittsburgh. Their intention was to coax the more thoughtful protesters to reconsider plans both to burn Pittsburgh and war with the American government.

Fearing he might lose control of the mob to the peacemakers, Bradford responded by calling a meeting of representatives from all the area's townships. More than two hundred delegates appeared on August 14, the very day the President's commission arrived in Pittsburgh. Bradford's supporters called out for "a declaration of independence." Another demanded, "Are you for Congress or for liberty?"[2] When word reached the camp that Washington had issued a proclamation drafting troops to attack the protesters, Bradford's men howled with rage and demanded an immediate declaration of war against the government.

Suddenly, Gallatin, the cool Swiss legislator, mounted a small platform and waited in haughty silence for the crowd's attention. As Brackenridge worked the group, soothing members with seductive whispers of empathy for their plight, Gallatin's imposing reserve and icy, aristocratic stare quieted them. Using every debating skill he had learned in the U.S. Senate, he appealed to the logic of moderate, undecided members, saying that if the commissioners had come to declare war, they would have brought the army with them.

In a move to split the gathering, he urged the assembly to appoint a committee to demonstrate "western good manners" and good faith by meeting with the commissioners—not to yield, but to ascertain the government's intentions and report back to Braddock Field rebels. At the very least, he argued, the meeting would give insurgents more time to prepare a successful battle strategy.

Bradford was too sly a lawyer not to see through Gallatin's clever words. Although he angrily protested the motion, Gallatin's logic won the day. As the militia retreated to the confines of Fort Fayette, Gallatin and Brackenridge moved for adjournment and immediately began selecting a sixty-member committee to meet with the Philadelphia commissioners. As an insidiously clever gesture of conciliation, they selected Bradford first—a move that automatically raised suspicions among Bradford's most radical followers about his loyalty to the rebellion.

After three days of negotiations, the commission refused all compromise, warning that the federal government would crush insurgents mercilessly unless they agreed to "perfect and entire acquiescence" to the whiskey tax by September 1. Unable to obtain any concessions from the commissioners, the committee voted 34 to 23 against yielding to government demands.

On September 9, President Washington abandoned hopes for peaceful settlement, and, buoyed with confidence by Wayne's victory at the Battle of Fallen Timbers, he ordered Hamilton to assemble the fighting force. Ten days later, nearly 13,000 troops, militia, volunteers, draftees,

*President George Washington, noticeably aged after eight years as President, refused to run for a third term, setting a precedent that all his successors observed until 1940, when President Franklin D. Roosevelt sought and won election to a third term.*
(LIBRARY OF CONGRESS)

and paid substitutes from four states began converging on Carlisle and Bedford, Pennsylvania.

At 10 a.m. on September 30, to Martha Washington's dismay and cries of protest, the President prepared to take command of the army in the field—the first and last American president ever to do so. No longer the tall, imposing young warrior of '75, he was in too much pain from arthritis—and indeed too fat—to mount his horse, and he climbed unsteadily into a carriage outside his Philadelphia residence. At his left sat Hamilton, who had first served Washington as a twenty-two-year-old captain seventeen years earlier during the Revolutionary War. It, too, began as a protest against taxes. Now, as Treasury secretary, Hamilton had imposed—and Washington had endorsed—a tax that provoked a similar rebellion that the two old comrades-in-arms were determined to crush.

The irony of the situation was not lost on either man: The leader of the first American Revolution setting out to crush a second—along the very road he had traveled as a young Virginia colonel to engage the French and Indians in the mid-1750s.

On October 4, the presidential carriage crossed the Susquehanna River; the Pennsylvania Light Horse awaited on the far bank to escort Washington and Hamilton westward beyond Harrisburg to Carlisle, where state militia had assembled for the march to Pittsburgh.

By evening, the various commanders had gathered to pay homage to Washington—many of them old comrades-in-arms from the Revolutionary War: General Henry Lee, the legendary "Light-Horse Harry," who was now governor of Virginia; Pennsylvania Governor Thomas Mifflin, the quartermaster general during the unforgettable winter at Valley Forge; General (now doctor) Edward Hand, a heroic colonel and battalion commander in the Trenton-Princeton campaign; and Major General Daniel Morgan, whose Virginia riflemen had overwhelmed the Redcoats at Saratoga, New York, and at Cowpens on the border between the two Carolinas. Morgan had retired in ill health to his Virginia estate, but came out of retirement to serve his old commander in chief one last time.

They were all there: the great old men of the Revolution, gallant soldiers all, brave commanders, close friends, at a loss for words, engulfed by memories, gripping each other's hands, throats choking with emotion, barely able to utter each other's names, not daring to embrace, saddened at the evident toll that age had taken on their faces and bodies. Virginia Governor Henry Lee outranked them all except Washington; Mifflin, Hand, and Daniel Morgan were next in the chain of command.[3]

On October 9, two emissaries arrived from Pittsburgh to ask the President to delay his attack while Pittsburgh's civic leaders attempted to obtain full compliance with the whiskey tax law. The President rejected the request, saying it had come too late, that the insurrection had gone on too long. "Nothing short of the most unequivocal *proofs* [his italics] of absolute submission," he insisted, "would retard the march of the army into the western counties." Washington pledged that "the government could and would enforce obedience to the laws," but that the military would not exact vengeance in the case of unconditional surrender. "There could be no answering for consequences," he warned, "if the insurgents fired their guns."[4]

Three days later, the President and his entourage of military and political figures set off for Fort Cumberland, where Washington had led 386 survivors of the Braddock massacre to safety in 1755. On October 20, Washington ordered the army to march to Pittsburgh in forty-eight hours and split into two wings before converging on Braddock's Field. After Hamilton convinced him that he was too valuable to the nation to risk his life in battle, Washington reluctantly ceded command to Lee and prepared to return to Philadelphia.

In a farewell message to the troops, the President complimented them on their "enlightened and patriotic zeal for the Constitution and the laws which have led them cheerfully to quit their families and homes and the comforts of private life . . . to perform a long and fatiguing march and to encounter the hardships and privations of a military life."[5]

The long, hard journey over the mountains, however, quickly converted the "enlightened and patriotic zeal" of the troops into rage—and a determination to exact brutal revenge on the rebels responsible for the torturous expedition. The two army divisions reached Braddock's Field the following month, and, thirsting for blood, charged out of the surrounding woods prepared to massacre the rebel encampment. To their astonishment, however, the rebels, having heard of Wayne's victory in Ohio, had vanished abruptly, ending their revolution without firing a shot.

Infuriated at having made so arduous a journey for nothing, the troops scoured the countryside in a vain attempt to round up rebels. They managed to find only twenty sleeping drunks—most of them homeless, displaced farmworkers, whom the troops chained onto carts and carried back to Philadelphia, where they paraded their pathetic "captives" down Market Street. Instead of cheering, however, onlookers watched in silence before turning away in disgust.

Most Whiskey Boys were either tenant farmers or frontiersmen who owned no property and therefore had no vote. Washington had crushed the most vulnerable of America's citizens—men, with few rights, already crushed by poverty and government inequity. Of the twenty, the court dismissed charges of treason against eighteen for lack of evidence, and Washington pardoned the other two, one of whom was clearly demented.

The Whiskey Rebellion proved a stunning victory for both victors and vanquished. Without firing a single shot—indeed, without even showing his face on the field of battle—President Washington had crushed a rebellion and clearly established the prerogatives and authority of all three branches of the federal government—executive, legislative, and judiciary. Together with his victory in the Indian wars, he established and reinforced presidential powers not granted by the Constitution over both "the sword and the purse."

In establishing the president's right to call up troops to enforce the law and keep the peace, Washington not only raised another pillar of presidential power—federal law enforcement—he reinforced powers of the two other branches of government: the power of Congress to legislate federal taxes without the consent of state legislatures and the power of the federal judiciary to try and punish those who disobey the laws of Congress.

Executive law enforcement powers added a sixth pillar of power to the presidency, complementing executive appointments, foreign policy, military affairs, government finances, and legislation by proclamation.

The rebels did not flee without scoring a significant victory of their own, however. Their uprising forcefully demonstrated the enormous, potentially deadly risks of government attempts to disenfranchise any segment of the citizenry. Moderates like Brackenridge and Gallatin in

Pennsylvania and their equivalents in Virginia, the Carolinas, Georgia, and elsewhere returned to their state legislatures to fight for and win legislation that gave the rural inland population more equal representation in state legislatures and greater access to courtrooms.

One key to ensuring equality was the transfer of state capitals from the centers of wealth and influence in coastal cities to the geographical centers of each state, Columbia replacing Charleston as the capital of South Carolina, Raleigh replacing Wilmington in North Carolina, and Harrisburg eventually replacing Philadelphia as capital of Pennsylvania.

In the end, the Whiskey Rebellion was part of a second revolution that transformed the American government from an ideal on paper into a practical, functioning apparatus for governing free, but imperfect human beings. It helped make the United States "a *more* perfect union"— though still far from perfect. Although Washington had crushed western Pennsylvania secessionists, he by no means crushed secessionism as a form of protest against oppressive state and federal rule. Within a decade, New York, New Jersey, and five New England states would renew calls for secession, in favor of an independent Northern Confederacy.

In 1798, Thomas Jefferson, by then Vice President, went a step farther, proclaiming the Constitution only "a compact" between *sovereign* states, which, he insisted, retained authority to restrain federal government actions that exceeded its constitutional mandate. Jefferson rode to Kentucky to introduce the "Kentucky Resolution" and convince a legislative majority that any federal government exercise of powers not specifically delegated by the Constitution was, by definition, unconstitutional and, therefore, subject to nullification by state governments. Although Kentuckians removed the word "nullification," they agreed with the principle of Jefferson's resolution and approved it.

James Madison, also an advocate of states' rights by then, would win a similar resolution in the Virginia legislature, which added a state's right "to interpose" its authority to prevent "the exercise of . . . powers" by the federal government not granted by the Constitution.[6] Although all the other states rejected similar resolutions, fifty-three years later, eleven southern states would secede over the issue of state sovereignty and plunge the nation into civil war.

Even in the late twentieth century, some state leaders continued threatening to "nullify" federal laws and federal court rulings they considered unconstitutional. In the early twenty-first century a small group of tax protesters launched a harmless campaign for the five boroughs that make up New York City to secede from New York and form a new, fifty-first state.

Although he had triumphed over the whiskey rebels, President Washington's victory cost him the aura of immortality he had earned in the American Revolution. Americans continued to love and cherish the mythic *General* George Washington as "Father of Our Country"—and they celebrated his birth night each year as a national holiday. But they no longer idolized *President* George Washington as a divinely inspired, quasi-monarch and would never again regard him—or any other president—as other than mortal. At a public dinner in Virginia, one critic proposed a toast that would have been unthinkable a decade earlier: "A speedy death to General Washington."[7]

The change in public perception wounded the President deeply. He grew more distant, appeared at fewer receptions; his solemn mood discouraged others from visiting the presidential mansion, and attendance at his levees thinned. "I can religiously aver," he complained, "that no man was ever more tired of public life, or more devoutly wished for retirement, than I do.[8] Washington learned it was all but impossible to be an effective president and retain the love of all the people.

Still another crisis awaited, however, to reinforce that lesson.

# CHAPTER TWELVE

## The Final Pillar

With the new year of 1795, Henry Knox and Alexander Hamilton resigned from Washington's cabinet, leaving the aging President to run the nation without the men he trusted most. They were men with whom he had fought side by side through the Revolutionary War to establish American independence and through the political wars to overturn the confederation, write a new constitution, and establish a new government.

When they had first met two decades earlier, all were British subjects, each from a different, independent British colony. To Washington, the term "my country" meant Virginia; to Knox, it meant Massachusetts; to Hamilton, New York—and they were no different from other Americans. Nor did independence from Britain change the thinking of most Americans; the Revolutionary War left each of the former colonies an independent sovereign state with its own constitution and government—and no legal ties or obligations to the twelve other colonies.

The war did, however, change the thinking and allegiances of men like Washington, Knox, Hamilton, and tens of thousands of other Continental Army officers and troops who had worked, fought, and died together. Unlike state militia, whose men came from the same regions and fought as homogeneous state units during the war, the Continental Army blended men from all the states into a heterogeneous corps. As they marched, fought, slept, and bled together, they quickly discovered that they all bled red, regardless of their home states. Together, they and the others in the Continental Army metamorphosed into "Americans." When they uttered the term "My Country," they meant the United States of America.

Continental Army veterans, however, represented but a minority of Americans, and, even after ratification of the Constitution and almost eight years of the Washington Administration, most Americans continued to cling to parochial allegiances to their respective states. Except for veterans, most Americans had never traveled far from home, let alone out of state. Property qualifications had permitted fewer than 25 percent of white male adults to vote for or against the Constitution, leaving the vast majority of Americans either indifferent or opposed to the national government.

Even as the First Congress adjourned in March 1791, Rhode Island Senator Joseph Stanton, Jr., reported to the governor of his state that "on a review of what we have done and the manner it has been done in the course of two years, I think we may return to our countries without a blush." For Stanton and most other senators, their states remained "our countries," where, in Stanton's words, "different laws, customs, and habits of thinking . . . prevailed."[1]

None of the crises that Washington had faced during his eight-year presidency exposed those differences more than the controversy over the Jay Treaty. When John Jay returned home in the winter of 1795, both he and Washington recognized the treaty as a diplomatic triumph—not only for the concessions Jay had won, but for Britain having dealt with the United States as an *equal* and independent sovereign state for the first time. But Washington and Jay both knew the treaty would provoke a storm of controversy for what it did not accomplish—especially among myopic states' rights advocates and Anglophobes. They were correct.

When the public learned the terms of the treaty in March 1795, a tide of acrimony swept across the nation—in Congress, the press, and in the streets. Although its origins were unclear and its leadership invisible, a massive opposition formed to condemn the President. Although Washington loyalists hailed him for averting another brutal war with England, Francophiles and Anglophobes pilloried him for pro-British bias. One newspaper charged that Washington "insidiously aims to dissolve all connections between the United States and France, and to substitute a monarchic for a republican ally."[2]

Southerners—especially Virginians—still railed at the prospects of paying debts to British merchants incurred before the Revolutionary War, while receiving no compensation for the losses of their slaves. Most claims by British merchants were against Virginians, who, as owners of the nation's largest plantations, had also lost the most slaves. Washington loyalists in the Senate, however, outnumbered treaty opponents, and the Senate ratified it on June 24—ironically, just as Jay himself slipped away from the fray, resigning as chief justice of the Supreme Court to run for the governorship of his home state of New York.

Senate ratification did not calm the furor, however. Provoked by newspaper advertisements and editorials by French ambassador Fauchet, Francophiles across the nation organized petitions demanding that Washington not sign it. Westerners joined the opposition, claiming that British withdrawal behind the Canadian border would not prevent their arming and inciting Indians to attack American settlers.

In the East, Fauchet provoked Anglophobes to protest any treaty with Britain as a "deal with the devil." In Boston, a mob burned a British privateer, while New York mobs celebrated Independence Day on July 4 by shouting down John Jay, their new governor. Two weeks later, foes of the treaty organized a "Town Meeting" in New York City, where 5,000 workers spent their normal noontime dinner hour booing, shouting, and hurling stones at Alexander Hamilton as he tried to explain provisions of the treaty.

Wisely, Washington returned to his sanctuary in Mount Vernon and waited until the heat of August forced Congress to recess and drive any men of consequence out of Philadelphia. Equating opponents of the treaty to mad dogs, he returned to the empty capital just long enough to sign the treaty into law without fanfare and rode back to Mount Vernon to complete his summer recess with no one in America aware that the Jay Treaty had become the law of the land.

No sooner had he signed the treaty, however, when a courier arrived with a letter from Massachusetts Senator George Cabot: Sixteen-year-old George Washington Lafayette—Lafayette's only son and Washington's godson—was in Boston with his tutor, at Cabot's home and asking help in reaching the Washingtons. American Ambassador James Monroe had arranged for Adrienne de Lafayette's release from prison and helped her and her two daughters flee to neutral Denmark, but at her insistence he had secreted her son and his tutor onto a ship bound for America and the safety of his godfather's home at Mount Vernon. His arrival could not have come at a worse time, as Washington explained in his reply to Cabot.

"Let me in a few words, declare that I *will be his friend*," Washington wrote, "a father, friend, protector, and supporter, but the manner of becoming so, considering the obnoxious light in which his father is viewed by the French government and my own situation as Executive of the United States requires more time to consider."

To avoid the appearance of harboring the son of an enemy of the French government, Washington urged the boy to enroll in college until Washington finished his term in office and could receive him as a private citizen. "To give him all the advantages which education can bestow," Washington told Cabot, "he should enter as a student at the University in Cambridge [Harvard] although it should be for a short time *only*. The expence of which, as also every mean for his support, I will pay."[3]

Fearing the boy's presence would further inflame passions over the Jay Treaty, he asked that Lafayette use his patronymic family name "Motier," rather than Lafayette.

Although opponents of the Jay Treaty were furious when they learned how the President had outflanked them, a series of unrelated events combined to silence their voices and quell the national anger. A British frigate had captured a French vessel carrying the furnishings and personal effects of retiring French ambassador Fauchet back to France. Among Fauchet's private papers was a copy of a letter he had sent to his foreign minister reporting that Secretary of State Edmund Randolph, an avowed Francophile, had solicited bribes to try to defeat the Jay Treaty.

News of the letter staggered Washington, who had known and trusted Randolph for years—considered him a close personal friend. Scion of one of Virginia's oldest, most "aristocratic" families, Randolph had been governor of Virginia and an ally of Washington in the fight for ratification of the Constitution in the Virginia ratification convention. A wealthy plantation owner like Washington, he had been Washington's aide-de-camp in Boston at the beginning of the Revolutionary War in 1775. Washington all but broke down in tears as he confronted Randolph with the letter and came to the inescapable conclusion that Randolph had pocketed thousands of dollars from Fauchet. He demanded and received Randolph's immediate resignation.

Pro-Washington newspapers called the letter final proof of treachery by the French government and the Democratic Societies that had supported Genet's conspiracy "to separate the western country from the Atlantic states."[4]

Revelation of Randolph's apparent treachery left the Franco-American Treaty of 1778 in shreds. The French government called the Jay Treaty a violation of "the alliance which binds the two peoples." After repudiating the treaty with America, the French government sent warships to attack American shipping. In the course of the year, French ships captured and sold more than three hundred American ships and their cargoes, without compensating owners. The French executed many of the captured American seamen on the spot and tossed the rest into chains in the forbidding Bordeaux prison.

Just as American affection for France was cooling, news arrived from the West that defused much of the residual anger against the British. Not only had the British pulled their troops back into Canada, their former ally, Chief Little Turtle, who headed the Northwest Confederation of Indian tribes, signed a treaty ceding most of Ohio, Indiana, Illinois, and Michigan to the United States. The treaty ended the bloody Indian forays on American settlements and opened a vast new territory to settlement along the Ohio River and Mississippi River valleys northward to the Great Lakes.

Adding to the euphoria was news that Spain had agreed to grant free navigation "privileges" to Americans on the Mississippi River for three years. The Spanish also granted Americans the "privilege" to deposit goods in New Orleans for export overseas. Negotiated by Thomas Pinckney of South Carolina, the treaty carefully avoided the word "rights," but did offer conditional renewal privileges after the first three years.

Elated at the economic opportunities that would certainly follow peace with the Indians, British troop withdrawal, and access to the Mississippi, westerners all but forgot the reasons for their rancor towards the Jay Treaty and Washington's Neutrality Proclamation. In fact, America's neutral status combined with the Jay, Pinckney, and Wayne treaties to set off an economic boom that reaped unprecedented profits for American states, who crouched behind the shield of neutrality to fill nonmilitary needs of the warring states in Europe. Washington's masterful management of American foreign affairs had, at last, muted opponents of the Jay Treaty, and as merchants and farmers across the land reaped the profits of foreign trade generated by the treaty, opposition to the agreement vanished.

"If the people of this country have not abundant cause to rejoice at the happiness they enjoy," Washington exulted to his friend Gouverneur Morris, "I know of no country that has.

> We have settled all our disputes and are at peace with all nations. We supply their wants with our superfluities and are well paid for doing so.

The earth, generally, for years past, has yielded its fruits bountifully. No city, town, village, or even farm, but what exhibits evidences of increasing wealth and prosperity.[5]

Although Washington's victory elated Federalists in Congress, it left a gang of Jeffersonian Republicans in the House of Representatives humiliated—indeed, seething with anger. They decided to exact revenge by using their constitutional authority over appropriations to refuse funding for the Jay Treaty's joint arbitration commission until they examined all of Jay's and Washington's papers to see if Jay had colluded with the British. Their action set off a series of bitter constitutional debates that would last for nearly two months, with some issues, amazingly, still unresolved to this day.

The first issue concerned the constitutional authority of the House to thwart implementation of any foreign treaty. There was no question that only the House could originate appropriations bills, but only the Senate had authority to reject or approve treaties. House control over appropriations, however, now seemed to give it joint control over treaties with the Senate—something the framers of the Constitution had not envisioned or sanctioned.

The second issue was the right of the House to access the President's secret and confidential papers. Jefferson's Democratic-Republicans in the House argued that secrecy in government was a threat to republican government. Federalists countered that the President's constitutional role as commander in chief obligated him to withhold certain documents and information to protect national security—an argument still used today. Washington's opponents pressed ahead, passing a resolution demanding to see all the Washington-Jay papers "excepting such of said papers as any existing negotiation may render improper to be disclosed."[6]

Infuriated by what he considered congressional overstepping of its authority into executive affairs, Washington refused. In one of the fiercest rebukes any sitting president has ever administered to Congress, Washington essentially amended the Constitution with a new principle not envisioned by its framers or contained in its language: the existence of three *separate* and *equal* branches of government. He told Congress it had no business poking its collective fingers into *any* presidential papers.

"It is essential to the due administration of the government," he declared, "that the boundaries fixed by the Constitution between the different departments should be preserved. It does not occur that the inspection of the papers asked for can be relative to any purpose under the cognizance of the House of Representatives."

Washington went on to give Congress a stern lecture on the Constitution:

> Having been a member of the general convention and knowing the principles on which the Constitution was formed, I have ever entertained but one opinion . . . that the power of making treaties is exclusively vested in the President, by and with the advice and consent of the Senate . . . and that every treaty so made and promulgated became the law of the land . . . [and] they become obligatory. In this construction of the Constitution every House of Representatives has heretofore acquiesced. . . . As therefore it is perfectly clear to my understanding that the assent of the House of Representatives is not necessary to the validity of a treaty . . . a just regard to the Constitution and the duty of my office . . . forbids a compliance with your request.[7]

All but calling its members disobedient schoolboys, Washington told the House that it had no choice but to obey the terms of the treaty and appropriate the necessary funds or openly flout the law.

Only Washington, with his enormous prestige and popularity, could have addressed Congress with such demeaning language. In doing so, however, Washington not only crushed the attempts of the House to assert itself into foreign affairs and treaty negotiations, he asserted full control over those two areas for future presidents and established a number of extra-constitutional principles that are still in place today. One was the principle of executive prerogatives and privileges, which remains in force, despite continuing demands by House and Senate committees to see at least some of every President's private papers.

A second Washington accomplishment was the establishment of firm, all-but-impenetrable boundaries between the executive and legislative branches. It was a monumental achievement that completed the construction of the basic presidential structure, with the raising of a seventh, and final, pillar of power: executive privilege based upon separation of government powers. The presidency now stood apart from the legislative and judicial branches of government, its seven enormous pillars of power supporting a mighty separate *and* equal branch of government.

## CHAPTER THIRTEEN

# Farewell from a Friend

In an astonishing effort to ensure and perpetuate the republican character of the American presidency, George Washington climaxed his second term in office with this announcement:

> The period for a new election . . . to administer the executive government of the United States being not far distant . . . it appears to me proper . . . that I should now apprise you of the resolution I have formed to decline being considered among the number of those out of whom a choice is to be made.[1]

With those opening words of his farewell address to the nation, the President limited his service in office to two terms—a precedent that no succeeding president would violate until 1939, when Franklin D. Roosevelt announced he would campaign for a third term the following year. After Roosevelt ran for election and won a fourth term four years later, mounting concern over the lack of presidential term limits provoked enactment of the Twenty-Second Amendment to the Constitution in 1951, limiting the president to no more than two full terms in office.

Washington sent his farewell address for publication to the *American Daily Advertiser* on September 19, 1796, in the form of a letter to the American people. In it he tried to establish broad precedents for his successors in the conduct of national and foreign affairs. He railed against political parties at home and urged binding the regions of the nation into "fraternal union"; in foreign affairs, he urged keeping the United States a perennially neutral nation, with no long-term ties to any foreign nations.

Warning Americans against "the baneful effects of the spirit of [political] party," he argued that political parties "agitate the community with ill-founded jealousies and false alarms, kindle the animosity of one part against another, foment occasional riot and insurrection . . . [and] open the door to foreign influence and corruption.

> However combinations of associations . . . may now and then answer popular ends, they are likely . . . to become potent engines by which cunning, ambitious, and unprincipled men will . . . subvert the power of the people and usurp for themselves the reins of government, destroying afterwards the very engines which have lifted them to unjust dominion. . . . They . . . put in place of the delegated will of the nation, the will of the party, often a small but artful and enterprising minority.[2]

Rather than turning to a political party to right "any particular wrong," he urged "that it be corrected by an amendment in the way which the Constitution designates."

Washington cited as "a matter of serious concern" the efforts of rabble rousers "to excite a belief that there is a real difference of local interests and views" between geographical regions.

"One of the expedients of party to acquire influence within particular districts," he declared, "is to misrepresent the opinions and aims of other districts. . . . They tend to render alien to each other those who ought to be bound together by fraternal affection."

In foreign affairs, Washington warned against "the insidious wiles of foreign influence.

> I conjure you to believe me, fellow citizens, the jealousy of a free people ought to be constantly awake, since history and experience prove that foreign influence is one of the most baneful foes of republican govern-ment. . . . The great rule of conduct for us, in regard to foreign nations, is in extending our commercial relations to them with as little political connection as possible.[3]

Aware of the growing immigrant population, Washington con-demned "a passionate attachment of one nation for another," saying it produced "a variety of evils. Sympathy for the favorite nation . . . gives to ambitious, corrupted, or deluded citizens (who devote themselves to the favorite nation) facility to betray or sacrifice the interests of their own country.

> Nothing is more essential than that permanent, inveterate antipathies against particular nations and passionate attachments for others should be excluded. . . . The nation which indulges towards another an habit-ual hatred or an habitual fondness is in some degree a slave. It is a slave to its animosity or to its affection, either of which is sufficient to lead it astray from its duty or interest . . . into a participation in quarrels and wars . . . without adequate inducement or justification.[4]

Washington then proclaimed what he hoped would be inscribed as the defining words on the foreign policy pillar of his presidency: "'Tis our true policy to steer clear of permanent alliances with any portion of the foreign world."[5]

The presidential structure that Washington built was far from com-plete when he left office nor did it ensure its future occupants of success or stability. Indeed, many of his successors failed miserably—especially weaker men who were unable to control members of their cabinets or prevent political divisions and infighting between cabinet members, political factions in Congress, or factions in their political parties. Even Washington had difficulties controlling Jefferson and Hamilton during their bitter feud.

Washington's major failure as President, however, was, by his own admission, his inability to unite Americans and convince them all to embrace the nation as "my country." His failure to teach, coax, or cajole Americans into abandoning loyalties to individual states, regions, countries of origin, and economic and political factions would, of course, eventually evolve into civil war. Many Americans today—especially the newly arrived—remain more intent on cementing or reestablishing ties to their countries of origin than voting or learning the history and laws of the United States. Americans with such divided loyalties necessarily impede national progress and subvert national interests.

Political-party rivalries all but paralyze state legislatures in many states, as well as in Congress. In recent years, senators and representatives from both political parties have routinely ignored national priorities in their rage to block every action—good or bad—by their political opponents. Regional rivalries have provoked construction of costly sports stadiums and arenas, while ignoring construction of efficient public transport that would promote George Washington's cherished unity and fraternity of the American people. High-speed rail service—a basic element of the infrastructure in most industrialized nations—remains all but unknown in the United States.

Meanwhile, other basic services of every civilization—public education, health care, housing, and the public infrastructure—deteriorate in the United States to levels that fall below the standards of many third-world countries.

Washington's plea for neutrality in world affairs helped keep the United States out of foreign wars for almost a century, during which time America focused on building new industries and creating a national infrastructure that surpassed every nation on earth. Colossal projects in the nineteenth and early twentieth centuries expanded and modernized the American infrastructure, uniting the nation with an intercontinental railway network and, later, an interstate highway system. Government and private investments harnessed the nation's resources with such massive projects as the Hoover Dam and other daring achievements.

Since World War II, however, Washington's successors have ignored or forgotten his words, pouring ever-increasing amounts of American resources into foreign soil and leaving American soil proportionately less fertile—even barren. Although some foreign investments—the Marshall Plan after World War II, for example—yielded beneficial returns to the United States, many overseas investments spilled into economic black holes—primarily wars without finite, achievable goals in Vietnam, Iraq, Afghanistan, and elsewhere. As Washington warned his successors and the American people, "Avoid the necessity of those overgrown military establishments which under any form of government are inauspicious to liberty and which are to be regarded as particularly hostile to republican liberty.

"'Tis our true policy," Washington declared, "to steer clear of permanent alliances with any portion of the foreign world. . . . There can be no greater error than to expect or calculate upon real favors from nation to nation." Although he was referring to Europe at the time, Washington believed that foreign nations have "primary interests which to us have no or a very remote relation." He called it "unwise" to tie the United States to foreign governments.

"Our detached and distant situation," he declared, "invites and enables us to pursue a different course.

> If we remain one people under an efficient government, the time is not
> far off when we may defy material injury from external annoyance;
> when we may take such an attitude as will cause the neutrality we may

at any time resolve upon to be scrupulously respected; when belligerent nations, under the impossibility of making acquisitions upon us, will not lightly hazard giving us provocation; when we may choose peace or war as our interest guided by our justice shall counsel.

"Why forego the advantages of so peculiar a situation?" Washington asked. "Why quit our own to stand upon foreign ground?"

Washington warned sternly against "interweaving our destiny" with the ambitions, rivalries, interests, or caprices of foreign nations, saying such ties would inevitably threaten, if not destroy, America's "peace and prosperity."

"In offering to you, my countrymen, these counsels of an old and affectionate friend," he concluded,

I dare not hope they will make the strong and lasting impression I could wish; that they will control the usual current of passions or prevent our nation from running the course which has hitherto marked the destiny of nations. But if I may even flatter myself that they may be productive of some partial benefit, some occasional good; that they may now and then moderate the fury of party spirit, warn against the mischiefs of foreign intrigue, guard against the impostures of pretended patriotism; this hope will be a full recompense for the solicitude of your welfare by which they have been dictated.

Washington included this prayer for his countrymen in his address: "that heaven may continue to you the choicest tokens of its beneficence; that your Union and brotherly affection may be perpetual."[6]

# CHAPTER FOURTEEN

~❦~

# *First in the*
# *Hearts of His Countrymen*

"If ever a nation was debauched by a man," wrote the *Aurora*, the viciously Antifederalist, pro-French newspaper, "the American nation has been debauched by Washington." Owned by Benjamin Franklin's grandson Benjamin Franklin Bache, the *Aurora* had fought since ratification to stem the inexorable growth of federal authority. "If ever a nation has suffered from the improper influence of a man," Bache railed, "the American nation has suffered from the influence of Washington. If ever a nation was deceived by a man, the American nation has been deceived by Washington."[1]

Although the press attack saddened the President, enough Americans— even his political opponents—ignored the *Aurora*'s insults at the approach of Washington's last birthday in office in February 1797. Christmas had been especially joyful at Mount Vernon at the end of 1796. Young Lafayette had arrived from Cambridge, and Washington's aide Tobias Lear appeared a few days after that, with four toddlers in tow. The mansion was so crowded that the Washingtons had to stuff at least four people and a few infants in every room and set pallets on the attic floor for assorted relatives who arrived unexpectedly.

Ever the farmer, Washington resumed his daily routine of rising with the sun to ride through the fields. "If my hirelings are not in their places at that time," he explained, "I send them messages expressing my sorrow for their indisposition . . . by the time I have accomplished these matters, breakfast (a little after seven o'clock.) is ready. This over, I mount my horse and ride around my farms, which employs me until it is time to dress for dinner."[2]

Always home for dinner at three, he came to the table in a plain blue coat, his hair dressed and powdered. He never knew whom to expect at the table—family relatives, "characters of distinction," or boorish intruders and curious travelers with the gall to barge in. Some insisted they had served under the general—sometimes in battles he never fought, such as Saratoga. "I rarely miss seeing strange faces come, as they say, out of respect to me," Washington complained.[3] Martha was more understanding. "I cannot tell you, my dear friend," she wrote to Secretary of War Henry Knox's wife Lucy,

> how much I enjoy home after having been deprived of one for so long, for our dwelling in New York and Philadelphia was not home, only a sojourning. The General and I feel like children just released from school or from a hard taskmaster, and we believe nothing can tempt us to leave the sacred roof-tree again except on private business or pleasure. We are so penurious with our enjoyment that we are loath to share it with anyone but dear friends, yet almost every day some stranger claims a portion of it, and we cannot refuse.[4]

The Washingtons had to leave "the sacred roof-tree" one last time, however, to celebrate his birthday in Philadelphia on February 22, 1797, and attend the inauguration of Washington's successor to the presidency, Vice President John Adams, the following month. A national holiday by then, Washington's Birthday began with church bells ringing, cannons firing, and militiamen marching to the music of parading bands. Flags flew from every perch in every city, town, and village in the nation. Americans rejected the harsh words of the *Aurora* and the rest of the opposition press. Evidently, they had tired of arguments and riots.

In the days that preceded and followed his birthday, Washington received testimonies of appreciation for his service to the nation from each of the state legislatures, as well as thousands of citizens. Most were content to live in an ordered society free of the anarchic upheavals that had once plagued America and were still plaguing Europe.

The President and First Lady attended an "elegant entertainment" on his birthday evening, with supper and dancing for 1,200, lasting well past midnight. According to one guest, "Mrs. Washington was moved even to tears with the mingled emotions of gratitude for such strong proofs of public regard and the new prospect of uninterrupted enjoyment of domestic life. . . . I never saw the President look better, or in finer spirits, but his emotions were too powerful to be concealed. He could sometimes scarcely speak."[5]

Washington and his wife spent their last nights in Philadelphia at theater, concerts, and other festivities, and, on March 2, two days before he was to leave office, he wrote his last letters as President. One went to Henry Knox in Boston, the retired Secretary of War who had served Washington faithfully since their first days with the Continental Army at Cambridge more than twenty years earlier:

"Although the prospect of retirement is most grateful to my soul," Washington told his old friend, "yet, I am not without my regrets at parting with (perhaps never more to meet) the few intimates whom I love, among these, be assured you are one."[6]

On the eve of Washington's departure from office, he and Martha entertained for the last time in the presidential residence. "Ladies and gentlemen," the President raised his glass to the political notables there, "this is the last time I shall drink your health as a public man. I do so with sincerity, and wishing you all possible happiness." According to one witness, tears ran down the cheeks of those present as they tried to sip from their glasses.[7]

Just before noon the next day—Saturday, March 4—President Washington walked to Congress Hall, dressed in a black suit, a military hat, his hair powdered as usual. Greeted by thunderous applause, he climbed the speaker's platform and took his seat. The new Vice President, Thomas Jefferson, the loser to former Vice President John Adams in the presidential election, followed without expression and sat between Washington and the Speaker's chair. President-elect Adams appeared last, sat momentarily in the Speaker's chair, then rose to take the oath of office.

None of Jefferson's supporters uttered a word of protest. The presidential structure that Washington had built stood rock solid; the crowd of onlookers was orderly, watching the peaceful transition of an elected government administration with deep, silent respect, knowing that they themselves had raised the new President to power without firing a shot. It was one of the most remarkable moments in world history.

"A solemn scene it was indeed," President Adams wrote to his wife, Abigail, the next day, "and it was made affecting to me by the presence of the general, whose countenance was as serene and unclouded as the day. He seemed to me to enjoy a triumph over me. Methought I heard him say, 'Ay! I am fairly out and you fairly in! See which of us will be happiest!'"[8]

After the ceremonies, Washington—a private citizen for the first time in eight years—called on the new President before attending a lavish farewell dinner. The vicious *Aurora*, however, would not let Washington retire in peace: "If ever there was a period for rejoicing this is the moment. Every heart, in unison . . . ought to beat high with exultation that the name of Washington ceases from this day to give currency to political iniquity and to legalize corruption."[9]

While President Adams lodged at a hotel, the huge Washington family—including young Lafayette and his tutor—tried assembling their effects for the move to Mount Vernon, separating government from family property, then deciding which family property to keep and which to sell. Washington needed nearly one hundred boxes, fourteen trunks, forty-three casks, and thousands of yards of cord and baling wire to pack his things—and a sloop to carry them to Virginia. He ended up giving away many furnishings, including a chandelier, a mirror, and his private desk.

On March 9, the Washingtons, their granddaughter Nelly Custis, and young Lafayette and his tutor climbed into the family coach with a dog and Nelly's parrot and began what the Washingtons hoped would be their last ride home to Mount Vernon. Six days later, they pulled into the Mount Vernon drive in time for dinner.

On September 19, 1797, five years after they had taken him prisoner, the Austrians released Lafayette from his dungeon cell, and, after hearing the news, his son immediately left Mount Vernon to return home to France. A week later, Washington received a letter attesting to the boy's safe arrival at Alexander Hamilton's home in New York and his imminent departure for France:

> I have the hope of being after so long and cruel a separation united with my parents and sisters. . . . If anything can soften the pain of all their sufferings, it will be to hear . . . what a tender interest you took in them, what efforts you made to alleviate them and that the friendship with which you always honored the father has induced you to receive the son under your roof with so much goodness! In your house I have been as happy as I could be separated from my family, and the time which I passed with you will never be forgot.[10]

A year after Washington's return home to Mount Vernon, a letter from President Adams initially sent the former president into gales of laughter.

"If the Constitution and your convenience," Adams wrote, "would admit of my changing places with you or of my taking my old station as your lieutenant, I should have no doubts of the ultimate prosperity and glory of the country."[11]

What followed, however, turned Washington's smiles into frowns—and sent Martha flying from the room in tears. Adams was raising an army; relations with France had deteriorated into undeclared war on the high seas and Adams feared it would expand into open warfare if the French tried to invade the American mainland. In the years since Washington had signed the Jay Treaty with England, the French had sunk or captured upwards of eight hundred American vessels in retaliation and all but paralyzed American trade. Although Adams had sent a commission to Paris to discuss peace, French Foreign Minister Talleyrand had refused to negotiate unless the American envoys paid a substantial bribe. Outraged by the French response, Adams asked Congress to strengthen national defenses.

"In forming an army," he wrote to Washington, "I am at an immense loss whether to call out all the old generals or appoint young ones. If the French come here, we must learn to march with a quick step, and to attack, for in that way only they are said to be vulnerable. I must tap you. Sometimes for advice. We must have your name, if you, in any case will permit us to use it. There will be more efficacy in it, than in many an Army."[12]

On July 2, Congress named Washington commanding general of the armed forces, and five days later abrogated the alliances with France from the Revolutionary War. A few days later, the Secretary of War sent Washington his formal commission from the President.

A personal note from President Adams accompanied the commission with "all the apologies I can make" for asking Washington to return to public life. "My reasons for this measure, will be too well known to need any explanation to the public. Every friend and every enemy of America, will comprehend them. . . . As I said in a former letter, if it had been in my power to nominate you to be President of the United States, I should have done it with less hesitation and more pleasure."[13]

On November 5, Washington broke the solemn promise he had made to himself and to Martha to retire and left for the capital by carriage accompanied by his secretary Tobias Lear (now assigned the rank of colonel) and an entourage of aides and servants. Troops of light horse met their carriage at the Philadelphia city line, where General Washington and Colonel Lear mounted their horses and rode into the nation's capital to the tolling of church bells and cheers of thousands.

Washington remained in the capital six weeks, during which time he effectively organized an army—on paper. He estimated he would need twelve infantry regiments and a corps of artillery men and engineers to defend the nation against a French invasion. He named Alexander Hamilton second in command and promoted him to major general. Despairing of squeezing into his old uniform, Washington designed a new one—"a blue coat, with yellow buttons and gold epaulettes (each having three silver stars) linings cape and cuffs buff, in Winter, buff vest and breeches, in summer, a white vest and breeches of nankeen [brownish-yellow coarse cotton]." He ordered a white plume as "a further distinction" for the commander in chief's hat, as well as those of his staff.[14] Then, as he prepared to go to war, he ordered a new set of teeth from the dentist before returning to Mount Vernon for Christmas.

As the last year of the eighteenth century began, Washington grew annoyed with the War Department's failure to begin recruiting troops for his army, but six weeks later, just after his birthday, electrifying news reached Mount Vernon that made recruiting unnecessary. The American ship *Constellation* had captured the incomparable French Navy frigate *Insurgente*; the humiliation cowed the French government into suing for peace and ending its outrages against American shipping. American preparations for war ended, and, by the end of May, Washington could once again call Mount Vernon "the seat of my retirement; where I rather hope . . . to spend the remnant of my life in tranquility;

if one may judge from the appearance of both external, and internal causes, which present themselves to our present view."[15]

As spring blossoms embraced Mount Vernon, Washington learned that his old friend Patrick Henry had died at sixty-three. A staunch supporter of the war against Britain, Henry had been Washington's fiercest opponent in the fight to ratify the Constitution and establish a strong central government. Washington responded to Henry's death by drawing up a lengthy will and preparing for his own death. He would not have to wait long. On December 12—a cloudy morning—he set out on his usual ride. "About 1 o'clock it began to snow," he noted in his diary, "soon after to hail and then turned to cold rain. Mercury 28 at night."[16]

Tobias Lear recalled the day in his journal:

> When he came in . . . I observed to him that I was afraid he had got wet, he said no. . . . He came to dinner without changing his dress. A heavy fall of snow took place on Friday, which prevented the General from riding out as usual. He had taken cold . . . and complained of having a sore throat—he had a hoarseness, which increased in the evening; but he made light of it. He would never take anything to carry off a cold; always observing, "let it go as it came."[17]

He was sicker the following morning, worsened during the day and night, and died the following day, despite—or because of—ministrations by four doctors, who left him dehydrated and in hemorrhagic shock after extracting eighty-two ounces, or more than five pints of blood. When no more blood would flow, they fed him a mercurous chloride purgative and a tartar emetic—both now known to be poisonous—that ensured his immediate death. George Washington died just after 10 on the evening of December 16, 1799.

"While we were fixed in silent grief," Lear wrote, "Mrs. Washington asked, 'Is he gone?' I could not speak, but held up my hand as a signal that he was. 'Tis well' said she in a firm voice. 'Tis all now over. I have no more trials to pass through. I shall soon follow him!' I kissed the cold hand, which I had 'till then held, laid it down, went to the fire and was for some time lost in profound grief. . . . About 12 o'clock, the corpse was brought down and laid out in the large room."[18]

Four days later, on December 18, a procession of friends, relatives, military officers, freemasons from Alexandria, and other admirers escorted Washington's coffin from the mansion to the vault on the grounds of his beloved Mount Vernon. Lear cut a lock of his hair as a keepsake for Martha.

Congress set December 26 as a day of mourning in the capital, which held a funeral procession with an empty coffin, led by a riderless horse with boots reversed in its stirrups. With no other way to participate, cities, towns, and villages across the nation followed suit, staging mock funerals to display their grief. President Adams ordered the Army to wear black sleeve bands for six months, then issued a formal message: "For his fellow-citizens, if their prayers could have been answered, he would have been immortal."[19] The Senate declared, "Ancient and modern names are diminished before him. . . . Let his countrymen consecrate the memory of the heroic General Washington, the patriotic statesman and the virtuous sage. Let them teach their children never to forget that the fruit of his labors and his example are their inheritance."[20]

For the formal religious service, Congress elected Henry "Lightfoot Harry" Lee, Washington's heroic comrade in the Revolutionary War, to give the eulogy whose ending would echo in the hearts of Americans for generations:

> First in war, first in peace and first in the hearts of his countrymen, he was second to none in the humble and endearing scenes of private life. Pious, just, humble, temperate and sincere—uniform, dignified and commanding. . . . Such was the man for whom our nation mourns.[21]

Martha Washington died about two and a half years later, on May 22, 1802, but the powerful presidential structure her husband built still stands, strong and stable—many critics say too stable, too strong. While the anarchy Washington feared and despised reigns in endless countries around the globe—even in Greece, the birthplace of democracy—Americans have lived under one constitution and gone to the polls peacefully for more than two centuries, electing forty-four different presidents to office. Until the passage of a constitutional amendment limiting presidential terms in office, all but one observed the precedent set by Washington by voluntarily leaving the White House after no more than eight years. Even in the face of foreign wars, a civil war, presidential assassinations and attempted assassinations, economic collapse, and terrifying natural (and man-made) disasters, every presidential transition in American history has proceeded seamlessly, calmly, without violence or popular upheavals, because of the stable presidential structure George Washington built.

# Appendix

## *The Pillars of Presidential Power and President Washington's Precedents*

George Washington assumed the presidency of the United States without any of the powers he had sought at the Constitutional Convention. Unwilling to serve in a ceremonial post, he demanded and won from Congress or simply assumed executive powers not granted by the Constitution and converted the presidency into the most powerful office in American government—a separate *and* equal branch. Here are the seven pillars of power on which Washington built the presidential edifice.

### 1. FOREIGN POLICY

(August 1789)

***Constitutional Powers:*** The President *shall have power, by and with the advice and consent of the Senate, to make treaties, provided two-thirds of the senators present concur; and he shall nominate, and by and with the advice and consent of the Senate, shall appoint ambassadors, other public ministers. . . .*

***Restrictions:*** The Senate of the First Congress argued that the "advice and consent" restriction required the President to obtain Senate approval of every aspect of foreign policy—from the initial contacts with a foreign power to the actual ratification of an agreement or treaty.

***Resolution:*** "In a fret," the President insisted the framers had purposely placed the advice-and-consent phrase between commas in Section 2 of the

235

Constitution, thus rendering it parenthetical to his expressly stated power "to make treaties." When the president exercises that power—and indeed the power of appointments—he declared, the Senate "is evidently only a council to the President, however its concurrence may be to his acts."[1]

## 2. EXECUTIVE APPOINTMENTS

(May 1790)

**Constitutional Powers**: The President *shall nominate, and by and with the advice and consent of the Senate, shall appoint . . . officers* [i.e., department executives] *of the United States. . . .*

**Restrictions:** The Constitution withheld from the President any direct authority over department executives, including the power to discharge them.

**Resolution:** With Vice President John Adams casting the tie-breaking vote in the U.S. Senate, President Washington demanded and won passage of a congressional act giving him the right to dismiss any officer of the executive branch of government without "the advice and consent" of the Senate. In effect, the act stripped Congress of authority over the executive branch and placed it in the hands of the President.

## 3. GOVERNMENT FINANCES

(February 1791)

**Constitutional Powers:** None.

**Restrictions:** *The Congress shall have the power to lay and collect taxes, duties, imports and excises, to pay the debts . . . of the United States . . . to borrow money on the credit of the United States. . . .*

**Resolution:** At President Washington's and Treasury Secretary Alexander Hamilton's behest, Congress authorized establishment of the Bank of the United States, which gave the Treasury (and the President, in effect) the power to borrow "on the credit of the United States" and bypass direct authority of Congress when spending government funds.

## 4. MILITARY AFFAIRS

(May 1792)

**Constitutional Powers:** *The President shall be commander in chief of the army and navy of the United States, and of the military of the several states, when called into actual service of the United States.*

**Restrictions:** *The Congress shall have the power to . . . provide for the common defense . . . declare war . . . raise and support armies . . . provide and maintain a* *navy . . . provide for calling forth the militia to execute the laws of the union, suppress insurrections and repel invasions . . . provide for organizing, arming and disciplining the militia, and for governing such part of them as may be employed in the service of the United States.*

**Resolution:** Faced with Indian attacks on American settlers in the West, President Washington, in the absence of Congress, unilaterally assumed extra-constitutional powers to send troops to war. Rather than face public wrath by withholding the President's right to defend Americans and American territory, Congress passed the Militia Act, giving the President powers to draft state militia into a federal force to fulfill his constitutional obligation to "take care that the laws be faithfully executed." Although the Act initially required consent of a federal judge, Congress later removed that restriction, giving the President all-but-unfettered powers to call up troops and send them into conflicts without the consent of Congress. Of more than a dozen wars that the United States has waged with other nations, Congress has issued formal declarations of war in but five of them—against Britain in the War of 1812, Mexico in 1846, Spain in 1898, Germany and Austria-Hungary in World War I, and Japan and Germany in World War II. A presidential order sent the nation into all other conflicts.

## 5. LEGISLATION BY PRESIDENTIAL PROCLAMATION AND EXECUTIVE ORDER

(April 1793)

**Constitutional Powers:** None.

**Restrictions:** None, other than statements of the framers that, as Connecticut's Roger Sherman put it, "The powers vested in the federal government are particularly defined, so that each State still retains its sovereignty . . . and a right to exercise every power of a sovereign state not particularly delegated to the government of the United States."[2] Reiterated in the Tenth Amendment, the restrictions on the President (and the rest of the federal government) were clear: *The Powers not delegated to the United States by the constitution . . . are reserved to the states respectively, or to the people.* The Constitution gives the President no power to issue proclamations with the force of law.

**Resolution:** President Washington assumed the power to issue proclamations with the force of law when he saw fit. In the case of the Neutrality Proclamation, Congress later gave the President's proclamation legislative sanction, but in other cases, the President's Proclamations stood on their own as the law of the land without consent of the legislature.

## 6. FEDERAL LAW ENFORCEMENT

(July 1794)

***Constitutional Powers:*** The President *shall take care that the laws be faithfully executed.*

***Restrictions:*** The Constitution fails to give the President a law enforcement arm or any other means of executing the laws.

***Resolution:*** In unilaterally sending troops to war against Indian marauders in the West and then calling up troops to crush tax protests in western Pennsylvania, Washington assumed powers to use troops to enforce laws and protect Americans. In its acquiescence, Congress essentially ceded powers to the President to use troops to suppress domestic insurrections, as well as repel invasions by foreign troops, and, by extension, the power to combat any violations of federal law.

## 7. EXECUTIVE PRIVILEGE

(March 1796)

***Constitutional Powers:*** None.

***Restrictions:*** None, other than the previously stated admonition of the framers that "powers vested in the federal government are particularly defined," and, without any mention of executive privilege in the Constitution, the President had none.

***Resolution:*** President Washington unilaterally assumed executive privilege, refusing to turn over to the House of Representatives his own confidential notes and those of John Jay, his envoy to Britain. Implying that public inspection of such documents might endanger national security, he asserted a new principle of separation of powers between the branches of government. Although the Constitution says nothing about separation of powers, Washington insisted that "the boundaries fixed by the Constitution between the different departments should be preserved."

## PRESIDENT WASHINGTON'S PRECEDENTS

Open White House; open government; government officials as "servants" of the people rather than rulers; touring the nation to see, hear, and touch the people and their lives; prohibiting appointment of a government official's relatives and friends to government posts; regional representation in executive appointments; the cabinet meeting, bringing all department heads together; presidential control of executive-branch decisions; restriction of presidential appearances to joint sessions of Congress; the annual state-of-the-union address; senatorial courtesy in judicial appointments; presidential discretion in sending troops to war to defend national interests without congressional approval; the "farewell address"; self-imposed two-term limit on presidential service (made mandatory in 1951 under the Twenty-Second Amendment).

# Notes

## INTRODUCTION

1. [Philadelphia] *Aurora*, December 23, 1796; November 20, 1795.

2. Worthington C. Ford et al., eds., Continental Congress, *Journals, 1774–1789* (Washington, D.C.: 1921–1926, 8 vols.), 1:109.

3. George Washington [hereafter GW] to Bryan Fairfax, July 20, 1774, W. W. Abbott, Dorothy Twohig, Philander D. Chase, and Theodore J. Crackel, eds., *The Papers of George Washington, Revolutionary War Series, June 1775–April 1778* (Charlottesville: University of Virginia Press, 1984–[multi-volumes in progress]), 10:128–131. [Hereafter PGWR.]

4. Thomas P. Slaughter, *The Whiskey Rebellion: Frontier Epilogue to the American Revolution* (New York: Oxford University Press, 1986), 122.

5. James Madison, *Notes of Debates in the Federal Convention of 1787 Reported by James Madison* (New York: W. W. Norton, 1987), 46. [Hereafter Madison, *Notes.*]

6. Patrick Henry to the Virginia Convention, June 5, 1788, Merrill Jensen, John P. Kaminski, Gaspare Saladino, Richard Leffler, and Charles H. Schoenleber, eds., *The Documentary History of the Ratification of the Constitution* (Madison: State Historical Society of Wisconsin, 1976–[multi-volumes in progress]), 9:943–968. [Hereafter DHRC.]

7. GW to Major General Daniel Morgan, October 8, 1794, in John C. Fitzpatrick, ed., *The Writings of George Washington, from the Original Manuscript Sources, 1745–1799* Washington, D.C.: U.S. Government Printing Office, 1931–1944, 39 vols.), 33:522–524. [Hereafter, Fitzpatrick, *Writings.*]

241

8. GW Circular to the States, June 8, 1783, Fitzpatrick, *Writings,* 26:483–496.

9. Arthur M. Schlesinger, Jr., *The Imperial Presidency* (Boston: Houghton, Mifflin, 1973).

10. Carl Van Doren, *The Great Rehearsal* (New York: Viking Press, 1948), 264.

11. DHRC, 9:929–931.

12. Madison, *Notes,* 651.

13. Ibid.

14. DHRC, 9:929–931; William Wirt Henry, *Patrick Henry: Life, Correspondence, and Speeches* (New York: Charles Scribner's Sons, 1891, 3 vols.), 3:568.

15. Henry Lee to James Madison, April 3, 1790, in Richard R. Beeman, *Patrick Henry: A Biography* (New York: McGraw-Hill, 1974), 174.

16. GW to James Madison, November 5, 1786, W. W. Abbott, Dorothy Twohig, *The Papers of George Washington, Confederation Series, January, 1784–September, 1788* (Charlottesville: University Press of Virginia, 1992–1997, 6 vols.), 4:331–332. [Hereafter PGW Confed.]

## PROLOGUE

1. John Adams to Abigail Adams, December 19, 1793, in John Bartlett, *Familiar Quotations,* 16th ed. (Boston: Little, Brown, 1992), 338n12.

2. John Ferling, *John Adams: A Life* (New York: Henry Holt, 1992), 53.

3. John Adams to Abigail Adams, May 29, 1775, June 2, 1775, ibid., 206–209.

4. GW to George Augustine Washington, March 31, 1789. W. W. Abbot, ed., *The Papers of George Washington, Presidential Series* (Charlottesville: University Press of Virginia, 1987–[multi-volumes in progress]), 1:472–476. [Hereafter PGWP]

## CHAPTER ONE

1. GW to Philip Schuyler, January 30, 1780, in Fitzpatrick, *Writings,* 17:464–468.

2. GW to the Magistrates of New Jersey, January 8, 1780, in Fitzpatrick, *Writings,* 17:363.

3. Henry Lee, *Memoirs of the War in the Southern Department of the United States* (Philadelphia, 1812, 2 vols.), 2:361.

4. GW to the Officers of the Army, March 15, 1783, Fitzpatrick, *Writings,* 26:222–227.

5. Ibid., 222n.

6. George-Washington Lafayette [Gilbert Motier, Marquis de Lafayette], *Mémoires, Correspondence et Manuscrits du Général Lafayette, publiés par sa famille* (Bruxelles: Société Belge de Librairie, Etc., Hauman, Cattoir et Compagnie, 2 vols., 1837), 1:26.

7. Fitzpatrick, *Writings*, 26:222n.

8. Douglas Southall Freeman, *George Washington: A Biography* (New York: Charles Scribner's Sons, 1948–1957, 7 vols., completed by John Alexander Carroll and Mary Ashworth), 5:433–435, citing "The Journals of Major Samuel Shaw . . . with a Life of the Author by Josiah Quincy."

9. GW Circular to the States, June 8, 1783, Fitzpatrick, *Writings*, 26:483–496.

10. Benson J. Lossing, *Mary and Martha, the Mother and the Wife of George Washington* (New York: Harper & Brothers, 1886), 168–171.

11. GW Address to Congress on Resigning His Commission, December 23, 1783, Fitzpatrick, *Writings*, 27:284–285.

12. James Tilton to Gunning Bedford, December 25, 1783, in Fitzpatrick, *Writings*, 27:285n.

13. GW to Lafayette, February 1, 1784, PGW Confed., 1:87–90.

14. GW to David Stuart, July 1, 1787, PGW Confed., 5:239–241.

15. John J. McCusker, *How Much Is That in Real Money? A Historical Commodity Price Index for Use as a Deflator of Money Values in the Economy of the United States* (Worcester, Mass.: American Antiquarian Society, 2001), 34.

16. Richard B. Morris, *Witnesses at the Creation: Hamilton, Madison, Jay, and the Constitution* (New York: Holt, Rinehart and Winston, 1985), 171.

17. Lee to GW, October 1, 1786, PGW Confed., 4:281–282.

18. Lee to GW, October 17, 1786, ibid., 4:295–296.

19. DHRC, 13:25.

20. William Short [citing Henry] to Thomas Jefferson, May 15, 1784, in Robert Douthat Meade, *Patrick Henry, Practical Revolutionary* (Philadelphia: J. B. Lippincott, 1969), 273.

21. GW to Jonathan Trumbull, Jr., January 5, 1784, Fitzpatrick, *Writings*, 27:293–295.

22. Madison, *Notes*, 7.

23. Benjamin Franklin to James Parker, March 20, 1750, Leonard W. Labaree et al., *Papers of Benjamin Franklin* (New Haven, Conn.: Yale University Press, 1959–[multi-volumes in progress]), 4:117–121.

24. John Steele Gordon, *An Empire of Wealth: The Epic History of American Economic Power* (New York: Harper Collins, 2004), 61–63.

25. Henry Knox to GW, January 31, 1785, in PGW Confed., 2:301–306.

## CHAPTER TWO

1. GW to Benjamin Harrison, October 10, 1784, PGW Confed., 2:86–99.

2. George Washington to Jacob Read, November 3, 1784, Fitzpatrick, *Writings*, 27:489.

3. GW to James Madison, November 30, 1785, PGW Confed., 3:419–421.

4. Van Doren, *The Great Rehearsal*, 264.

5. GW to Henry Knox, February 3, 1787, ibid., 7–9.

6. Freeman, *George Washington*, 6:44.

7. Thomas Jefferson to Walter Jones, January 2, 1814, John P. Kaminski, ed., *The Founders on the Founders: Word Portraits from the American Revolutionary Era* (Charlottesville: University of Virginia Press, 2008), 519–520.

8. John Adams to Benjamin Rush, November 11, 1807, ibid., 515–516.

9. Madison, *Notes*, 34.

10. Ibid., 35.

11. Ibid., *Notes*, 42–43.

12. Max Farrand, ed., *The Records of the Federal Convention of 1787* (New Haven: Yale University Press, 1911, 4 vols.), 1:501.

13. Ibid., 103.

14. DHRC, 1:241.

15. Madison, *Notes*, 502.

16. Ibid., 45–47.

17. Ibid., 46.

18. Ibid., 49.

19. Ibid., 51–55.

20. Farrand, 1:529–531.

21. Ibid.

22. Madison, *Notes*, 129–139.

23. GW to the Marquis de Lafayette, August 17, 1787, Freeman, *George Washington*, 6:105; GW to George Augustine Washington, May 27, 1787, ibid., 196–199.

24. Madison, *Notes*, 98.

25. John Yoo, *Crisis and Command: A History of Executive Power from George Washington to George W. Bush* (New York: Kaplan Publishing, 2009), 401.

26. DHRC, 15:280–283.

27. Madison, *Notes*, 68.

28. DHRC, 15:613.

29. Ibid., 280–283.

30. Madison, *Notes*, 651.

31. Van Doren, *The Great Rehearsal*, 189–190.

32. Madison, *Notes*, 652–654.

33. GW to Patrick Henry, Benjamin Harrison, and Thomas Nelson, September 24, 1787, PGW Confed., 5:339–340.

34. GW to Dr. James Anderson, December 24, 1795, in Fitzpatrick, *Writings*, 34:405–410.

35. Richard Henry Lee to George Mason, October 1, 1787, Richard Henry Lee, *The Letters of Richard Henry Lee* (Danvers, MA: General Books [reprint], 2009, 2 vols.), 2:323–324.

36. DHRC, 9:1050–1072.

37. Ibid.

38. *Massachusetts Centinel*, November 17, 1787, DHRC, 4:259–262.

39. Centinel I, Philadelphia *Independent Gazetteer*, October 5, 1787, ibid., 13:326–337.

40. Philadelphia *Freeman's Journal*, September 26, 1787, ibid., 13:243–245.

41. Philadelphia *Independent Gazetteer*, January 12, 1788, ibid., 5:817.

42. Louis-Guillaume Otto to French minister of foreign affairs, comte de Montmorin, October 10, 1787, Correspondence politique, États-Unis 32, 368 ff., Archives du Ministre des Affaires Étrangères, Paris.

43. Henry, *Patrick Henry*, 3:579.

44. DHRC, 9:931–936.

45. Ibid., 1036.

46. John Parke Custis to George Washington, June 10, 1776, in PGWR, 4:484–486.

47. Henry Knox to GW, March 19, 1787, PGW Confed., 5:95–8.

48. GW to Henry Knox, April 1, 1789, in W. W. Abbott, Dorothy Twohig, Philander D. Chase, and Theodore J. Crackel, eds., PGWP, 2:2–3.

49. Alexander Hamilton to GW, September [30], 1788, PGWP, 1:23–25.

50. Alexander Donald to GW, February 28, 1789, ibid., 1:347–348.

51. GW to Henry Knox, April 1, 1789, PGWP 2:2–3.

52. Martha Washington to Mercy Otis Warren, December 26, 1789, Benson J. Lossing, *Mary and Martha, the Mother and Wife of George Washington* (New York: Harper & Brothers, 1886), 223–224.

53. Martha Washington to John Dandridge, April 20, 1789, in Joseph E. Fields, *Worthy Partner: The Papers of Martha Washington* (Westport, CT: Greenwood Press, 1994), 213–214.

54. Donald Jackson and Dorothy Twohig, eds., *The Diaries of George Washington* (Charlottesville: University Press of Virginia, 1976–1979, 6 volumes), 5:445. [Hereafter, *Diaries*.]

55. GW to Edward Rutledge, May 5, 1789, PGWP, 2:217–218.

### CHAPTER THREE

1. Benjamin Huntington to Governor Samuel Huntington, March 11, 1789; Elias Boudinot to Hannah Boudinot, May 15, 1789; in Charlene Bangs Bickford and Kenneth R. Bowling, *Birth of the Nation: The First Federal Congress, 1789–1791* (Lanham, MD: Madison House Publishers, 1989), 15–16 and 10, respectively.

2. John Adams to Benjamin Rush, July 24, 1789, in Bickford and Bowling, *Birth of the Nation*, 28.

3. Representatives and senators received identical compensation until 1983, when Congress awarded members of the House higher *per diem*s than senators, but permitted senators to earn unlimited income from nonconflicting outside projects.

4. Freeman, *George Washington*, 6:206n., 416–417, citing *Journal of the United States House of Representatives* (9 vols.), 1:43; *Journal of the Senate of the United States* 1:30.

5. [Washington's parentheses], Freeman, *George Washington*, 6:183.

6. PGWP, 2:154–155, citing Tobias Lear's diary.

7. Ibid.

8. First Inaugural Address, April 30, 1789, ibid., 152–177.

9. George Fisher Ames to George Richard Minot, May 3, 1789, in "Introductory notes to 'First Inaugural Address,'" ibid., 152–156.

10. GW to Henry Knox, January 29, 1789, Fitzpatrick, *Writings*, 30:183.

11. *Daily Advertiser*, April 24, 1789.

12. *Gazette of the United States*, April 25, 1789.

13. GW to David Stuart, June 15, 1790, Fitzpatrick, *Writings*, 31:49–55.

14. GW to Edward Rutledge, May 5, 1789, PGWP, 2:217–218.

15. GW to James Madison, May 5, 1789, ibid., 2:216–217.

16. Martha Washington to Fanny Bassett Washington, June 8, 1789, in Fields, *Worthy Partner*, 215–216.

17. Ibid., 282.

18. Ibid., 355.

19. Freeman, *George Washington*, 6:211.

20. *Daily Advertiser*, June 15, 1789, as cited in Freeman, *George Washington*, 6:213.

21. Freeman, *George Washington*, 6:213, citing Abigail Adams to her sister Mary Cranch, June 28, 1789, in Stewart Mitchell, ed., *New Letters of Abigail Adams, 1788–1801* (Boston: Houghton Mifflin, 1947).

22. Freeman, *George Washington*, 6:213–14.

23. Fitzpatrick, *Writings*, 30:280–281.

CHAPTER FOUR

1. GW to John Jay, June 8, 1789, Fitzpatrick, *Writings*, 30:455.

2. William Maclay, *Journal of William Maclay*, Edgar S. Maclay, ed. (New York: D. Appleton & Co., 1890), 128–132.

3. Ibid.

4. Conference with a Committee of the United States Senate, PGWP, 3:400–403.

5. Maclay, *Journal*, 128–132.

6. "Sentiments delivered by the President at a second conference with the Senate," August 10, 1789, PGWP, 3:408–410.

7. Ibid.

8. Ibid., January 8, 1790, 543–549.

9. Ibid.

10. Maclay, *Journal*, 128–132.

11. *Congressional Register*, 1:557.

12. Ibid., 531.

13. Ibid.

14. Charlene Bangs Bickford et al., eds., *The Documentary History of the First Federal Congress* (Baltimore: Johns Hopkins University Press, 1992–1998, 17 vols.), 9:5. [Hereafter DHFFC.]

15. Charles Francis Adams, ed., *The Works of John Adams* (Boston: Little, Brown, 1850–1856, 10 vols.), 6:232–281.

16. John Steele to Joseph Winston, May 22, 1790, in Bickford and Bowling, *Birth of the Nation*, 41.

17. GW to Gouverneur Morris, October 13, 1789, PGWP, 4:176–179.

18. Forrest McDonald, *The Presidency of George Washington* (Lawrence: University Press of Kansas, 1974), 41.

19. Thomas Jefferson to John Melish, January 13, 1813, in Kaminski, *Founders*, 518–519.

20. McDonald, *Presidency*, 41.

21. GW to Bushrod Washington, July 27, 1789, Fitzpatrick, *Writings*, 30:366.

22. Christian Theodor Sigismund von Molitor and Georg Hermann Vulteius to GW, May 18, 1789, PGWP 2:323–324.

23. GW to Christian Theodor Sigismund von Molitor and Georg Hermann Vulteius, May 21, 1789, ibid., 2:358–359.

24. Mary Wooster to GW, May 8, 1789, PGWP, 2:234–235.

25. GW to Mary Wooster, May 21, 1789, ibid., 2:327–328.

26. GW to James Bowdoin, May 19, 1789, ibid., 2:235–236.

27. Benjamin Lincoln to GW, February 20, 1789, ibid., 1:330–333.

28. GW to Robert R. Livingston, May 31, 1789, ibid., 417–418.

29. Bickford and Bowling, *Birth of the Nation*, citing Thomas Lloyd, *The Congressional Register* (New York: 1789–1790, 4 vols.), 1:299.

30. Freeman, *George Washington*, 6:351.

## CHAPTER FIVE

1. GW to John Adams, May 10, 1789, PGWP, 2:245–250.

2. *Diaries*, 5:452–453.

3. Ibid., 470–471, 479–480.

4. GW to William Washington, January 8, 1791, PGWP, 7:211–213.

5. *Diaries*, Friday, October 16, 1789, 5:462.

6. GW to David Stuart, June 15, 1790, PGWP, 5:523–528.

7. Edmund Randolph to GW, February 12, 1791, ibid., 7:330–340.

8. Edenton *State Gazette of North Carolina*, November 26, 1790.

9. Richmond *Virginia Independent Chronicle*, July 7, 1790.

10. Henry Lee to James Madison, April 3, 1790, in Beeman, *Patrick Henry*, 174.

11. GW to David Stuart, June 15, 1790, Fitzpatrick, *Writings*, 31:49–55.

12. Thomas Cushing to Benjamin Goodhue, April 17, 1790, 68; John Adams to Stephen Higginson, March 14, 1790; both citations in Bickford and Bowling, *Birth of the Nation*, 68.

13. Oliver Wolcott to Oliver Wolcott, Jr., April 23, 1790, ibid.

14. Julian P. Boyd et al., eds., *The Papers of Thomas Jefferson* (Princeton, NJ: Princeton University Press, 1950–[multi-volumes in progress]), 16:429.

15. Freeman, *George Washington*, 6:260n, S. Ogden to Henry Knox, May 22, 1790.

16. Boyd, *op. cit.*

17. Martha Washington to Mercy Otis Warren, June 12, 1790, Fields, 225–227.

18. "Sydney," *Philadelphia National Gazette*, April 23, 1790; Baltimore *Maryland Journal*, July 9, 1790; *New York Packet*, June 1, 1790.

19. Moses Seixas, warden of the Congregation of Yeshuat Israel of Newport, Rhode Island, to GW, August 18, 1790, in PGWP, 6:286n.

20. GW to the Hebrew Congregation in Newport, Rhode Island, August 18, 1790, ibid., 284–286.

21. GW Circular to the States, June 8, 1783, Fitzpatrick, *Writings*, 26:483–496.

22. GW to Rochambeau, August 10, 1790, PGWP, 6:231–232.

## CHAPTER SIX

1. Richard B. Morris, ed., *Encyclopedia of American History* (New York: Harper & Brothers, 1953), 123.

2. DHRC, 10:1537.

3. DHFFC, 6:1844–1845.

4. Thomas Jefferson to GW, February 15, 1791, ibid., 348–353.

5. McDonald, *The Presidency of George Washington*, 64.

6. Alexander Hamilton to GW, February 23, 1791, ibid., 422–452.

7. GW to Patrick Henry, December 27, 1777, PGWR, 13:17–18.

8. Ibid.

9. GW to David Humphreys, July 20, 1791, PGWP, 8:358–361.

10. Ibid.

11. Ibid., U.S. Senate to GW, October 27, 1789, ibid., 9:138–139.

12. Thomas Jefferson to James Madison, February 17, 1826, John P. Kaminsky, *The Founders on the Founders*, 387.

13. Patrick Henry to Virginia Ratification Convention, June 14, 1788, Henry, *Patrick Henry*, 3:527–528.

14. John P. Kaminski, ed., *The Quotable Jefferson* (Princeton, NJ: Princeton University Press, 2006), 390–391.

15. Ron Chernow, *Alexander Hamilton* (New York: Penguin Press, 2004), 216.

16. Ibid., 399, citing *Anas of Thomas Jefferson*, in Paul Leicester Ford, ed., *The Writings of Thomas Jefferson* (New York: G. P. Putnam's Sons, 1892–1899. 10 vols.), 1:51.

17. Ibid., 399.

18. John Adams to Benjamin Rush, January 25, 1806, Kaminski, *Founders*, 208.

19. Chernow, *Alexander Hamilton*, 398.

20. "Catullus" No. 3, *Gazette of the United States*, September 29, 1792.

21. *Gazette of the United States*, July 25, 1792, in Chernow, *Alexander Hamilton*, 403.

22. New York *Daily Advertiser*, March 21, 1788.

23. Tobias Lear to David Humphreys, April 12, 1791, PGWP, 8:361.

24. John Dos Passos, *The Men Who Made the Nation* (Garden City, NY: Doubleday, 1957), 225.

25. GW to David Humphreys, July 20, 1791, PGWP, 8:358–361.

26. Thomas Jefferson to Robert R. Livingston, February 4, 1791, Paul Leicester Ford, ed., *The Writings of Thomas Jefferson* (New York: G. P. Putnam's Sons, 1892–1899, 10 vols.), 5:274.

## CHAPTER SEVEN

1. "The Memorial of the Inhabitants of the Country West of the Allegheny Mountains," Historical Society of Pennsylvania, cited in Slaughter, *The Whiskey Rebellion*, 33.

2. GW to Major General Daniel Morgan, October 8, 1794, Fitzpatrick, *Writings*, 33:522–524.

3. GW to John Cannon, June 15, 1794, Fitzpatrick, *Writings*, 33:409.

4. Memorial of Levi Allen, November 22, 1786, Public Archives of Canada, Ottawa, Q. 28:7.

5. Dr. John White to Don Estevan Miro, Governor of Louisiana, April 18, 1788, cited in Archibald Henderson, "The Spanish Conspiracy in Tennessee," *Tennessee Historical Magazine* 3 (1917), 232; William Jay, *The Life of John Jay: With Selections from His Correspondence and Miscellaneous Papers* (New York, 1833, 2 vols.), 1:170–172.

6. Jay, *The Life of John Jay*, 1:170–2.

7. *Pittsburgh Gazette*, September 7, 1791.

8. Alexander Hamilton to GW, September 1, 1792, PGWP, 11:59–60.

9. Freeman, *George Washington*, 6:329.

10. St. Clair's dispatch to Knox, November 9, 1791, PGWP, 9:276n–279n.

11. GW to the Senate and the House of Representatives, December 12, 1791, ibid., 274.

12. Patrick Henry to the Virginia Ratification Convention, June 14, 1788, Henry, *Patrick Henry*, 3:527–528.

13. Henry Knox to the hostile Indian nations, April 4, 1792, PGWP, 10:186n–189n

14. Ibid., 186n–187n.

15. GW Memorandum on General Officers, March 9, 1792, ibid., 74. See also ibid., 71.

16. PGWP, 9:505.

17. GW to Lafayette, February 1, 1784, ibid., 1:87–90.

18. GW to Edward Newenham, June 22, 1792, PGWP, 10:493–495.

19. GW to James Madison, May 20, 1792, ibid., 399–403.

20. Alan and Donna Jean Fusonie, *George Washington, Pioneer Farmer* (Mount Vernon, VA: The Mount Vernon Ladies' Association, 1998), 22.

21. Fitzpatrick, *Writings*, 33:268–71, GW to William Pearce, February 16, 1794.

22. Ibid.

23. Chernow, *Alexander Hamilton*, 401.

24. GW to Thomas Jefferson, PGWP, 10:28–32.

25. Thomas Jefferson to Archibald Stuart, January 4, 1797, Kaminski, *The Quotable Jefferson*, 435.

26. Chernow, *Alexander Hamilton*, 403–404, citing the *Gazette of the United States*, July 25 and August 4, 1792.

27. GW to Alexander Hamilton, August 26, 1792, PGWP, 11:38–40.

28. Thomas Jefferson conversation with GW, July 10, 1792, ibid., 10:535–537.

29. Alexander Hamilton to GW, July 30–August 3, 1792, ibid., 10:594–596.

30. GW to Thomas Jefferson, August 23, 1792, ibid., 11:28–32.

31. GW to Alexander Hamilton, August 26, 1792, ibid., 38–40.

32. With most of the nation engaged in farming, Americans could not afford to leave the fields and livestock during the day to celebrate Washington's birthday. Instead, they celebrated his birth night.

## CHAPTER EIGHT

1. Edmund Burke, *Reflections on the Revolution in France, 1790*, in Louis I. Bredwold and Ralph G. Ross, eds., *The Philosophy of Edmund Burke* (Ann Arbor: University of Michigan Press, 1967), 231–255.

2. GW to the President of the National Assembly of France, January 27, 1791, PGWP, 7:292–293.

3. Harlow Giles Unger, *Lafayette* (Hoboken, NJ: John Wiley & Sons, 2002), 236–237.

4. Dumas Malone, *Jefferson and the Rights of Man* (Boston: Little, Brown, 1951), 214.

5. Ibid., xvii.

6. Unger, *Lafayette*, 227.

7. Chernow, *Alexander Hamilton*, 459.

8. George A. Peek, Jr., ed., *The Political Writings of John Adams* (New York: The Liberal Arts Press: The American Heritage Series, 1954), 194.

9. Thomas Jefferson to Joel Barlow, January 24, 1810, in Kaminski, *Founders*, 209–210.

10. *National Gazette*, cited in Chernow, *Alexander Hamilton*, 433; Thomas Jefferson to Lafayette, April 2, 1790, in Kaminski, *The Quotable Jefferson*, 2006, xlvi.

11. Alexander DeConde, *Entangling Alliance* (Durham, NC: Duke University Press, 1958), 181; Dumas Malone, *Jefferson and the Ordeal of Liberty* (Boston: Little, Brown, 1962), 97.

12. Meade Minnigerode, *Jefferson—Friend of France* (New York: G. P. Putnam & Sons, 1928), 205.

13. GW to Thomas Jefferson, April 12, 1793, PGWP, 12:448–449.

14. Thomas Jefferson to GW, April 7, 1793, ibid., 419–420.

15. Freeman, *George Washington*, 7:36.

16. Archives des Affaires Étrangères, Ministère des Affaires Étrangères, Quai d'Orsay, Paris, France. Volume 38, Dossier *Correspondence Consulaire: Genet.*

17. Thomas Jefferson to French Foreign Minister Comte de Vergennes, November 20, 1785, in Frederick A. Schminke, *Genet: The Origins of His Mission to America* (Toulouse: Imprimerie Toulousaine Lion et Fils, 1939), 31.

18. Minnigerode, *Jefferson—Friend of France*, 221.

19. *Boston Gazette*, April 29, 1793.

20. Minnigerode, *Jefferson—Friend of France*, 221.

21. Ibid., 207.

22. *Instructions to Citizen Genet, Minister Plenipotentiary from the French Republic to the United States, from the Executive Council*, Archives des Affaires Étrangères, Paris, Volume 38, Dossier *Correspondence Consulaire: Genet.*

23. *Kentucky Gazette* (Lexington), April 5, 1794.

24. Archives des Affaires Étrangères, Volume 38, Dossier *Correspondence Consulaire: Genet.*

25. Richard Harwell, *An Abridgment in One Volume of the Seven Volume George Washington by Douglas Southall Freeman* (New York: Charles Scribner's Sons, 1968), 622.

26. Not until 1856, with the Declaration of Paris, would the world's leading maritime powers agree to codify the rights of neutrals and belligerents on the high seas. The Hague Conventions of 1908 added further clarification and codification of the rights and obligations of neutrals.

27. Harlow Giles Unger, *The Life and Times of Noah Webster, an American Patriot* (New York: John Wiley & Sons, 1998), 71, 183.

28. Henry Ammon, *The Genet Mission* (New York: W. W. Norton, 1973), 70.

29. Minnigerode, *Jefferson—Friend of France*, 223.

30. John Adams to Thomas Jefferson, June 30, 1813, in Lester J. Cappon, ed., *The Adams-Jefferson Letters: The Complete Correspondence Between Thomas Jefferson and Abigail and John Adams* (Chapel Hill: University of North Carolina Press, 1959), 346–347.

31. Minnigerode, *Jefferson—Friend of France*, 184.

32. Archives des Affaires Étrangères, Volume 38, Dossier *Correspondence Consulaire: Genet.*

## CHAPTER NINE

1. Malone, *Jefferson and the Ordeal*, 97.

2. Ibid., 81.

3. Minnigerode, *Jefferson—Friend of France*, 183.

4. Ammon, *The Genet Mission*, 91; George Washington to Virginia Governor Henry Lee, October 16, 1793, Fitzpatrick, *Writings*, 33:132–133.

5. Minnigerode, *Jefferson—Friend of France*, 282.

6. GW to Frances Bassett Washington, February 24, 1793, in PGWP, 12:264–265.

7. Donald H. Stewart, *The Opposition Press of the Federalist Period* (Albany: State University of New York Press, 1969), 132.

8. Ibid., 312.

9. Archives des Affaires Étrangères, Volume 38, Dossier *Correspondence Consulaire: Genet.*

10. *Greenleaf's New York Journal*, August 28, 1793.

11. *Boston Columbian Centinel*, August 17, 1793.

12. John Adams to Thomas Jefferson, June 30, 1813, Cappon, *The Adams-Jefferson Letters*, 346.

13. John Adams to Abigail Adams, February 23, 1794, cited in DeConde, *Entangling Alliance*, 398.

14. Minnigerode, *Jefferson—Friend of France*, 362.

15. Genet died at the age of seventy-one, on Bastille Day, July 14, 1834, having fathered six children by Cornelia Clinton. One of his great-great grandsons, Edmund Charles Clinton Genet, was the first American aviator killed in World War I—ironically, in the skies over France with the Lafayette Escadrille, a group of American fliers who volunteered to fight with the allies before the United States entered the war.

## CHAPTER TEN

1. The Navy remained part of the U.S. Army until 1798, when it became a separate branch of the military.

2. Ammon, *The Genet Mission*, 28; Jean Tulard, Jean-François Fayard, and Alfred Fierro, *Histoire et Dictionnaire de la Révolution Française, 1789–1799* (Paris: Editions Robert Laffont, S.A., 1987, 1998), 349.

3. Ibid., 98.

4. Washington to Henry Lee, August 26, 1794, Freeman, *George Washington*, 7:181–182; DeConde, *Entangling Alliance*, 262.

5. John C. Miller, *The Federalist Era* (New York: Harper & Brothers, 1960), 161.

6. James Carnahan, "The Pennsylvania Insurrection of 1794, Commonly Called the Whiskey Insurrection," *New Jersey Historical Society Proceedings* 6 (1853), 115–152, cited in Freeman, *George Washington*, 7:185–186. Carnahan was a student at Canonsberg Academy in 1794 and witnessed events he described.

7. Leland D. Baldwin, *Whiskey Rebels: The Story of a Frontier Uprising* (Pittsburgh: University of Pittsburgh Press, 1968), 141.

8. Ibid., 145.

9. Ibid., 42.

10. Chernow, *Alexander Hamilton*, 471.

11. Freeman, *George Washington*, 7:186–187.

12. Joseph J. Ellis, *His Excellency George Washington* (New York: Alfred A. Knopf, 2004), 224.

## CHAPTER ELEVEN

1. GW to Edmund Randolph, October 10, 1791, PGWP, 9:68–69.

2. Baldwin, *Whiskey Rebels*, 186.

3. Donald Jackson and Dorothy Twohig, *Diaries*, 6:186–187.

4. Ibid., 6:185–186.

5. Ibid., 6:195–186.

6. Morris, *Encyclopedia of American History*, 130.

7. Seth Ames, ed., *Works of Fisher Ames* (Boston: T. B. Wait, 1809, 2 vols.), 1:161.

8. Fitzpatrick, *Writings*, 34:98–101, GW to Edmund Pendleton, January 22, 1795.

## CHAPTER TWELVE

1. Joseph Stanton, Jr., to Arthur Fenner, February 17, 1791, Bickford and Bowling, *Birth of the Nation*, 99.

2. DeConde, *Entangling Alliance*, 427n, citing "Americanus" in the *Virginia Herald and Fredericksburg Advertiser*, July 24, 1795.

3. GW to George Cabot, September 7, 1795, Fitzpatrick, *Writings*, 34:299–301.

4. Ibid., 416.

5. GW to Gouverneur Morris, March 4, 1796, Fitzpatrick, *Writings*, 34:482–484.

6. McDonald, *The Presidency of George Washington*, 172.

7. GW to the House of Representatives, March 30, 1796, Fitzpatrick, *Writings*, 35:2–5.

## CHAPTER THIRTEEN

1. GW Farewell Address, September 19, 1796, Fitzpatrick, *Writings*, 35:214–238, esp. 214–215.

2. Ibid., esp. 256–227.

3. Ibid., esp. 233.

4. Ibid., esp. 232–235.

5. Ibid.

6. Ibid.


## CHAPTER FOURTEEN

1. *Philadelphia Aurora*, December 21 and 23, 1796, Stewart, *The Opposition Press*, 533.

2. GW to the Secretary of War [James McHenry], May 29, 1797, Fitzpatrick, *Writings*, 35:455–456.

3. Ibid.

4. Martha Washington to Lucy Flucker Knox [undated], Fields, *Worthy Partner*, 303–304.

5. Freeman, *George Washington*, 7:432, citing Judge Airedale to Mrs. Airedale, February 24, 1797.

6. GW to Henry Knox, March 2, 1797, Fitzpatrick, *Writings*, 35:408–410.

7. Freeman, *George Washington*, 7:436, citing the recollections of Philadelphia's Bishop William White in William Spohn Baker, *Washington After the Revolution, 1784–1799* (Philadelphia: J. B. Lippincott, 1898).

8. Freeman, *George Washington*, 7:457, citing John Adams to Abigail Adams, March 5, 1797, in Charles Francis Adams, ed., *Letters of John Adams Addressed to His Wife* (Boston: 1841, 2 vols.), 2:244.

9. Stewart, *The Opposition Press*, 533–534, Philadelphia *Aurora*, March 5, 1797.

10. George Washington Motier Lafayette to GW, October 22, 1797, Dorothy Twohig, ed., *The Papers of George Washington, Retirement Series, March, 1797–December, 1799* (Charlottesville: University Press of Virginia, 1998–1999, 4 vols.), 1:421.

11. John Adams to GW, June 22, 1798, ibid., 2:351–352.

12. Ibid.

13. John Adams to GW, July 7, 1798, ibid., 2:389.

14. GW to James McHenry, December 13, 1798, ibid., 3:250n–265n.

15. GW to Gouverneur Morris, May 26, 1799, Fitzpatrick, *Writings*, 37:214–215.

16. *Diaries*, 6:377–378.

17. Tobias Lear's Narrative Account of the Death of George Washington, December 15, 1799PGW, Ret. 4:542–546.

18. Ibid.

19. Freeman, *George Washington*, 7:650, citing A. B. Hart, ed., "Tributes to Washington," 25–26.

20. Ibid., citing Hart, 21.

21. Freeman, *George Washington*, 7:651, citing *Annals of 7th Congress*, 1:1310.

## APPENDIX

1. "Sentiments delivered by the President at a second conference with the Senate," August 10, 1789, PGWP, 3:408–410.
2. DHRC, 15:280–283.

# Bibliography

Abbot, W. W, and Dorothy Twohig, eds. *The Papers of George Washington, Colonial Series, 1748–August 1755.* 10 vols. Charlottesville: University Press of Virginia, 1983–1995.

———. *The Papers of George Washington, Confederation Series, January, 1784–September, 1788.* 6 vols. Charlottesville: University Press of Virginia, 1992–1997.

Abbot, W. W., Dorothy Twohig, Philander D. Chase, and Theodore J. Crackel, eds. *The Papers of George Washington, Presidential Series, September, 1788–May, 1793.* Charlottesville: University of Virginia Press, 1987–[multi-volumes in progress].

———. *The Papers of George Washington, Revolutionary War Series, June 1775–April 1778.* Charlottesville: University of Virginia Press, 1984–[multi-volumes in progress].

Adams, Charles Francis, ed. *Letters of John Adams Addressed to His Wife.* 2 vols. Boston: Little, Brown, and Company, 1841.

———. *The Works of John Adams.* 10 vols. Boston: Little, Brown and Company, 1850–1856.

———. *Writings of Albert Gallatin.* 3 vols. Philadelphia: J. P. Lippincott & Company, 1879.

Ames, Seth. *Works of Fisher Ames.* Boston: T. B. Wait, 1809.

Ammon, Henry. *The Genet Mission.* New York: W. W. Norton, 1973.

Baldwin, Leland D. *Whiskey Rebels: The Story of a Frontier Uprising.* Pittsburgh: University of Pittsburgh Press, 1968.

Beeman, Richard R. *Patrick Henry: A Biography.* New York: McGraw-Hill, 1974.

Bickford, Charlene Bangs, and Kenneth R. Bowling. *Birth of the Nation: The First Federal Congress, 1789–1791.* Lanham, MD: Madison House Publishers, 1989.

Bickford, Charlene Bangs, et al., eds. *The Documentary History of the First Federal Congress.* 17 vols. Baltimore: Johns Hopkins University Press, 1992–1998.

Boyd, Julian P., et al., eds. *The Papers of Thomas Jefferson.* Princeton, NJ: Princeton University Press, 1950–[multi-volumes in progress].

Brackenridge, Henry Marie. *History of the Insurrection in Western Pennsylvania, Commonly Called the Whiskey Insurrection, 1794.* Pittsburgh: W. S. Haven, 1859.

Bredwold, Louis I., and Ralph G. Ross, eds. *The Philosophy of Edmund Burke.* Ann Arbor: University of Michigan Press, 1967.

Cappon, Lester J., ed. *The Adams-Jefferson Letters: The Complete Correspondence Between Thomas Jefferson and Abigail and John Adams.* Chapel Hill: University of North Carolina Press, 1959.

Chernow, Ron. *Alexander Hamilton.* New York: The Penguin Press, 2004.

Davenport, Beatrix Cary, ed. *A Diary of the French Revolution by Gouverneur Morris.* 2 vols. Boston: Houghton Mifflin Company, 1939.

DeConde, Alexander. *Entangling Alliance.* Durham, NC: Duke University Press, 1958.

Dos Passos, John. *The Men Who Made the Nation.* Garden City, NY: Doubleday, 1957.

Ellis, Joseph J. *His Excellency George Washington.* New York: Alfred A. Knopf, 2004.

Farrand, Max, ed. *The Records of the Federal Convention of 1787.* 4 vols. New Haven, CT: Yale University Press, 1911.

Ferling, John. *John Adams: A Life.* New York: Henry Holt, 1992.

Fields, Joseph E. *Worthy Partner: The Papers of Martha Washington.* Westport, CT: Greenwood Press, 1994.

Fitzpatrick, John C., ed. *The Writings of George Washington, from the Original Manuscript Sources, 1745–1799.* 39 vols. Washington: U.S. Government Printing Office, 1931–1944.

Ford, Paul Leicester, ed. *The Writings of Thomas Jefferson.* 10 vols. New York: G. P. Putnam's Sons, 1892–1899.

Ford, Worthington C., et al., eds. Continental Congress, *Journals, 1774–1789.* 8 vols. Washington, D.C., 1921–1926.

Freeman, Douglas Southall. *George Washington.* 7 vols. Completed by John Alexander Carroll and Mary Wells Ashworth. New York: Charles Scribner's Sons, 1957.

Fusonie, Alan, and Donna Jean. *George Washington, Pioneer Farmer.* Mount Vernon, VA: The Mount Vernon Ladies' Association, 1998.

Genet, [Edmond Charles] Citizen. *The Correspondence between Citizen Genet, Minister of the French Republic to the United States of North America, and the Officers of the Federal Government; to which are prefixed the Instructions from the Constituted Authorities of France to the Said Minister.* Philadelphia: Benjamin Franklin Bache, 1793.

Genet, George Clinton. *Washington, Jefferson, and "Citizen" Genet, 1793.* New York, privately published, 1899.

Gordon, John Steele. *An Empire of Wealth: The Epic History of American Economic Power.* New York: Harper Collins Publishers, 2004.

Harwell, Richard. *An Abridgment in One Volume of the Seven Volume George Washington by Douglas Southall Freeman.* New York: Charles Scribner's Sons, 1968.

Henry, William Wirt. *Patrick Henry: Life, Correspondence, and Speeches.* 3 vols. New York: Charles Scribner's Sons, 1891.

Idzerda, Stanley J., and Robert Rhodes Crout, eds. *Lafayette in the Age of the American Revolution: Selected Letters and Papers, 1776–1790.* 5 vols. Ithaca, NY: Cornell University Press, 1983.

Jackson, Donald, and Dorothy Twohig, eds. *The Diaries of George Washington.* Charlottesville: University Press of Virginia, 1976–1979, 6 vols.

Jay, William. *The Life of John Jay: With Selections from His Correspondence and Miscellaneous Papers.* 2 vols. New York, 1833.

Jensen, Merrill. *The New Nation: A History of the United States During the Confederation, 1781–1789.* New York: Alfred A. Knopf, 1950.

Jensen, Merrill, John P. Kaminski, Gaspare Saladino, Richard Leffler, and Charles H. Schoenleber, eds. *The Documentary History of the Ratification of the Constitution.* 21 vols. Madison: State Historical Society of Wisconsin, 1976–[multi-volumes in progress].

Kaminski, John P., ed. *The Founders on the Founders: Word Portraits from the American Revolutionary Era.* Charlottesville: University of Virginia Press, 2008.

———. *The Quotable Jefferson.* Princeton, NJ: Princeton University Press, 2006.

Labaree, Leonard W., et al. *Papers of Benjamin Franklin.* 38 vols. New Haven, CT: Yale University Press, 1959–[in progress].

Lafayette, George-Washington *[Gilbert Motier, Marquis de La Fayette], Mémoires, Correspondence et Manuscrits du Général Lafayette, publiés par sa famille.* Paris: H. Fournier, 6 vols., 1837; Bruxelles: Societé Belge de Librairie, Etc., Hauman, Cattoir et Compagnie, 2 vols., 1837.

Lee, Henry. *Memoirs of the War in the Southern Department of the United States*. 2 vols. Philadelphia: 1812.

Lee, Richard Henry. *The Letters of Richard Henry Lee*. 2 vols. Danvers, MA: General Books [reprint], 2009.

Link, Eugene P. *The Democratic-Republic Societies, 1790–1800*. New York: Octagon Books, 1942.

Lipsky, Seth. *The Citizen's Constitution: An Annotated Guide*. New York: Basic Books, 2009.

Lossing, Benson J. *Mary and Martha, the Mother and the Wife of George Washington*. New York: Harper & Brothers, 1886.

Maclay, William. *Journal of William Maclay*. Maclay, Edgar S., ed. New York: D. Appleton & Co., 1890.

Madison, James. *Notes of Debates in the Federal Convention of 1787 Reported by James Madison*. New York: W. W. Norton, 1987.

Malone, Dumas. *Jefferson and the Rights of Man*. Boston: Little, Brown, 1951.

———. *Jefferson and the Ordeal of Liberty*. Boston: Little, Brown, 1962.

McCusker, John J. *How Much Is That In Real Money? A Historical Commodity Price Index for Use as a Deflator of Money Values in the Economy of the United States*. Worcester, MA: American Antiquarian Society, 2001.

McDonald, Forrest. *The Presidency of George Washington*. Lawrence: University Press of Kansas, 1974.

Meade, Robert Douthat. *Patrick Henry, Practical Revolutionary*. Philadelphia: J. B. Lippincott, 1969.

Miller, John C. *The Federalist Era*. New York: Harper & Brothers, 1960.

Minnigerode, Meade. *Jefferson—Friend of France*. New York: G. P. Putnam & Sons, 1928.

Mitchell, Stewart, ed. *New Letters of Abigail Adams, 1788–1801*. Boston: Houghton Mifflin, 1947.

Morris, Richard B. *Witnesses at the Creation: Hamilton, Madison, Jay, and the Constitution*. New York: Holt, Rinehart and Winston, 1985.

Peek, George A., Jr., ed. *The Political Writings of John Adams*. New York: The Liberal Arts Press: The American Heritage Series, 1954.

Raddin, George Gates, Jr. *Caritat and the Genet Episode*. Dover, NJ: The Dover Advance Press, 1953.

Schlesinger, Arthur M., Jr. *The Imperial Presidency*. Boston: Houghton, Mifflin, 1973.

Schminke, Frederick A. *Genet: The Origins of His Mission to America*. Toulouse: Imprimerie Toulousaine Lion et Fils, 1939.

Slaughter, Thomas. *The Whiskey Rebellion: Frontier Epilogue to the American Revolution*. New York: Oxford University Press, 1986.

Stewart, Donald H. *The Opposition Press of the Federalist Period*. Albany: State University of New York Press, 1969.

Tagg, James. *Benjamin Franklin Bache and the Philadelphia Aurora*. Philadelphia: University of Pennsylvania Press, 1991.

Tulard, Jean, Jean-François Fayard, and Alfred Fierro. *Histoire et Dictionnaire de la Révolution Française, 1789–1799*. Paris: Editions Robert Laffont, S.A., 1987, 1998.

Twohig, Dorothy, ed. *The Papers of George Washington, Retirement Series, March, 1797–December, 1799*. Charlottesville: University Press of Virginia, 1998–1999, 4 vols.

Unger, Harlow Giles. *America's Second Revolution: How George Washington Defeated Patrick Henry and Saved the Nation*. Hoboken, NJ: John Wiley & Sons, 2007.

———. *Lafayette*. Hoboken, NJ: John Wiley & Sons, 2002.

———. *The Life and Times of Noah Webster, an American Patriot*. New York: John Wiley & Sons, 1998.

Van Doren, Carl. *The Great Rehearsal*. New York: Viking Press, 1948.

———. *The Journals of the Proceedings of the President, 1793–1797*. Edited by Dorothy Twohig. Charlottesville: University Press of Virginia, 1981.

Yoo, John. *Crisis and Command: The History of Executive Power from George Washington to George W. Bush*. New York: Kaplan Publishing, 2009.

## MONOGRAPHS

Brackenridge, Hugh H. *Incidents of the Insurrection in the Western Parts of Pennsylvania, in the Year 1794*. Philadelphia: John McCulloch, 1795.

Carnahan, James. "The Pennsylvania Insurrection of 1794, Commonly Called the 'Whiskey Insurrection.' A Paper Read before the New Jersey Historical Society, September 8th, 1852." *New Jersey Historical Society Proceedings* 6, 1853.

Findley, William. *History of the Insurrection in the Four Western Counties of Pennsylvania in the Year M.DCC.XCIV, with a Recital of the Events Specifically Connected Therewith; and an Historical Review of the Previous Situation of the Country*. Philadelphia: Samuel Harrison Smith, 1796.

Fontaine, Edward. "Patrick Henry—A Patrick Henry Essay by Patrick Henry's Great-Grandson." Published by the Patrick Henry Memorial Foundation, 2008.

Henderson, Archibald. "The Spanish Conspiracy in Tennessee." *Tennessee Historical Magazine* 3 (1917).

## ARCHIVES

*Archives des Affaires Étrangères, Ministère des Affaires Étrangères, Dossier Correspondence Consulaire*, Quai d'Orsay, Paris France.

*Journal of the Senate of the United States of America* (Library of Congress).
*Journal of the United States House of Representatives* (Library of Congress).
Thomas Lloyd, *The Congressional Record*. New York: 1789–1790, 4 vols.


## REFERENCE WORKS

Bartlett, John. *Familiar Quotations*, 16th edition. Boston: Little, Brown, 1992.
Morris, Richard B., ed. *Encyclopedia of American History*. New York: Harper & Brothers, 1953.
*The New Cambridge Modern History*. Cambridge: Cambridge University Press, 1965.


## PERIODICALS

*Aurora* (Philadelphia)
Boston *American Herald*
*Charleston Evening Gazette*
*Freeman's Journal* (Philadelphia)
*Gazette of the United States*
*Massachusetts Centinel*
*National Gazette* (Philadelphia)
*New York Journal*
*New York Packet*
*Pennsylvania Packet*
*Providence Gazette*

# Index